Run of the Red Queen

Run of the Red Queen

Government, Innovation, Globalization,

and Economic Growth in China

Dan Breznitz
Michael Murphree

Yale UNIVERSITY PRESS

NEW HAVEN AND LONDON

Published with assistance from the foundation established in memory of Philip Hamilton McMillan of the Class of 1894, Yale College.

Yale University Press books may be purchased in quantity for educational, business, or promotional use. For information, please e-mail sales.press@yale.edu (U.S. office) or sales@yaleup.co.uk (U.K. office).

Set in Adobe Garamond type by The Composing Room of Michigan, Inc.
Printed in the United States of America.

Library of Congress Cataloging-in-Publication Data

Breznitz, Dan.
    Run of the red queen : government, innovation, globalization, and economic growth in China / Dan Breznitz, Michael Murphree.
        p. cm.
    Includes bibliographical references and index.
    ISBN 978-0-300-15271-5 (cloth : alk. paper)
    1. China—Economic policy.   2. Industrial policy—China.   3. Technological innovations—China.   4. New products—China.   5. Economic development—China.   I. Murphree, Michael, 1981–   II. Title.
    HC427.95.B748 2011
    338.951—dc22

                                                        2010036483

A catalogue record for this book is available from the British Library.

This paper meets the requirements of ANSI/NISO Z39.48–1992 (Permanence of Paper).

10 9 8 7 6 5 4 3 2 1

To Shiri, Mika, and Tom, for reminding me every day, and every minute
of the day, why
And to the memory of Hatuli, who in his last days sat with us
as we wrote the very first draft of this book
—DB

To Nana, for making my life a joy
And to Danny, for teaching me how to write and giving me this chance
—MM

Contents

Acknowledgments

This book is based on extensive and extended fieldwork. Therefore, it is not possible to thank all those who appeared at just the right moments to help with our field travels, data analysis, drafting, and the seemingly endless agonizing process of rewriting and revising (books, it should be said, are not written—they are rewritten and revised many more times than we care to admit). Nonetheless, a few individuals have given us extensive help, and without them, none of this would have been possible.

In China, first and foremost we thank Shanghai Jiaotong University and the School of International and Public Affairs for their support, partnership, and guidance throughout this project. Without their help as early as April 2007, this project would have never gotten off the ground. Frank Tan of the Zhongguancun Representative Office in Silicon Valley helped with initial contacts before the project even officially began. Special thanks are also due to the People's Government of Dongguan, the People's Government of Shenzhen, and the Zhongguancun Administrative Committee. Their openness and candor, assistance in arranging site visits and interviews, and great willingness to tell us flatly when we were wrong are greatly appreciated. We are deeply grateful to all of the following: the Chinese Academy of Sciences; Professor Otto C. C. Lin, for many hours of discussions and help in the field; Hong Kong University of Science and Technology; Beijing University of Posts and Telecommunications; Professor John C. Chiang, of Beijing University, and recently of USITO (the U.S. Information Technology Office), for sharing his almost limitless, deep knowledge of the history of the Chinese IT industry; Dean Weiying Zhang, of the Guanghua School of Management at Beijing University; Dr. Patrick Keating, of Cisco Systems; the Georgia Tech China Alumni Network; and the American Chamber of Commerce in Shanghai, for its hospitality, assistance, feedback, and mentorship in the field.

Above all else, we are forever in debt to the entrepreneurs, officials, executives, employees, and academics who so generously gave of their time to speak with us. We hope our research can be as advantageous and profitable for you as interviewing you has been for us. We deeply thank you.

For all their assistance, company, and good eats in China, we thank Nancy Chen, Huang Ming, Huang Qi, Robert Liu, Liu Xielin, Sheng Huanye, Ye Jiang, Yan Maosi, Zhang Aihua, Zhang Wei, and John Zhu. For their help with the long interviews and the longer process of transcribing and translating, we greatly appreciate the services of Philip Hu, Liu Bo, Irainy Liu, Ren Xiaopeng, Tan Yan, and Endymion Zhuang. Field research can be a lonely process, and their company was greatly appreciated. To the taxi drivers, wait staff, and hotel floor managers whose sense of humor, openness, generosity of spirit, and free offer of good conversation made our long trips possible in more ways than one, we are forever grateful. In Atlanta, special thanks to Siwan Cillian Liu for her endless patience, hard work, and assistance with analysis, translation, GIS (geographic information system) mastery, and graphics.

And of course, we thank Hua Jiao for everything.

For support on the second home front, many laughs, and great memories, special thanks to the faculty and staff of the Interlingua School in Guiyang and Zunyi. They forever have a special place in Michael's heart for enabling and then showing him how wonderful it is to live in China.

The arguments of this book were extensively improved thanks to the work of many. We thank all the participants in the inaugural meeting of the Kauffman Foundation International Innovation and Entrepreneurship Scholars Network in April 2008 in Atlanta as well as those at the Harvard Business School International Research Conference in May 2009, in particular Jordan Siegel. Special thanks should be given to our former hosts and good friends at Stanford University, especially to Henry S. Rowen, William F. Miller, Marguerite Gong Hancock, Rafiq Dossani, and George Krompacky of the Stanford Project on Regions of Innovation and Entrepreneurship (SPRIE). Many people gave us extensive comments on drafts of the text at various stages of our work, including William J. Long, Adam Segal, Minyuan Zhao, Andrea Herrmann, Scott Kennedy, Suzanne Berger, Dick Samuels, Barry Naughton, Susan Walcott, Martin Kenney, Fei-Ling Wang, John Garver, Doug Fuller, Mark Zachary Taylor, Edward Steinfeld, Adam Stulberg, and John Zysman, all of whom not only went far beyond the call of duty, but also made sure that even when we thought we could not move the argument forward anymore, we did. We would also like to thank our many beloved teachers, friends, and mentors along the way, from Ehud Harari, who was the first to open our eyes to the importance of comparative political economy, to our colleagues and teachers at the Georgia Institute of Technology, MIT, and elsewhere. The influence of many discussions we had with Amos Zehavi, Gerald McDermott, Carsten Zimmermann, Andrew Schrank, Woody Powell, Jason Owen-Smith, Richard Doner, John Walsh, Crystal Chang, and Frank Giarratani appears in every page of the book. Danny would also like to thank the following: Suzanne, for introducing him to the painful joy of book writing; Dick, for showing him the model and giving a personal example; Mike, for reminding him why it is important to be a social scientist; the faculty of the Sam Nunn School, for allowing and helping him to write, be agonized, and be joyful; and John, who might find it strange to be thanked for keeping him sane.

In the initial editing, both Marilyn Levine and Deborah Chasman made sure that our book could be read by people other than our close family. At Yale University Press, we would like to thank our editor, Michael O'Malley, for his enthusiasm and immense help; Alex Larson and Niamh Cunningham, for keeping the project on track; and Margaret Otzel for superbly managing the editing of the manuscript; thanks also to Kip Keller, a master wordsmith, for working his copyediting magic, and Marcia Carlson for superb indexing.

The research for this book was made possible by generous grants from the Kauffman and Sloan foundations; as befitting such foundations, their help went further than just granting us funds. For that, we are deeply in debt to their personnel, especially Gail Pesyna at the Sloan Foundation and Robert Strom, Lesa Mitchell, Robert Litan, Dave Kaiser, and Glory Olson at the Kauffman Foundation. At the Georgia Institute of Technology Sam Nunn School of International Affairs, Wanda Moore, Marilu Suarez, Angela Levin, Benjamin Powell, and Vince Pedicino made sure not only that we could do our work, but also that we did not go crazy along the way.

The ups and downs of book writing were shared not only by the authors, but also by their families, in an unfair exchange. We got both pain and joy, while our families mostly got just the pain. Michael would therefore like to thank his family for their support, love, and understanding in all of his endless wanderings. Patrick and Marcus, you always call me back to earth and keep the good times rolling. Momma and Daddy, thank you for everything, especially for supporting me over the long course of this project. Mama and Baba, thank you for making me your own and encouraging me always. Meimei, keep smiling for big brother. Finally, and most of all, thanks to my amazing wife, Nana; having you in my life is the greatest blessing I could ever ask for. You make me a better man. Thank you, honey.

Danny would like to thank his family: Marcel and Jina, who had to suffer me at my worse in Ashdod; Rinat, Ben, Matan, and Adi, for reminding him what life and growing up is all about; Doda Ada, Tom, and Noga, for love and surprise meetings in Jerusalem and Berlin; Assaf, although most of these thanks should go to Nevo and Shiri; Shlomo, Zvia, Ruthy, and Nurit; and above all, Dafna and Ima, for reminding me for the last four decades what family is all about—may you forever keep smiling. Last but certainly not least, my thanks and love to Shiri, my wife and true companion for so many years that we no longer truly remember when and how it started—every day I am amazed that you still put up with me; and to Mika—you are still too small to read this book, but you made sure that it took at least eighteen more months, spent in the pure joy of holding you and not my laptop, to finish it.

To the memory of Hatuli, a firm mentor, stern intellectual master, brave soul, and good friend.

Abbreviations

2G	second-generation mobile communications
3G	third-generation mobile communications
4G	fourth-generation mobile communications
AVD	Advanced High Density Disc System
CAE	Chinese Academy of Engineering
CAS	Chinese Academy of Sciences
CATR	China Academy of Telecommunications Research
CATT	China Academy of Telecommunications Technology
CCP	Chinese Communist Party
CDMA	Code Division Multiple Access
CEIBS	China Europe International Business School
CEO	chief executive officer
CTO	chief technical officer
DVD	digital versatile (or video) disc
EVD	Enhanced Versatile Disc
FDI	foreign direct investment
FRAND	fair, reasonable, and nondiscriminatory
GDP	gross domestic product

GSM	Global System for Mobile Communications
HD-DVD	High-Definition Digital Video Disc
HDV	high-definition video disc
HTDZ	high-technology development zone
HVD	High-Clearness Video Disc
IC	integrated circuit
ICP	Internet communications protocol
ICT	Institute of Computing Technology
IPO	initial public offering
IPR	intellectual property rights
ISO	International Organization for Standardization
IT	information technology
ITU	International Telecommunications Union
KMT	Kuomintang
LAN	local area network
M&A	mergers and acquisitions
MBA	master of business administration
MEI	Ministry of Electronic Industry
MII	Ministry of Information Industry
MITI	Ministry of International Trade and Industry (Japan)
MNC	multinational corporation
MOST	Ministry of Science and Technology
MPT	Ministry of Posts and Telecommunications
NDRC	National Development and Reform Commission
NIE	newly industrialized (or industrializing) economy
NPC	National People's Congress
OBM	original brand manufacturing (or manufacturer)
ODM	original design manufacturing (or manufacturer)
ODP	original design product
OECD	Organization for Economic Cooperation and Development
OEM	original equipment manufacturing (or manufacturer)
OSS	open-source software
PHS	personal handy-phone system
PRC	People's Republic of China
PRD	Pearl River Delta
PTIC	Posts and Telecommunications Industry Corporation
R&D	research and development
RMB	renminbi

S&T	science and technology
SASAC	State-owned Assets Supervision and Administration Commission
SCDMA	Synchronous Code Division Multiple Access
SEZ	special economic zone
SHIP	Shenzhen High-Tech Industrial Park
SIM	subscriber identity module
SME	small- and medium-sized enterprise
SMIC	Semiconductor Manufacturing International Corporation
SOE	state-owned enterprise
SSTC	State Science and Technology Commission
SZVU	Shenzhen Virtual University
TD-LTE	Time Division–Long-Term Evolution
TD-SCDMA	Time Division–Synchronous Code Division Multiple Access
TSMC	Taiwan Semiconductor Manufacturing Company
TVE	township and village enterprise
UMC	United Microelectronics Corporation
UPS	uninterruptible power supply
VA	volt-ampere
VC	venture capital
VCD	video compact disc
VHS	Video Home System
WAPI	Wireless Local Area Network Authentication and Privacy Infrastructure
WTO	World Trade Organization
XLT	*xiaolingtong*
ZGC	Zhongguancun Science Park
ZTE	Zhongxing Telecom

Run of the Red Queen

Introduction An Invention of My Own

"I see you're admiring my little box," the Knight said in a friendly tone. "It's my own invention—to keep clothes and sandwiches in. You see I carry it upside-down, so that the rain can't get in."

"But the things can get *out,*" Alice gently remarked. "Do you know the lid's open?"

"I didn't know it," the Knight said, a shade of vexation passing over his face. "Then all the things must have fallen out! And the box is no use without them." He unfastened it as he spoke, and was just going to throw it into the bushes, when a sudden thought seemed to strike him, and he hung it carefully on a tree. "Can you guess why I did that?" he said to Alice.

Alice shook her head.

"In hopes some bees may make a nest in it—then I should get the honey."

"But you've got a bee-hive—or something like one—fastened to the saddle," said Alice.

"Yes, it's a very good bee-hive," the Knight said in a discontented tone, "one of the best kind. But not a single bee has come near it yet. And the other thing is a mouse-trap. I suppose the mice keep the bees out—or the bees keep the mice out, I don't know which."

"I was wondering what the mouse-trap was for," said Alice. "It isn't very likely there would be any mice on the horse's back."

"Not very likely, perhaps," said the Knight; "but if they *do* come, I don't choose to have them running all about."

"You see," he went on after a pause, "it's as well to be provided for *everything*. That's the reason the horse has all those anklets round his feet."

"But what are they for?" Alice asked in a tone of great curiosity.

"To guard against the bites of sharks," the Knight replied. "It's an invention of my own."

—*Lewis Carroll,* Through the Looking-Glass and What Alice Found There

This book rebuts two myths.

The first concerns the relationship between innovation and economic growth. A pervasive misconception among policy makers and academics has made excellence in innovation—defined solely as the creation of new technologies, services, and products—the holy grail of economic growth.

The second myth addresses the misframed debate about China's unprecedented rate of economic growth—10-plus percent of gross domestic product (GDP) annually for twenty years (OECD 2006). Many scholars judge China's success against the model followed by other developed industrial powers. They look for the fabled creature of "true" innovation, a novel-product innovation-based industry resembling Silicon Valley.[1] If they see it, they declare the Chinese central government's industrial innovation policies a success; failing to find it, they warn that China's growth is not sustainable (Cao 2004; Ernst and Naughton 2007; Huang and Qian 2008; Segal 2003; Steinfeld 2004). A prominent Chinese scholar even warned that the fate of China's high-technology industry might be to lapse into a "premature senility" because too many high-tech enterprises were not fully transforming themselves into operations driven by technology and innovation (Cao 2004).

We argue that policy makers and academics put too much faith in the notion that states and societies must create novel technologies in order to secure long-term growth and enhance national welfare. Indeed, for China, excelling in other kinds of innovation has been the key to economic growth.

Furthermore, we argue that China's current system of innovation is sustainable for the medium and long term, thanks to the changes in the global production of services and products. Globalization has spatially fragmented industries and services; thus, activities, not necessarily entire industries, are now geographically clustered. This global reorganization of production and services offers a new logic of value creation as well as a new set of specialization and innovative capacities; hence, we must rethink what innovation means and what the best national strategies for long-term prosperity might be (Breznitz 2007b; Rodrik 2007).

This book documents the coevolution of public policy and industrial strategy in China, which accidentally created two innovation systems, one national and one regional.[2] These parallel systems have so far precluded novel-product innovation, but have allowed China to thrive in second-generation, production, and process innovation. We call this course of development China's "run of the Red Queen," a reference to the world of Lewis Carroll's Red Queen in *Through the Looking-Glass and What Alice Found There*, who, in order to even stay in the same place, had to run as fast as she could (Carroll 2001). China shines by keeping its industrial-production and service industries in perfect tandem with the technological frontier. Like the Red Queen, it runs as fast as possible in order to remain at the cusp of the global technology frontier without actually advancing the frontier itself.

This Red Queen analogy has produced a flurry of intellectual activity. So-called Red Queen games have been the subject of many papers in economics and management. This stream of research describes an innovation arms race in which one company's innovation forces other companies to innovate, which then forces the first company to innovate even faster. While this literature considers the unintended effects of the games on consumer welfare or on the market position of specific companies, in our view, the run of the Red Queen is a sustainable strategic goal for national economic growth, not the accidental result of an escalating arms race.[3]

As the technology frontier continues to advance, China has found that running fast enough to keep in step is extremely beneficial. Within an international economic system of globally fragmented production, China can excel in a wide array of innovative activities that might not advance the technological frontier but can certainly transform how the global economy works. It is important to reflect here on two historical facts. First, the Japanese gained dominance in the car industry not by novel-product innovation but by developing a superior system of production, one formulated around the specificities of the Japanese political-economic system (Streeck 1996; Womack et al. 1990). Second, we should remember that Alice, the little girl coming from Queen Victoria's great empire, might have been baffled by the behavior and perspective of the Red Queen, but in the mirror land, the Red Queen was The Queen. Thus, although other countries may be advancing the technological cutting edge, China continually grows in importance as a critical location for innovations built upon these discoveries.[4]

The notion that late developers, or follower countries, should concentrate first on imitation, utilizing economies of scale and scope to excel by using the latest technologies developed elsewhere, goes as far back as the work of Gerschenkron (1962). Gerschenkron and his followers viewed this only as a stage that backward countries need to master before they can develop the capabilities to excel in novel-product innovation and become true economic powers. This has been the main argument of scholars looking at Asia's newly industrialized economies (NIEs, also known as tigers or dragons) and at Japan (Amsden 1989, 2001; Amsden and Chu 2003; Cheng 1990; Fields 1995; S. Hong

1997; Johnson 1982; Kim 1997; Levi-Faur 1998; Noble 1998; Wade 1990; Woo-Cumings 1991). We argue that this perspective might have been true in a world of vertically integrated, co-located industries and a stable product cycle, à la Akamatsu (1962), Krugman (1979), and Vernon (1966). However, in an era of fragmented production in which each country specializes not only in specific industries but also in specific stages of production, and in which truly novel products are produced or sourced globally without being produced in the countries where they were developed, there are many modes of innovation that contribute to sustainable long-term economic growth. Furthermore, each mode confers competitive advantages relating to some stages of production but not others.

As China has become the global center for many different stages of production, it has also developed a formidable competitive capacity to innovate in different segments of the research, development, and production chain that are as critical for economic growth as many novel-product innovations, and perhaps even more so. In addition, taken together, China's regional and national systems have developed varied capabilities that amount to a specific and highly successful, though inadvertently created, national model. China's accomplishment has been to master the art of thriving in second-generation innovation—including the mixing of established technologies and products in order to come up with new solutions—and the science of organizational, incremental, and process innovation. Thus, China's innovation capabilities are not solely in process (or incremental) innovation but also in the organization of production, manufacturing techniques and technologies, delivery, design, and second-generation innovation. Those capabilities enable China to move quickly into new niches once they have been proved profitable by the original innovator. An example of such second-generation innovation is Baidu, the dominant search engine in China, founded in 2000. Baidu's Web page bears an undeniable resemblance to Google's. But the resemblance does not end with the visual representation; Baidu's business model and interface mirror those of Google and take advantage of the defined market space and pathway it has blazed since the late 1990s. Nonetheless, Baidu is not solely an imitator: it has its own innovation capabilities and design strengths. Baidu has built its own proprietary Chinese-language search software and has taken full advantage of local market openings.

We must emphasize that China and its "run of the Red Queen" model differ from the former Asian NIEs' fast-follower model. First, unlike those countries where governments had specific policies with clearly defined goals and the pathways to get there, China developed its Red Queen run by accident, partly as a result of local experimentation, and the outcome looks quite different from the declared goals of the central government. Second, the world has significantly changed since the early 1980s. In the past, late developers relied on national champions in the form of conglomerates that tried to master every stage of production. Today, in a world of fragmented production, successful Chinese information-technology (IT) companies have gained global prominence by specializing in specific stages of production and a tighter industrial focus. Furthermore, China, unlike previous NIEs, does not need to master novel-product innovation in order to achieve sustained economic and industrial growth. Last but not least, unlike South Korea, Taiwan, or newer emerging economies such as Vietnam, China has a massive and rapidly growing internal market. It is for this area that China's leading firms have developed their capabilities and produced their strongest second-generation or localized innovations. Although all other Asian NIEs, by necessity, used a development model focused extensively on export-oriented industries, China has become one of the world's largest exporters as well as one the most important markets, and one that is still rapidly growing.

To show that China has been following the "run of the Red Queen" path to development, we analyze the evolution and growth of the Chinese IT industry, utilizing multiple analytical approaches and data sources and relying on extensive fieldwork, including interviews with 209 representative actors in the three industrial regions at the heart of China's IT industry: Beijing, Shanghai, and the Pearl River Delta.[5] These three regions contain the most advanced cities in China and their spheres of influence. They account for 33.5% of China's annual research spending from all sources (NSBPRC 2007), 38.22% of research funding from local and provincial government sources, and 47.5% of China's Internet domains.[6] In addition, the regions around Beijing, Shanghai, and Guangdong province are responsible for 61% of China's high-technology exports.[7] All the top Chinese IT hardware and software companies, as well as all the major foreign multinational corporations, are headquartered in those areas (MOST 2006a, 2006b, 2006c; Y. Zhou 2005; Y. Zhou and Tong 2003).

In addition to being the largest and most globalized high-technology industry worldwide, the IT industry is far and away the most developed and important high-technology industry in China. For example, in 2007, the IT hardware subsector accounted for 94.9% of all high-technology exports (life science and biotechnology accounted for 2.7%, and all other technologies, 2.4%). This means that, with regard to economic growth, *the IT industry is the Chinese high-technology industry,* as can be seen in figures I.1 and I.2 below (NSBPRC 2008b).[8] Furthermore, the IT-hardware subsector accounted for 27.17% of all China's exports in 2006, with revenues of $263.764 billion, making it clear that the IT industry's importance for the Chinese economy is immense (MOST 2008a). Accordingly, an understanding of the IT industry is critical for understanding China's high-technology industries and the economic implications of its industrial-innovation system.

For the leading cities, the importance of the IT industry is even more pronounced than for the country as a whole. In the Pearl River Delta (PRD) city of Shenzhen, 98% of the high-technology exports from the Shenzhen High-Tech Industrial Park (SHIP) are in IT. The park itself accounts for 18% of Shenzhen's total industrial output (SHIP 2003). For Shenzhen as a whole, the manufacturing of communications equipment, computers, and other electronic equipment accounts for 49% of all industrial value-added (SSB 2008). In Beijing, 27.2% of industrial output comes from computers and communications equipment (HKTDC 2007a). In Shanghai, the IT industry accounts for 38.3% of all industrial output (HKTDC 2007b). Furthermore, China's IT industry continues to increase its influence on global markets and research-and-development (R&D) strategies, making China an indispensable link in the global IT-industry chain (*IHT* 2006; OECD 2006; OECD 2007).

By conducting our comparative study in Beijing, Shanghai, and the PRD, we were able to observe three very different regional political-economic-innovation systems operating within the constraints of the overall national one. China's first-tier cities, while successful at generating economic growth, have done so using quite different political, economic, and policy models.

Significantly, the Chinese high-technology development path has been drastically different from the one planned and hoped for by the Chinese central government.[9] The idealized research paradigm set out by the Chinese Communist Party (CCP) and government ministries has been to build a strong, independent innovative capacity.[10] A recent example of the strength of this research paradigm among national policy makers and politicians can be seen in President Hu Jintao's speech to the Seventeenth National Congress of the Chinese Communist Party in October 2007: "[We must] enhance China's capacity for independent innovation and make China an innovative country. This is the core of our national development strategy and a crucial link in enhancing the overall national strength" (Hu 2007b).

We maintain that two of the main threats to the viability of the current Chi-

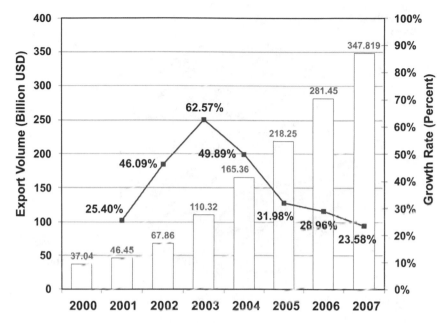

Figure I.1—Chinese Exports of High-Technology Products, 2000–2007
Source: MOST 2008a; NSBPRC 2008b

nese system are the technology security concerns and the political-economic ideology of China's central government, which still views independent mastery of novel-product innovation and new-technology creation as necessary for national wealth and economic security (authors' interviews; Cao et al. 2006; Serger and Breidne 2007). Our fear for China is that by focusing too much on producing novel-product innovation by any means possible, the central government might harm the pillars of China's sustained economic growth. In time, China will come to master novel-product innovation. We argue that instead of forcing itself to conform to foreign models developed over long periods of time within economic systems organized around institutions that are drastically different from its own, China will do significantly better to understand its own path of development when imagining its future (Zysman et al. 2007). Furthermore, we argue that there is no urgency for China to master novel-product innovation—quite the opposite, if the aim is sustained economic growth. This is especially so since the central government's concern for technology security is anachronistic, failing to take into account the economic interdepen-

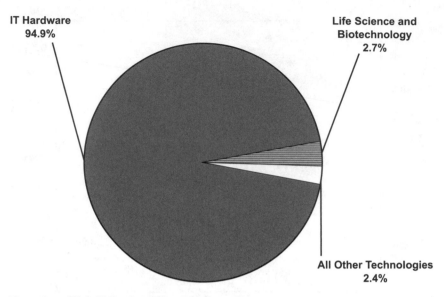

Figure I.2—High-Technology Exports by Sector, 2007
Source: NSBPRC 2008b

dencies established between China and the rest of the world, which have become only more apparent since the financial crisis of 2008.

The realities of China's growth trajectory, and the discrepancies between
state objectives and industrial reality, suggest that an institutional-political-
economic explanation is relevant for understanding China's idiosyncratic, but
highly effective, industrial-innovation strategy.

Our work builds on the argument of Adam Segal in his book *Digital Dragon:
High-Technology Enterprises in China* (2003), which contends that the IT sector of China's economy should not be analyzed as one homogenous economic
entity but rather as a multitude of regional systems. In the same way, Eric
Thun's research (2006) focuses on regional systems in an attempt to explain
the Chinese car industry. Unlike Segal (and later Thun), we argue that, collectively, these regional systems combine to form a unique, de facto *national* innovation system and that without understanding this system and how it interacts with the regional system, we will fail to understand China.[11] A study by
Yu Zhou and others (2010) of the IT industry in Beijing, Shanghai-Suzhou, and
Shenzhen-Dongguan similarly concludes that different regions have strikingly
different industrial structures, path dependences, and capabilities. Understanding how the regions differ in their international and domestic orienta-

tions helps explain their role in China's overall economy and the national capabilities. Furthermore, following the arguments of Shirk (1993), Naughton (1995), Huang (2003), Gutherie (2002), and Steinfeld (2004), we claim, and show in our empirical findings, that China should not be analyzed in the same way as developed, free-market, capitalist national economies because, simply put, it is not free, capitalist, or, as a matter of fact, truly national. In addition, we add to the literature that outlines China's pattern of "playing to the provinces," by arguing that China's specific development pattern, while allowing for regional dynamism in many decentralized policy domains, puts other domains critical for R&D under the direct control of the significantly more conservative and ineffective center.

An underlying assumption of this book is that in the new global system of fragmented production, an increasing percentage of the economic growth generated by novel-product technological innovation is reaped outside the locality in which it originated. Furthermore, building on the work of economists of innovation and growth, we contend that the acts of innovation that translate into economic growth are to be found at least as much in diffusion, application, incremental, organizational, and process innovation as in the development of completely new technologies and products. It is now generally accepted that the international economy is growing ever more global and that production and services are increasingly more modular and diffused. In this light, the argument of this book is that nations can sustain high rates of growth by developing the capability to transform technological innovation into things that are bought and sold, things that improve productivity, or both.

Chapter 1 The White Knight Avoided: Economic Reforms and Innovation for Growth in China

"I've cut off several slices already, but they always join on again!"

"You don't know how to manage Looking-glass cakes," the Unicorn remarked. "Hand it round first, and cut it afterwards."

This sounded nonsense, but Alice very obediently got up and carried the dish round, and the cake divided itself into three pieces as she did so.

"*Now* cut it up," said the Lion, as she returned to her place with the empty dish."

—*Lewis Carroll,* Through the Looking-Glass and What Alice Found There

This book argues that the pattern and trajectory of Chinese development, which we refer to metaphorically as the run of the Red Queen, allow China to develop unique capabilities that, coupled with the vastness of the Chinese market and labor force and its specific sociopolitical and economic institutions, make China a highly advanced, perhaps even the ultimate, workshop of the world. This position, thanks to an impressive array of innovational capabilities and a multitude of competing dynamic regional models within China, not only is sustainable for the medium and long term but also has continually prompted rapid economic growth and new job creation in multiple locations —the exact needs of a huge emerging economy.

For the purposes of this book, we define "sustainability" as the ability of the Chinese economy to continue to grow at a high rate for the next fifteen to twenty years. Sustainable growth does not necessarily mean equitable growth, as recent statistics of income inequality in China attest. But the opportunities afforded to both low-skilled workers (in factories producing electronic or IT hardware) and high-skilled workers (in start-ups and the IT-services industry) will continue to enable millions to rise into the Chinese middle class. Since around six hundred million Chinese still live in poverty, the first order for Chinese economic growth is job creation for the rural and urban masses (Whittaker et al. 2008).

Two questions arise immediately as a consequence of this theory: How did this development path come about? And how deeply is it institutionalized and, hence, not amenable to change? We argue that the Chinese development trajectory is the direct result of the politics, and the sociopolitical structure, of economic growth—specifically, political action that transferred the main loci of reforms from the center to the regions. In addition, we argue that one of the most important institutional features of the Chinese political economy is the consistent presence of what we term "structured uncertainty." As has been argued extensively, and as Chapters Two to Five show to be especially true in the case of science, technology, and innovation policy, China is unique in being persistently uninstitutionalized (Lieberthal 2004). Starting with Mao's obsessive efforts to fight institutionalization, Chinese policy making and implementation have been highly specific and personalized endeavors, a far cry from the routinized, professional, and bureaucratic procedures idealized by Weber (Weber 1952). Since 1976, there has been a significant amount of institutionalization and bureaucratization in the Weberian sense, but for reasons we analyze in Chapter Two, the Chinese system has, in many ways, remained less institutionalized and more ad hoc in its operations than other emerging or developed economies. The degree of structured uncertainty and its impact on the behavior of economic agents remain high. Nonetheless, as China grows, forces that aim to diminish structured uncertainty are on the rise; for example, top Chinese companies that aim to become global leaders, such as Huawei, Zhongxing Telecom (ZTE), and Lenovo, now view predictable policy making and legal enforcement as necessary for their own growth. Therefore, the dynamic of China's own growth is pushing indigenous constituencies to call for greater bureaucratization and regularization.

Consequently, to understand the economic behavior of actors, an institutional account of China must look at not only official institutions, organizations, and procedures, but also the spheres of structured uncertainty. We follow the Northian definition of institutions as formal and informal routinized patterns of behavior (North 1990). Thus, we define structured uncertainty as a part of the institutional system, although a part that prevents its "institutionalization" by ensuring that instead of patterns of behavior becoming routinized, a multiplicity of behaviors can be followed on a specific subject without any of the actors knowing in advance which behaviors are appropriate. In other words, structured uncertainty may be defined as an agreement to disagree about the goals and methods of policy, a condition leading to intrinsic unpredictability and, hence, to inherent ambiguity in implementation. This ambiguity leads to some tolerance of multiple interpretations and implementations of the same policy. Therefore, structured uncertainty is an institutional condition that cements multiplicity of action without legitimizing a specific course or form of behavior as the proper one.

China's capabilities developed as part of the rational reaction of economic actors to the incentives and restraints they faced, both internally and externally. Furthermore, we argue that while politics led to the development of very different regional systems (each of which should be analyzed and compared), thanks to national institutional constraints, none of these systems was ever inclined toward novel-product R&D, nor do they currently stimulate the development of such activities. As these regional systems and capabilities developed, however, they institutionalized an economic system that excels in utilizing and perfecting particular innovational capabilities in the production and adaptation of products and technologies developed elsewhere. The result, we contend, is that it would be quite difficult to change the trajectory of industrial R&D in China without detrimental economic consequences.[1]

Indeed, if there is a risk for the sustainability of the Chinese Red Queen model, it is the fixation of the central government on achieving technological independence at whatever cost. As stated by Liu Xielin of the Chinese Academy of Sciences concerning the government's goals in planning innovation and pushing novel-product research: "The most important factors behind the [five-year] plan are not market performance, but the breaking up the monopoly of multinationals and strengthening national security" (Liu 2006, 7). The current Chinese technology-standards policy shows both the perils and the limits of such attempts to plan innovation by the central government. A case in point was the attempted imposition of the Wireless Local Area Network Authentication and Privacy Infrastructure (WAPI) standard for wireless local area networks (LANs), which ended in failure; related to this is the heightened suspicion with which MNCs and foreign governments now view China's technology policies (authors' interviews; Kennedy 2006; Naughton and Segal 2003). As we discuss in detail in the conclusion, a much more prudent innovation policy should build on China's already impressive innovative capabilities and its power within the interdependent system of globally fragmented production.

For the remainder of this chapter, we briefly elaborate on our thesis, engaging with the literature and our empirical findings. We begin by positioning our argument within the growing literature on economic growth and innovation in a globalizing world. We then focus our attention solely on China, describing both our analysis of the current Chinese industrial innovation system and our political-economic view of how this system has developed and is sustained.

ECONOMIC GROWTH AND INNOVATION IN
A WORLD OF GLOBAL DECOMPOSITION

Since the late 1980s, scholars of economic growth have revived an old interest: the role played by R&D and industrial innovation in enhancing the long-run performance of the economy (Aghion and Howitt 1992; Baumol 2002; Edquist 1997; Helpman 1998; Helpman and Trajtenberg 1998; Lundvall 1992; Lundvall et al. 2002; Mowery and Rosenberg 1991; Nelson 1993; Romer 1990; Rosenberg 1983; Rosenberg and Birdzell 1986). Worldwide, politicians and policy makers lust after innovation, believing it to be the key to resolving all economic-development issues. R&D, along with the commercial innovations it generates, has been proclaimed the ultimate solution to every economic malady in both mature and emerging economies. This is a fascinating development, since for many years, technology was seen as an exogenous factor in economic theory (Solow 1956), and only a few renowned economists, such as Schumpeter, saw it as the main source of long-term economic growth (Schumpeter 1961).

It is now clear that technological development is the primary source of sustained economic development. However, under the conditions of intensified economic globalization and the fragmentation of production, it is no longer clear to what degree the economic-growth benefits of innovation remain within the locality of its origin. Hence, it is an open question as to where the sweet spot of economic growth lies on the long chain of innovation, from the creation of new technologies on one end, to changes in the organization of production and delivery on the other.

Policy makers often combine Schumpeter's insight that innovation and entrepreneurship are the main impetuses for long-term economic growth with Arrow's claim that inherent market failures lead firms to underinvest in R&D (Arrow 1962). Using this analysis, policy makers conclude that the government should play a substantial role in supporting the innovation creation process. But when policy makers place unconditional trust in the benefits generated by R&D investments, they commit the crucial logical fault of thinking that R&D focused primarily on new technologies automatically leads to innovation, which will, in turn, immediately translate into economic growth. Schumpeter himself pointed out that economic growth occurs only when entrepreneurs adapt inventions either to build new industries and improve the efficiency of the production process or to enhance the quality of existing products or services (Schumpeter 1961). Therefore, the process of the adoption of a new technology or using it as a way to create new industries is as important to economic growth as inventing it (Rosenberg 1983). This finer understanding of the mechanisms by which innovation leads to economic growth is a distinction often missing from current discussions about innovation.

In addition, in the last few decades, the world has witnessed a vast and accelerating increase in the fragmentation (also called decomposition, unbundling, or modularization) of productive activities. This means that the production of goods and services is no longer organized in vertically integrated hierarchical companies located in one country. Corporations increasingly break their activities into smaller, discrete modules and outsource or offshore them (Arndt and Kierzkowski 2001; Dossani and Kenney 2003; Gereffi et al. 2005; Gourevitch 2000; Kenney and Florida 2004; Sturgeon 2002, 2003). This process of fragmentation has changed the international economic system, leading different regions to specialize in specific stages of production for particular industries (Baldwin and Clark 1997, 2000; Berger 2006; Breznitz 2007b; Brown and Linden 2005; Ernst 2005; Fuller et al. 2003; Langlois 2002; Langlois and Robertson 1992; Linden et al. 2004; Sturgeon 2001, 2003; Sturgeon and Florida 2004; Sturgeon and Lester 2004; Zysman et al. 2007). Today, this spatial specialization in particular stages of production has led to an increased international interfirm (not just intrafirm) trade in components and services. Within the electronics industry, for example, there has been a major transformation in the way final products are manufactured and sold. Apple has never engaged directly in the production of its two most successful recent products, the iPod and iPhone.

Indeed, most of the design for the iPod, the iPhone, and the MacBook Air was bought as an outsourced service (Dedrick et al. 2008). Similarly, leading companies such as Dell, Sun, Cisco, and Microsoft's Xbox division do not have their own manufacturing facilities, but concentrate instead on R&D, high-level product design, sales, marketing, and, at most, final assembly. The rapid economic growth of India, based on its rise to prominence as a software and outsourced services hub, is a case in point (Dossani and Kenney 2007). Indeed, even components and subcomponents, such as hard-drives, are now manufactured in discrete stages in different locations around the world (Gourevitch 2000; Kenney and Florida 2004; McKendrick et al. 2000; Sturgeon 2000, 2003).[2]

These processes of fragmentation and regional specialization in different modes of innovation began as a result of changing cost structures, enabling technologies (such as information technology), and the opening of the international trade system. Once started, these processes become positively self-reinforcing because of the internal dynamics of modularization. The causes of these self-reinforcing dynamics are "production/service-stage economies of scope and scale" and "production/service-stage specialization and capability building" (Breznitz 2007b; Sturgeon 2002, 2003). These two dynamics are the main reasons for the rapid global decomposition of economic activities. Thus, understanding them is crucial to comprehending why the Chinese "run of the Red Queen" development path will be resilient for the long term.

"Production-stage economies of scale and scope" refers to the effect in which suppliers at each stage of a decomposed production chain pool the demand of many customers, creating economies of scope and scale that in-house divisions cannot (Breznitz 2007b). These economies of scope and scale enable suppliers to become more efficient and allow them to profitably operate on margins that are significantly lower than those achieved by in-house manufacturing divisions. This cost advantage allows them to lower their prices while offering products of the same or higher quality, additionally speeding the trend toward outsourcing of this stage's manufacturing or service-provision activities (Sturgeon 2000, 2002). The most famous example for such a scale and scope operation in China is Foxconn's 270,000-worker complex in the Bao'an District of Shenzhen in the Pearl River Delta, where the iPhone, iPod, and various Intel, Dell, Motorola, and Sony products are made (Dean 2007). Foxconn is one of Taiwan's largest private companies and the largest high-tech exporter in China. Apart from its gargantuan operation in Shenzhen, Foxconn employs another 200,000 workers at other sites in China. Foxconn's business strategy is built around the unique capabilities of the Chinese IT industry. For its development and operations in mainland China, Taiwanese ownership matters much less than the capabilities existing and developed in China that are not easily transferable. Accordingly, Foxconn is also a perfect example of how the particular innovational capabilities of China have made it a critical part of the global IT industry. While American companies formerly had the organizational and innovational capabilities to run such large-scale operations, even in its heyday the American production system was focused on mass production and could not flexibly produce such an array of products in the same place on the same production lines. Currently, capabilities of ultra mass-flexible production are unique to China.[3]

"Production-stage specialization" is the process by which companies develop superior capabilities in particular stages or components of the product or service network in response to product or service decomposition (Breznitz 2007b). Recent examples of this in the IT industry are Indian IT software consultancies such as TATA, Wipro, and HCL, which are by far the most efficient IT consultancies in the world, basing their competitive position on unique capabilities and tools they developed in project management (Arora and Gambardella 2005; Arora et al. 2001; Arora and Athreye 2002; D'Costa and Sridharan 2004). Such specialization enables companies to become better and more efficient in a narrow set of activities. It also helps them acquire specialized capabilities and knowledge that more vertically integrated firms cannot acquire. These capabilities, once acquired, enable firms to excel in innovation regarding the particular production or service stages and sets of components in which they specialize. Over time, these two related advantages, in skills and in innovation capabilities, provide these companies with even more advantages over the in-house divisions of vertically integrated companies. We observe this process in high-technology areas—for example, in software development or the manufacturing of specialized components such as graphic cards or memory chips —and in more traditional industries, such as bicycle companies, where product-chain fragmentation allowed one company, Shimano, to become the innovator and market leader in drive-train components (Galvin and Morkel 2001).

This, in turn, means that firms and countries need different modes of innovation in order to thrive in different stages of production. Furthermore, once a country starts to develop innovational capabilities that allow it to excel in a certain stage of production, a process of self-reinforcing sequences will then significantly increase the probability that its national industry will follow a particular trajectory of growth that utilizes these capabilities. This creates a situation of interdependency among firms that constitute global production networks, each set of which has unique innovational capabilities in some stages of production but not in others. Consequently, different nations can achieve rapid and sustainable growth by focusing their innovational activities on particular stages of production and thereby supplying unique outputs and services to global markets (Breznitz 2007b).[4] In addition, it is becoming apparent that each of these modes of innovation correlates not only with countries' retaining different fractions of the overall economic growth benefits of innovation, but also with different distribution of the fruits of growth within each society.

Certain innovative activities yield a widespread distribution of wealth, while others tend to concentrate it. In a former book, one of us showed that countries with apparently similar initial conditions of average income, educational attainment, and innovation capacity followed strikingly different yet successful industrial-innovation and entrepreneurship policies, each of which led to different outcomes in economic growth and wealth distribution (Breznitz 2007b). For instance, Israel chose to promote frontier technologies, but by and large neglected the creation of the institutional arrangements necessary for their dissemination throughout the domestic economy (Avnimelech and Teubal 2004, 2006; Breznitz 2005c, 2006, 2007a; Teubal 1983; Trajtenberg 2001). At the same time, Taiwan thought it best to draw upon novel technologies developed elsewhere in order to improve the production process or enhance the design of existing products (Amsden and Chu 2003; Berger and Lester 2005; Breznitz 2005a, 2005b; Cheng 1990; Fields 1995; Fuller 2007; Fuller et al. 2003; S. Hong 1997; Mathews and Cho 2000; Meany 1994; Park 2000). Today, Israel suffers from rapidly growing inequality and a widening gap between the few successful R&D-producing sectors and the rest of the economy, while Taiwan faces challenges relating to its novel-products innovational capacity (Breznitz 2007b).

Furthermore, and crucial to the story of China, this changed model of globalized production creates new dependencies between countries and industries. China's rise to prominence in the IT industry has been due, in large part, to the new opportunities in specific stages of production opened by the fragmentation of the IT industry. However, China's excelling in these stages has not only transformed China into a critical part of the global production networks of the IT industry, but has also created a new mutual dependency. On the one hand, the Chinese IT industry needs foreign novel-product-innovating companies to keep producing in China. On the other hand, foreign companies completely rely on Chinese companies to produce their novel products, a capability they no longer (or never did) possess. China needed Apple to develop the concept and definition of the iPod and the iPhone, but Apple cannot produce and sell these products without China. In the world of flexible mass production, the Red Queen country needs the novel-product innovators to keep churning out new ideas, and the novel-product-innovating countries need the Red Queen country to keep innovating on almost every aspect of production and delivery.

For these reasons, it is rather peculiar that most accounts of China presume that it must advance toward only one mode of innovation—new-technology development leading to the creation of new products and services—if it wants to ensure sustainable economic growth. For example, Porter and his coauthors (2009) give the most optimistic outlook on China, arguing, based on a rather specific reading of the data, that China may have already become the world's leading technology-based economy. Segal (2003), in his quest to look for a "Silicon Valley" in China, finds that, while some cities are more innovative than others, the educational, R&D, and entrepreneurial environment in Beijing ensure that China's capital will come to resemble Silicon Valley. S. H. Chen (2006) notes that China's national, Soviet-style research infrastructure enables it to excel at blue-sky research and innovation, offering the possibility of escaping the low-value-added trap that afflicts Taiwan (see also Chen and Chen 2006). Zhou and Tong (2003) note that the presence of foreign MNCs in China and their increasing R&D activities mean that China's enterprises are increasingly forced to innovate and compete on quality as well as price. Ernst and Naughton (2007), even more optimistic, argue that the IT industry is firmly on the road to ever more successful innovation and growth.

On the pessimistic side, scholars such as Cong Cao (2004) note that even in Beijing, the innovative bona fides of China are highly overstated, contending that China is doomed to remain mostly an assembler and processor of foreign technologies, forever trapped in lowest value-added activities. Looking at the evolution of global production networks in China, Steinfeld (2004) reaches a similarly bleak prediction. Finally, researchers for the Organization for Economic Cooperation and Development (OECD) concluded that while the Chinese IT industry is enormous, it is not innovative in terms of novel-product creation, remains dependent on imported high-value components, and is fully controlled by foreign MNCs, even in China's most advanced regions (OECD 2006).

We find this debate to miss the point. The question of whether China is as innovative in the creation of new technologies and products as Silicon Valley, while interesting, is specious regarding the question of how to sustain growth through innovation. We contend it is much more important to realize that within the new, fragmented international economic system, China has developed a remarkably profitable and sustainable model of innovation. This model makes China into a critical part of the world innovation system, but it does not rely on China excelling in cutting-edge novel-product R&D. However, we should quickly assert that this model, which was developed by trial and error based experimentation, is drastically different from the outcome envisioned by China's national planners, who have long intended to develop China into an independent and technologically advanced power. This desire arose initially in response to China's backwardness at the end of the Mao era and out of fear of military inferiority in the information age (authors' interviews). Despite repeated programs and investment by centrally directed research organs, China's high-technology industry has mostly emerged as a result of trial and error by local authorities and the enterprises themselves.[5] In time, China may yet develop novel-product innovation capabilities as institutional reforms address some of the central government-created obstructions to novel-product innovations we outline in Chapter Two. However, the question for Chinese policy makers should be how to develop such capabilities by building on, but not destroying, the highly successful "Red Queen run" innovation model it has hitherto utilized.

China's model of innovation, we argue, builds on its comparative advantages, operates under both internal and external competitive pressures that keep it extremely dynamic and resilient, and has made China into a critical location of international economic activity. Furthermore, policy choices in China have given its industry particular innovational capabilities, and because of the difficulty (even unlikelihood) of other countries' replicating these circumstances, those capabilities should be sustainable in the medium and long term. Unlike India or even Taiwan, China has used its size and the depth of its talent to specialize in many IT sectors at stages of production ranging from relatively high-level design through manufacturing, components assembly, trade, and logistics. This breadth of activity further strengthens China's hand in the global economy and enhances the benefits that accrue to China, regardless of where cutting-edge innovations are initially developed. In addition, the diverse regional strengths of China ensure that even if one of its regional systems suffers a downturn, China as a whole will continue to flourish. Hence, from the national point of view, the multitude of competing regional models should also be seen as conferring on the country the added benefits of redundancy and robustness.

Thus, it is evident that the lessons China offers to political leaders concerned with the development and welfare of their people is that seeking novel-product innovation is not the only highly successful strategy. Following the path of the Red Queen enables a country like China to achieve significant economic growth benefits from innovation activities, create a large number of new jobs, and simultaneously avoid taking the high risks necessary to thrive at the cutting edge. Such a model might be highly attractive to policy makers concerned with national welfare but not wedded to the de rigueur techno-fetishism of novelty in the West.

THE POLITICS OF CHINESE REFORM

Politics and its unintended consequences are the root cause of the particular form and trajectory of China's economic miracle. The institutions that govern China's economy, and the political battles that fashioned its evolutionary change, both stimulate and constrain the opportunities available to entrepreneurs and companies. Accordingly, China's miracle is not a story of a developmental state carefully orchestrating its industrial development; rather, it is a story of trial-and-error economic experimentation led by subnational entities but fashioned by political contestations between conservatives and reformers at the center, between influence-wielding interest groups within the Chinese Communist Party (CCP), and between the center and the provinces. These political debates informed the growth of the IT industry and have in turn been shaped by it. China's Red Queen run is, in essence, a story of political institutions and spheres of uncertainty shaping and enabling growth, facilitating certain types of innovation and R&D behavior, inhibiting others, and being shaped via a feedback loop by the particular economic changes they initiated.

We contend that the particular process of reform in China, within which the most extensive experimentation was delegated to the provincial level while the center stayed far more cautious, led to two sets of institutions that affect the behavior of Chinese economic actors. The first is the set of central government institutions that govern the national economy, specifically those presiding over the transition to China's current semicapitalist market economy. These institutions have been far less reform oriented than their counterparts at the provincial level.[6] Crucial among these national institutions are those that regulate property rights and other rights, as well as those that oversee critical infrastructure, education, and the science-and-technology (S&T) research infrastructure. It is these institutions that create the national framework within which China's local economies operate. As we will show in detail in Chapters Two to Five, one of the main impacts of these national institutions is to reduce long-term risk taking in both large and small companies, including both "protected" state-owned conglomerates and private companies. Consequently, national policies limit the development of new technology, one of the most high-risk economic activities undertaken by either public or private economic actors.

The second set of institutions includes those that effectively separated China into a series of regional economic fiefdoms, which both fiercely compete and cooperate with one another and with the center. This dynamic, in which each region develops a unique set of capacities, enables China to dominate at many stages of the fragmented global economy yet inhibits businesses and entrepreneurs from engaging in cutting-edge, and highly risky, novel-technology and products development. Thus, the dual-track nature of reform in China has had considerable impact on the particular development trajectory of its industries.

Last but not least, we argue that because of the political rationale of action in China, the dynamic development of these institutions occurred within a system imbued with structured uncertainty. Furthermore, as we explain in Chapter Two, while regions were given leeway to independently interpret reforms, the actual boundaries of these reforms and the institutions needed to implement and oversee such reforms were still fully controlled by the center, further installing structured uncertainty throughout the Chinese economy and in state-industry interactions. Hence, an institutional analysis of China, besides investigating institutions, policies, industries, and their coevolutionary development, must take into account the fact that high-level structured uncertainty in China ensures that a multitude of behavioral patterns will be followed in each particular domain, with none fully gaining legitimacy. Thus, to understand the development of the IT industry in China, we need to understand the formal and informal institutional environment, and the ways in which political battles around policy are settled, the spheres of "un-institutionalization," and the encompassing impact of structured uncertainty on the regions and the center.

We can see that the particular process of economic reform in China evolved as a result of political necessity. After the chaos of the Cultural Revolution, China's national leaders enacted policies designed to stimulate the growth of the national economy and shore up the legitimacy of CCP rule. These policies were intended to carry out the "Four Modernizations" in the areas of agriculture, industry, science and technology, and national defense.[7] As the first delegations of CCP leaders ventured abroad in the late 1970s, they became acutely aware of China's economic and technological backwardness. Convinced that China would not be able to become a technological and economic superpower by autarkic means, China's leaders opted to open the economy selectively through centralized policies. Channeled through existing political and economic institutions, these selective openings had the unintended consequence of fragmenting the national economy and the policy apparatus, decreasing the authority of the center. The result was the creation of a network of national institutions that constrain the ability of the center to govern the economy but also limit the choices available to entrepreneurs. These national institutions shape the market environment in which entrepreneurs operate and strongly influence their behavior.

DYNAMISM AT THE LOCAL LEVEL: REGIONALISM AND ITS INFLUENCE ON THE IT INDUSTRY

The institutions that have shaped the regional development trajectory of the IT industry—and, collectively, of China's economy as a whole—slowly developed through a process shaped by the institutional legacy of a "flexible state," local planning from the Mao era and the province-specific and piecemeal nature of reforms begun during Deng's era, coupled with the continued inability of the national government to implement its will at the local level (Zhu 2010). The central government pragmatically allowed regions to experiment with new economic structures and incentive systems but did not grant complete autonomy. The central government has, as discussed below, also retained the mechanisms necessary to influence or constrain regional authorities. Its interest in commanding the heights of the economy and critical domains such as high-technology development has increased in recent years as well. This conflict between pragmatic opening and a desire to retain control has played a major role in shaping the capabilities of China's enterprises and the policies of the regions where they are located.

As explored by Shirk (1993), Oi (1992, 1995, 1999), N. Lin (1995), Y.-L. Liu (1992), and Bachman (2001), the central leadership during Mao's later years continually expanded the role of local economic officials in planning the economy and implementing economic policies at the expense of centralized control. In practice, by the end of the 1960s, the center provided general directives for all but the largest strategic enterprises and left the provincial authorities to determine how to carry them out.[8] The result was that by 1977–1978, central planners allocated goods and revenues for only 50%–55% of industrial output. By 1980, only 3% of China's state-owned factories were directly administered by the industrial ministries of the central government (Shirk 1993). While the largest enterprises remained under central control, the vast majority of the industrial economy was now locally or provincially planned and managed. It is also important to note that in the Chinese system, the ranking and terminology of bureaucratic and political power is different from that used in Western systems. In the Chinese system, top provincial officials and national ministers have equal rank. Hence the head of a national ministry, such as the Ministry of Science and Technology, has no direct authority over provincial governors. Furthermore since some governors are also members of the Politburo, being national ministers does not guarantee that they have top authority even in their areas of responsibility.[9]

Scholars studying the emergence of China as an economic power since the 1980s have attributed much of its success to the decentralization of economic decision making, namely, the center allowing market forces a greater role in the allocation of goods (Chien 2007; Montinola et al. 1995; Naughton 1995; Qian and Weingast 1996; Shirk 1993; Weingast 1995; Xu and Zhuang 1998). Building upon the legacy of local planning from the Mao era, reformers gradually increased the authority of local officials, albeit in a piecemeal manner, to experiment, approve projects, and seek foreign investment. The impact of decentralization varied widely: some regions boomed, but others fell behind or adopted unsuccessful policies (Solinger 1996; Thun 2004). It should be noted, however, that not all scholars agree that decentralization was the cause of economic growth, attributing it instead to factional competition at the center in which rival officials sponsored growth in different regions to prove the correctness of their ideas (Cai and Treisman 2006).

Decentralization of authority took on several critical forms that would greatly impact the development of the IT industry in China. One of the first reforms under Deng, in 1980, was to permit localities to retain a portion of their revenues (Jin et al. 1999; Montinola et al. 1995; Oi 1992, 1999). Here it is important to point out, for readers more accustomed to Western terminology, that revenue sharing in the Chinese system refers to profits from locally run state-owned enterprises (SOE) in addition to locally collected national taxes. In essence, the fiscal reforms should be seen as a transfer of partial (or full) property rights from the center to the provinces. Local governments, while not always permitted to sell their stakes in companies and privatize them (although, in many cases, local governments have divested themselves from companies they took over in the 1980s), took full operational control over the enterprises. The rationale was that this would give local officials (as owners) strong incentives to run their companies more profitably and engage in large-scale entrepreneurial activities. The ability to retain local revenues within the local economy prompted cadres to become increasingly concerned with local development and the strength of local enterprises, especially since their advancement in the CCP was mostly locally controlled. This led to a deep fragmentation of the Chinese economy into competing economic blocks. As one region gained certain economic advantages or freedoms from the center and proceeded to grow rapidly, others soon clamored for similar rights for fear of being left behind.[10]

A second important impact on local institutions came from the fragmented and piecemeal nature of the reform process in the 1980s. As described in detail by many scholars, the 1980s were a story of gradually increasing economic or market freedoms in different localities (Naughton 1995, 2007; Qian 2003; Qian and Weingast 1996; Shirk 1993; Solinger 1996). The time at which a region received permission to begin certain market activities greatly shaped the form its high-technology economy would later take (Segal 2003; Solinger 1996; Thun 2004). The differing degrees of freedom given to the major regions, particularly the Pearl River Delta, Shanghai, and Beijing, also shaped their institutional evolution. This process, in which each region started its evolution at a different time under different regulations and with different endowments, critically affected the patterns of investment and the types of companies and R&D activities conducted in each region. However, one would do well to remember that, while these influences were critical in setting the terms for the initial political-economic debate and policy formation in each region, these debates, policy formulations, and industrial-development dynamics are very much alive today as politics continues to shape the particular trajectory of each province.

Furthermore, private companies were not legally recognized in China until relatively recently, and, hence, many companies were directly owned and managed by various local and provincial bureaucracies (Montinola et al. 1995; Naughton 2007; Oi 1995, 1999; Qian 2003; Walder 1995). For these reasons, many IT entrepreneurs needed to form a legal relationship with an administrative unit, and this arrangement gave the provinces, which were responsible for implementing the reform, great leeway to influence their industry's development. As Segal (2003) has noted, even after noncollective enterprises were no longer explicitly outlawed, it was up to the provinces to profit from this ambiguousness by crafting specific policies to stimulate high-technology growth.

As localities became directly responsible for their own revenues, and as their leaders increasingly had the chance to become personally wealthy, many of them became increasingly competitive and pursued their own parochial interests, largely independent of national ones (Chien 2007; Jin et al. 1999).[11] The result has been the creation of strongly policy-innovative and fiercely competitive regions within China. This forced many Chinese companies to think and act locally and offered foreign MNCs the ability to play one region off against another in order to secure the most favorable deal as local government officials competed to attract the largest number of foreign-investment projects in order to advance their own careers.

Career advancement in the Chinese bureaucracy usually happens solely within the same organization; only the top elites move among agencies and provinces. Out of a few million Chinese civil servants, only a few thousand cadre positions are selected through the central *nomenklatura* system, and the rest serve (and advance) solely within one organization.[12] As a result, the provincial political economies are strongly autonomous. Since cadres are promoted locally, their interests are best furthered by satisfying the desires of their local constituencies and superiors, not necessarily those of the central government.[13] Indeed, the central government expects bureaucrats to advance the interests of their own agencies (Lieberthal and Oksenberg 1988; Shirk 1993), and this ensures that local economic growth, job creation, and stability are of primary importance to any ambitious civil servant. In addition, on the national level, provincial government leaders are judged by the CCP's top leadership mostly on the economic growth of their regions. These achievements are measured by revenue and job growth. As recently as October 2007, President Hu Jintao, in his report to the Seventeenth National Congress of the Chinese Communist Party, reaffirmed the core principles of his administration and the mission of the CCP and government: "We must regard development as the top priority of the Party in governing and rejuvenating the country . . . We must firmly commit ourselves to the central task of economic development, concentrate on construction and developing the productive forces" (Hu 2007c).[14] Furthermore, Hu's second social-development objective for improving people's livelihoods addressed the specific question of employment: "Implement a development strategy that promotes job creation and encourage entrepreneurship to create more employment opportunities" (Hu 2007a).[15]

Even national-level S&T development zones, such as Zhongguancun, Zhangjiang, and the Shenzhen High-Tech Industrial Park, have effectively become local-government projects and the centers of local economic-development strategies. National plans are commonly disregarded in the interest of fostering the most rapid local development. Collectively, this leads to the creation of semiautonomous regional economies whose emphases, outlooks, planning, and behavior are explicitly local. Since these regions are the pillars on which national plans are supposed to be built, the result is that national plans remain mostly on paper.

National policies created diverse regional economic and innovation systems, but these regional innovation systems have not created identical regions. Beijing, Shanghai, and the Pearl River Delta, while subjected to the same decentralizing efforts, have developed very different industrial structures and innovational capabilities. And they continue to interact with, and be influenced by, the central authorities. Together, these three regions form the core of the Chinese national innovation system, accounting for the variety of innovational capabilities necessary to sustain its success and promote further growth. Each has built on the capabilities it inherited from the planned economy and adapted its skills to meet the desires of local planners and foreign and domestic customers. Like the Looking-glass cake that cannot be cut without joining back together, these three regions are distinct yet part of an inseparable whole. Indeed, their differences and unique capabilities can be fully appreciated only when viewed as part of the whole Chinese IT industry and innovation system.

We found Beijing to be a city of start-ups, state research labs, and R&D-based enterprises, both foreign and domestic. Government policy has pushed the city to deindustrialize, forcing companies either to adopt a services-only product line or to outsource production, most often to the Pearl River Delta. Beijing has built its IT enterprises upon the strongest human resources and educational resources in the country, but its ability to innovate and sustain novel businesses or research endeavors is constrained by a "unitist" culture that inhibits cooperation. Of the three regions, Beijing is the most strongly influenced by changes in central-government plans and interests. Enterprises here must carefully manage their relationships with the central government to ensure they are close to and cooperative with, but not captured by, the center. Beijing's R&D-intensive business models rely on the production prowess of the other two regions, and this makes Beijing a guiding force in the types of new ventures launched across China.

Shanghai has built a large-scale industrial structure of huge enterprises, state conglomerates, and foreign investment by using its existing industrial structure and foreign direct investment (FDI) as well as generous funds from the local government invested through locally owned state companies. The industries in which Shanghai excels, such as the production of integrated circuits, enable other regions to design circuits or to produce the hardware that uses them, at low costs that would be impossible to achieve without Shanghai. Shanghai also has a wealth of human resources, both through its university system and by attracting talent from abroad. However, the advantages arising from a concentration of educated workers and clustered overseas start-ups are muted by the purposeful dispersion of university campuses and industrial zones far from the urban core. Enterprises in the city are subject to an activist local planning authority that attempts to force small and large enterprises to conform to a planned vision for the city's development. This has restricted the impact of market forces and made the city function much like a developmental state. However, governmental plans do not necessarily accord with the actual needs of the city, a fact that has resulted in high unemployment and disillusionment among many educated youths.

Finally, the Pearl River Delta built its regional innovation and industrial system seemingly out of nothing. Since it lacked a large existing industrial base or an educational and research infrastructure, the region utilized investment from Hong Kong and overseas Chinese to build export-oriented production facilities. At the same time, local entrepreneurs used this industrial base to set up companies oriented toward the domestic market, conquering China's hinterlands with rugged low-cost technologies. Successful firms today continue to rely on a joint strategy. They market their own brands domestically and perform outsourcing or contract manufacturing for foreign customers on the global market. The clustering of related enterprises has made the PRD's industrial structure resilient in the face of rising costs and has increasingly enabled Chinese companies in Beijing and Shanghai to keep nearly the whole of their production chains, from design through logistics, within China. The PRD is the base upon which all other IT industry models in China are built.

CAUTION AT THE CENTER: STRUCTURES OF POLICY MAKING AND THEIR INFLUENCE ON THE IT INDUSTRY

While the process of reform was both dynamic and diverse regionally, in the domains that stayed under national control, reforms have been slower, less encompassing, and more overtly nationalistic. Political battles and the nature of policy reforms at the central level have impeded reforms. While policy reforms in most Western economies happen at the level of the ministry or agency, policy change in China requires that whole ministries and agencies be created or demoted (L. Chen 2005; Xia 2007b).[16] Furthermore, since open politics and elections are not avenues to advancement, policy reform is one of the key ways in which ambitious and entrepreneurial politicians advance their careers (authors' interviews; Shirk 1993). Hence, not only is the bureaucratic structure itself in constant flux, which makes it extremely difficult to concentrate the skills, knowledge, responsibility, authority, and power needed to implement reforms on the enormous national scale that is China, but these agencies and policies are also deeply tied to the personal fortunes of particular politicians (authors' interviews; L. Chen 2005; Xia 2007b). In addition, as noted above, even when a specific policy initiative is institutionalized in the form of a new ministry or agency, that ministry has no direct authority over the provinces.

The process of national policy formulation in China has improved, becoming more transparent and somewhat less arbitrary as more people have become involved in making it. However, many of the policy-mechanism shortcomings that plagued China in the past remain in effect, specifically the almost complete intermeshing of politics and policy (L. Chen 2008). This is especially true in the case of S&T industrial-policy development, which has been a top government priority since 1978. For example, in her study of the government's strategic plans to develop the semiconductor industry, Chen Ling found that these plans were particularly plagued by uncertainty and that the means of achieving an integrated and effective policy process in this arena has yet to be found (L. Chen 2005).[17]

Many scholars of the developmental state have emphasized the importance of a nodal, or pilot, agency that orchestrates industrial development.[18] The bureaucratic reality in China is as far removed from this ideal type as it can be while still being somewhat effective at promoting development. Thus, even with rapidly expanding R&D expenditure (see figure 1.1), the central government's push for more novel-product innovation has been less than effective.

There is no single central developmental agency in China that formulates or influences institutional changes in R&D policy. It is therefore best to look at the economic impact of the relevant institutions rather than their organizational power. The national institutions that matter most for industrial R&D activities are those that oversee property and social rights, the financial system, and education and research. Each will be considered below.

Much has been written about the importance of clearly defined property rights and social freedoms in fostering the development of a high-technology economy.[19] Indeed, in China, the lack of clearly defined property rights greatly

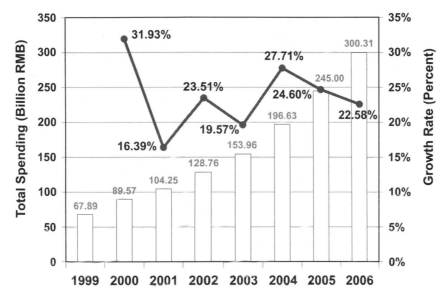

Figure 1.1—R&D Spending in China, 1999–2006
Source: MOST 2006c, 2008a

constrains the actions of the private economy and encourages a concentration on short-term time horizons. For example, until October 2007, China did not explicitly guarantee property rights to private entrepreneurs, homeowners, and businesses, leading many businesses to construct complex public-private or foreign joint ventures in order to legally conduct business. During our interviews, we found that many Chinese IT companies hailed as "ideal examples" of private entrepreneurship actually consist of a portfolio of many different kinds of companies in various localities, using different ownership structures to allow them to enter into certain deals and gain certain benefits in different markets or with the government. Indeed, many publicly listed IT companies have various state agencies or government holding companies as major stockholders, arrangements that emphasize the great influence that politics still has on the development of the IT industry in China.[20] This state of affairs, which requires entrepreneurs to spend significant resources and valuable time on managing their ambiguous ownership status and political relations, has been detrimental to high-risk and novel-product R&D. It has, however, enabled enterprises that adapt to the system to excel in second-generation innovation and business activities that generate short-term gains.

Since the 1990s, China's central government has belatedly taken steps to formalize property rights and enforce intellectual property rights (IPR). While some reforms, such as the Antimonopoly Law, were widely perceived as antiforeign and protectionist, others, such as the official sanctioning of private property in 2007, signaled a gradual decrease in structured uncertainty for private businesses. A perfect example of China's long-term blurred view of IPR can be seen in the experience of Baidu, the dominant Chinese search engine. Baidu owes its meteoric rise as China's most popular search engine not only to its quite impressive Chinese-language search technology but also to the fact that it offered users the ability to find and download musical files for free (this function was removed in January 2008). As with other areas of the IT industry, once Baidu began to reach abroad—in this case, into the Japanese market— and to achieve a certain critical mass as a company, the rules and regulations regarding its behavior moved more in line with established international practice.

The question of IPR is especially in flux with the recent wave of China-based standards, which have been written for almost every part of the IT industry, down to the level of mobile-battery design. These regulatory developments, together with changes in the high-technology certification system done specifically to foster "indigenous innovation" (自主创新), further raise questions about the commitment of China's national leaders to an open market economy.[21] In keeping with Arrow's analysis of the suboptimal resource allocation to R&D under free-market conditions, such legal uncertainty, which further decreases appropriability—specifically, many of the IT entrepreneurs we interviewed were not sure how much of the fruits of their success they would be allowed to retain in the future—limits the ability of firms to take long-term risks and forces firms and entrepreneurs to focus on short-term gains and profits (Arrow 1962). In such an environment, rational economic actors refrain from committing to extensive, cutting-edge R&D, which is deemed both high risk and long term.

Diminished social rights regarding freedom of movement and residence also constrain the development of certain capabilities in the IT industry, since they deter the movement of talent around China. Of particular importance is the household registration system, or *hukou* (戸口).[22] The hukou system organizes all Chinese citizens on the basis of their ancestral hometowns. Hukou affects employability as well as access to education (for oneself and one's children), social services, and a passport or permission to travel. In repeated interviews, engineers listed hukou as the primary influence on their choice among employment options. Cities impose different degrees of difficulty on those applying for a change of hukou and use it as part of their industrial policy. In Beijing and Shanghai, only the largest and best-connected companies can offer a change of hukou, putting new and more innovative start-ups at a disadvantage. In the PRD, the rules are specifically far more lax as part of a targeted policy to attract educated talent to the region.

China's national financial institutions have significant influence on the kinds of companies that can secure capital. China's banks remain state owned, and the laws defining the stock markets have only recently begun to open avenues of financial exit for venture capital (VC), and even those avenues are reduced by the lack of merger-and-acquisition (M&A) markets. One of the main reasons for the weak M&A market is that even after establishing "technology-oriented" boards on the stock exchanges of Shanghai and Shenzhen, government regulations made it illegal for companies to use stock to buy other companies, considerably lowering the number of acquisitions of Chinese IT companies by other Chinese companies. Second, a recent backlash against the foreign acquisition of Chinese companies has also significantly slowed the development of a thriving M&A market in China.

A recent example of such intervention by the Chinese central government is its decision to block the acquisition of the Xuzhou Construction Machinery Group Company by Caterpillar. The logic for blocking the acquisition was that China could not afford to lose the fruits of its own investment in engineering R&D to foreign powers. While the impact of these actions on the independence of indigenous industry is still undetermined, it is clear that for venture capitalists, the utilization of M&A as an instrument of financial exit is of limited use.

These feelings of techno-nationalism run deep. One of the most vivid examples we encountered in our research occurred at a dinner with a few professors from China's leading management schools, who highlighted the merits of top Western economic and management techniques, financial regulations, scholarship, and journals. Nonetheless, at the same time, and without any apparent awareness of a contradiction, they expressed the deep conviction that it would be unfair to allow MNCs to buy successful Chinese companies, since that "would leave China barren of these hard-earned achievements, since they will now belong to a foreign, already more powerful country" (authors' interview).

The VC industry also suffers from a legal ambiguity. Consequently, on average, venture capitalists behave more like private-equity firms and avoid investing in small start-up companies with novel R&D-based business models (authors' interviews; Fuller 2005b; Segal 2003). The preferred strategy of Chinese venture capitalists is to invest only in companies following proven models, such as those developing software applications, IT-enabled services, or copies of successful Western companies like Google or eBay. Interestingly, many Chinese branches of foreign VC funds are also following this much more cautious strategy (authors' interviews). In addition, the state-owned banks remain devoted to their primary charges—state-owned companies (Fuller 2005b; Naughton 1995; Steinfeld 1998). While companies established by Chinese returnees (also known as "sea turtles") are, on average, more technologically advanced than local start-ups, these companies still adhere to the Red Queen logic when choosing a business model for their companies (authors' interviews; Breznitz 2005a, 2007b; Chang 1992; Fuller 2005a; Fuller et al. 2003).

Apart from the banks and the venture capitalists, the largest single source of financing available for R&D comes from the government itself. Of the total governmental S&T investment in 2006, 59.8% came from central-government sources (NSBPRC 2007). Governmental organs (state research groups and universities) still conduct 28.9% of all R&D. Allocations of state funds to governmental and nongovernmental research organs remain political decisions, and are given to favored sectors and actors (Cao et al. 2006; Cyranoski 2004; Serger and Breidne 2007). New companies with innovative ideas find themselves out of the loop as the central government continues to pick what it sees as winners—the so-called national-banner enterprises—whether or not these preferred champions engage in novel R&D. This limits the scope of innovation and constrains business activities outside preferred sectors and companies.

Finally, at the national level, China's educational system and research infrastructure shape the formation and behavior of the national high-technology economy. If the pattern of economic reform in many other spheres has been to "play to the provinces" by offering them decentralized control and significant leeway to devise their own strategies, China's S&T infrastructure still retains many of the old Leninist structures of party committees and political control. Moreover, research and education may be the one domain in which the central government has strengthened its influence instead of relinquishing it, further slowing down changes in behavior, specifically in university-industry relationships.

PLAN OF THE BOOK

To reiterate: this book contends that, under conditions of intensified global-ization and the decomposition of economic activities, assumptions about the link between innovation and economic growth need to be reexamined. Further, this book demonstrates that the sweet spot of innovation-based economic growth might not be in novel-product innovation; the case of China, the world's largest and longest case of rapid, sustained economic growth, provides strong evidence that policy makers who care about growth, especially in emerg-ing economies, might not want to be enthralled by the current Western fixa-tion on novel-product R&D. Instead, policy makers might do better to con-centrate on how to transform other aspects of innovation into economic growth within their national borders.

In the pages ahead, we offer an in-depth understanding of the development of the Chinese high-technology industry and its relationship to the global IT industry, advancing the argument that China runs on a particular trajectory of industrial-technology development—the run of the Red Queen—a path that has given China significant and sustained economic growth coupled with wide-spread job creation. This is the best for which a huge emerging economy can hope. In analyzing how this development path came to be, and in looking closely at its specific resilience in China, this book emphasizes the importance of politics, specifically the politics of institutional reform, for the long-term performance of the economy. We thus narrate the story of China's dual-track (regional and national) high-tech economic development as an acute reminder that politics matter and that many different choices for successful economic growth are available to nations, regions, and firms. Consequently, this book aims to remind us that economic reform is a deeply contextual science, best practiced when it is tailored to local tastes and local capabilities.

The chapters are divided as follows. In Chapter Two we explain how poli-tics is crucial for understanding China's run of the Red Queen. We analyze the particularities of the Chinese political system and the mechanisms by which they affect specific behaviors of the IT industry. We use historical analysis as well as particular policy case studies to substantiate our argument that two prominent features of the Chinese political economy, in comparison with other rapidly growing emerging economies, are its very low level of institutionaliza-tion and the structured uncertainty that imbues it. In addition, the chapter an-alyzes the impact of the central government's delegating a great deal of re-sponsibility for the interpretation and implementation of reforms to the regions. Yet we also point out a condition that has received insufficient scholarly attention: while responsibility has been delegated to the provinces, the center firmly retains control over major institutional and technological features crucial to the development of high-technology industry.

Chapters Three to Five present our comparative findings from the three regions. Chapter Three focuses on Beijing, showing that the city has relied on a strategy of deindustrialization and extensive use of its rich human resources to attract the research facilities of leading IT multinational corporations (MNCs) and to encourage the development of technology spin-off enterprises. In Chapter Four, we consider Shanghai, contending that the region's approach to technology development, highly planned and resembling that of a local developmental state, while effective at attracting MNCs looking to establish large-scale facilities, has stifled technology entrepreneurship and limited the region's ability to innovate in the long run. Chapter Five analyzes the Pearl River Delta. Here we argue that the region, lacking the educational and research infrastructure of Beijing and Shanghai, has managed, through an emphasis on manufacturing and the acceptance of a broad definition of "indigenous innovation," to excel by building on its strong production capabilities. The PRD first developed its manufacturing prowess and only later moved into R&D, thus giving PRD companies such as Huawei and ZTE, not companies from Beijing or Shanghai, the innovative capacities to compete head-on with leading Western MNCs.

Finally, Chapter Six presents our conclusion. We first suggest ways in which China can learn from it current and past successes, and shun the techno-fetishist paradigm, when devising its innovation policies. We then consider the lessons, opportunities, and challenges that China's rise to economic prominence offers to the developed and developing world.

Chapter 2 Rules of the Run: The Politics of China's Institutions of Innovation

"I don't know what you mean by 'glory,'" Alice said.

Humpty Dumpty smiled contemptuously. "Of course you don't—till I tell you. I meant 'there's a nice knock-down argument for you!'"

"But 'glory' doesn't mean 'a nice knock-down argument,'" Alice objected.

"When *I* use a word," Humpty Dumpty said, in a rather scornful tone, "it means just what I choose it to mean—neither more nor less."

"The question is," said Alice, "whether you *can* make words mean so many different things."

"The question is," said Humpty Dumpty, "which is to be master—that's all."

—*Lewis Carroll,* Through the Looking-Glass and What Alice Found There

Politics is the key to understanding China's run of the Red Queen. Economic behavior in high-risk long-term activities such as R&D is extremely sensitive to the institutional environment in which it takes place. The Chinese system, massively transformed since 1978, has been constantly refashioned by political battles both at the center and between the center and the regions in a contest to determine the pace and shape of reforms. Understanding how these contestations are settled is crucial to understanding the path taken by the Chinese IT industry. The resolutions of these political confrontations have institutionalized specific incentives that stimulate particular sets of activities, the particular business models that firms utilize, and the development of certain capabilities while inhibiting others. In the case of the Chinese economy, the particular political dynamic of reform and policy debate has been even more important than the institutionalization of specific reforms in specific areas in shaping the development trajectory of the IT industry.

Structured uncertainty permeates the Chinese political-economic system. Structured uncertainty is inherent in a system such as China's, with its extensive cross-allegiances, tangled matrices of authority, numerous organizations with very little institutionalization, and the ensuing strong reliance on personal authority and network consensus. Therefore, uncertainties and the domains in which they reign have shaped the trajectory of the IT industry and its innovational capabilities, and they have done this at least as much as the institutionalized environment.

As has been argued extensively, and as we show to be the case particularly in science and technology (S&T), the Chinese political-economic system is unique in its great amount of persistent "un-institutionalization," especially in comparison with those in other Communist Party–led regimes (Lieberthal 2004).[1] Molded by Mao's single-minded effort to fight what he saw as the nemesis of revolution—namely, the process of institutionalization and bureaucratization—policy processes and actions in the Chinese state remain extremely personal even today. Admittedly, much progress in institutionalization and in the regularizing of procedures has taken place since 1976. However, in many cases, this has simply amounted to formalizing informal policy making and deal making among China's elites.

The rise and fall of individuals or groups of leaders also determines the rise and fall of different policy packages and political trends. A vivid example of the difference between true power and institutionalized organizational relations can be seen in the case of Deng Xiaoping, a leader who tried to encourage institutionalization across China's political system (Baum 1994; Lieberthal 2004; Shirk 1993). In 1992, when he conducted his Southern Tour, which rekindled economic reform efforts and opened China to the massive foreign-direct-investment (FDI) inflows it attracts to this day, Deng's sole official title was honorary chairman of the Chinese Bridge Association (which is devoted to the card game, not civil engineering). Such a system, as a matter of principle, involves significant amounts of uncertainty and ambiguity. Hence, we contend that to explain the economic behavior of actors, an institutional account of China must look not only at official institutions, organizations, and procedures, but also at the spheres of structured uncertainty.

However, this is not to say that political confrontations themselves and the ways in which they have been settled are not shaped by the political institutions of the Chinese system. China has a wide range of formal institutions and organizations responsible for the IT industry: the Ministry of Science and Technology (MOST), the Ministry of Information Industry (MII), the National Development and Reform Commission (NDRC), the Chinese Academy of Sciences (CAS), and a broad and active university system. Each of these units interacts with the others as well as with the overlying structure of the CCP while seeking to maximize its benefits without running afoul of the central, functional-area Leadership Small Groups and the *xitong* (systems) of top ministerial, agency, and departmental leaders (Lieberthal 2004).

Ergo, we need to understand the structure of uncertainty in China, the political contestations around specific reforms, and the institutions that shaped these political confrontations. Moreover, the reforms, once unleashed, created specific dynamics of development and added uncertainties and ambiguities. The new uncertainties and ambiguities, in turn, influenced the next set of political debates, which further informed the reform process. Accordingly, if we are to understand the particular trajectory of the Chinese IT industry, we must understand not merely the formal political institutions but also the coevolution of politics and economic opening. This chapter explains the political underpinnings of the behavior of China's IT industry by examining the dynamic between reforms and both the institutionalized certainties—most notably, the rewards for positive economic growth—and the particular structure of the uncertainties they produced.

First, we elaborate on the meaning of structured uncertainty, presenting the four features of the Chinese political economy that infuse the country with it, and consider the impact of structured uncertainty on the behavior of economic actors. We then focus our attention on the central government, delving into the particularities of reforms in China and mapping out areas of both certainties and uncertainties. To anchor our argument in a dynamic understanding of Chinese political economy, this section presents an analysis of two domains critical to the development of the IT industry—telecommunications and domestic technology standards. Following this analysis, we discuss local actors and institutions and their critical role in the differentiated development of the

IT economy in each of the three regions under study. To do this, we examine the development of science-based industrial parks and China's special category of nongovernmental IT enterprises, called *minying*.

Throughout this inquiry, we explore the critical tension between the economically and politically dynamic regional areas and the more conservative center. Of note here is the fact that, while the regions were designated as the loci of dynamic reforms, the center retained power over several domains critical to the development of innovation capabilities and business models in the IT industry. The powers reserved by the center, and the occasional strong exercise of central authority over regional or enterprise experiments, in effect bracketed the broad, locally based reforms that the center had first enabled. We illustrate these policy domains in our discussion of telecommunications and domestic technology standards. We illustrate regional coping mechanisms through an exploration of science-based industrial parks and minying enterprises.

STRUCTURED UNCERTAINTY: POLITICAL ECONOMIC ACTION IN THE CHINESE SYSTEM

As discussed in Chapter One, we define structured uncertainty as an agreement to disagree about the goals and methods of policy, which leads to intrinsic unpredictability and to inherent ambiguity in implementation. Thus, structured uncertainty is an institutional condition that cements multiplicity of action without legitimizing any specific course or form of behavior as the proper one. This ambiguity consequently leads to some tolerance for multiple interpretations and implementations of the same policy. In China, at the same time that a plurality of policy actions is tolerated, the punishment of those deemed transgressors can be severe, abrupt, and arbitrary. The limits of tolerance are undefined, which adds another layer of ambiguity. Furthermore, the multiplicity of actions and procedures themselves create more uncertainty, since no one is sure what the proper course of action is or where lines of authority and responsibility reside.

Thus, structured uncertainty can be analyzed as an institutional feature guaranteeing that a plurality of behaviors will be followed in a specific domain and that none of the actors will know in advance the appropriate ways to conduct themselves. Structured uncertainty exists to a certain degree in almost all policy domains in most countries. Indeed, it is the main reason why street-level bureaucracy is so important in every society (Wilson 1968). However, it takes on different qualitative and quantitative manifestations in the Chinese system because of the specificities of its transformation from a communistic, revolutionary society to a more organized, bureaucratic, rule-bound one.

As was succinctly argued by Kenneth Arrow (1962) in the case of R&D, under conditions of perfect market competition there is a tendency for private economic agents to underinvest in it, because of its inherent characteristics of indivisibility, inappropriability, and uncertainty. These three traits are significantly augmented by structured uncertainty, which leads to substantial negative incentives with regard to R&D. It is bad enough for technological entrepreneurs to work in an environment where their property rights are weak; it is immensely worse to work in an environment where these rights also keep changing and are applied arbitrarily; worse still, even the rights of businesses to operate in certain markets are never assured and always shifting. As we later elaborate in the case of telecommunications, central regulators are reluctant to clarify what technology they will permit to be implemented. Under such extreme structured uncertainty, the great puzzle for economic theory is why some Chinese companies do any R&D at all. The impact of China's extreme levels of structured uncertainty goes beyond simply an increase in risk. It encompasses all areas that tend to lead to underinvestment in R&D. We should note, however, that today there are strong and growing constituencies in China that demand change. Not least are established Chinese companies such as ZTE, Huawei, Lenovo, and Tencent, which have come to understand that in order to continue to be globally successful, they must impose more certainty onto the Chinese political economy. Nonetheless, as we explain below, since structured uncertainty has become a necessary condition for the Chinese political-economic system to work, fundamental change, though expected, will be a long and incremental process.

Structured uncertainty is not unique to China. The concept of structured uncertainty builds upon contributions from the political science debate about federalism and economic development. Much of this debate is concerned with formal structures of the government, such as the separation of powers, and the impact of these structures on economic behavior. China's situation is far more complex and fluid than that in even the most federalist Western countries. Some would argue that the United States, with its federal structure, also has a high degree of structured uncertainty. While a federal system provides opportunities for conflicting policies and interpretations, in general the division of powers is clearly defined, making the central government's policies superior to those of the many states. Moreover, the means by which the central and state governments can challenge each other's authority are defined in the courts. In China, the basic boundaries are unclear and constantly changing, and the ability of the center and the provinces to challenge each other is not institutionalized or governed. Furthermore, structured uncertainty permeates all levels of society and business in China and, compared to its working in other societies, is far more important to the daily incentives governing the behavior of economic actors.

There are four main features of the Chinese system that produce structured uncertainty: the need to launch reforms in a centrally planned socialist state, a bureaucracy organized so that different levels are not necessarily inferior or superior to others, the personalized nature of power and influence in China's governmental institutions, and, finally, the ambiguous, ill-defined, and ever-changing nature of the economic reforms themselves. These four features necessitate built-in vagueness with regard to policy decisions and policy "un-decisions," that is, to areas in which no formal policy decisions have taken place, and make China's degree of structured uncertainty much more intense than that in other political-economic systems.

The first feature of the Chinese political-economic system that produces structured uncertainty was the need to start reforms in the context of a strong conservative center and a ruling ideology of "socialism."[2] From the start, when Deng and his followers decided to enact economic reforms, they faced two significant obstacles. First, they needed to counteract the center, which was strongly influenced by conservative and veto-wielding vested interests (such as the industrial ministries) that wished to limit the scope of reform to restoring the primacy of centrally planned economic development.[3] Second, reformers needed to devise a strategy that would allow some degree of free-market competition to operate within a system infused with a strong communist ideology and overseen by a ruling party that historically legitimized its power by claiming to be the true agent of this ideology. The strategy that the reformers chose, which has since become institutionalized, was to authorize agents to experiment with their own interpretations of reforms within the limits of obscurely worded policies and pronouncements.

From the first reforms in 1978 to the present, China's central leaders never laid out detailed reform plans. Instead, they used vague terms to authorize regional and economic actors to experiment in certain policy or economic areas: first, between 1978 and 1981, in agriculture and SOE management; then, during the 1980s, in collective enterprises or township and village enterprises (TVEs); and finally, in 1988, in urban private enterprise (authors' interviews; Lieberthal 2004; Naughton 1995, 2007; Shirk 1993). After the center granted permission, regional leaders needed to decide whether to implement any changes at all. Authorities who opted for reform had to develop a particular interpretation of the ambiguous pronouncements made by the CCP leadership and the central government and to decide what actions the leadership actually desired and permitted. This interpretation would then be used as the basis of their specific regional policies. While successful experiments were often formally approved later, a too liberal interpretation, or one that ran afoul of a new direction of policy at the center, could lead to harsh recriminations (Kennedy 1997; Tsai 2002). For example, to raise capital, China Unicom pursued foreign investment, even though such financing was not permitted in telecommunications operations. Through a complicated system called China-China-Foreign, where Unicom would form a joint venture with another state entity that had a joint venture with a foreign company, Unicom covertly received injections of foreign capital. By 1998 there were forty-nine such collaborations completed or under negotiation when the Ministry of Posts and Telecommunications (MPT) abruptly declared three of them "illegal" and the remainder "irregular," which led to their immediate termination. What had been a creative interpretation of policy and a pragmatic route for business development was suddenly deemed a bridge too far and crushed by central authorities (DeWoskin 2001; Low 2005; Wu 2009).

Thus, while provinces, municipalities, and even creative enterprises became the loci of change and reform dynamism, risk and uncertainty for reformist regional leaders remained quite high. The only constant benchmark for policy was that successful rapid growth was favorably treated over and above long-term considerations or, usually, the particular means by which it was achieved (Lieberthal 2004). This condition continues to the present. In February 2008, one interviewee went so far as to state: "While the national government, which now worries about overheating, sets a goal of only 9% economic growth, an official who secures 15% growth [for his region] is still rewarded and promoted, even though he has completely ignored the central command, to the same degree that an official is punished for his failures if he manages to bring only 3% growth. It is clear that economic growth still trumps all other considerations" (authors' interview).

High uncertainty was further augmented by the fact that the time frame of the reforms was left unspecified, and changes in policy came unexpectedly and not infrequently. Furthermore, when conservatives managed to gain the upper hand in debates at the political center, new sets of changes often contradicted earlier reforms.

The imposition of sharp policy changes that contradict earlier trends continues today, even if not necessarily because of ideological shifts. In 2007 and 2008, the efforts to cool the economy by restricting credit, investment rates, and exports contradicted well-established national policies of the last twenty years. These attempts to cool and steer economic growth were then completely reversed when the global financial crisis began to sharply curtail export earnings and profits in exporting regions in the fall of 2008. Central leaders halted the appreciation of the renminbi (RMB—China's currency), encouraged loans to exporters, and subsidized threatened sectors.

This ever-changing environment of extreme uncertainty, with high risks and high gains, had a far-reaching effect on the behavior of actors. Rational actors opted to focus on securing short-term gains while trying to minimize risk. Since industrial R&D, especially novel-product development, is both long term and high risk, the particularities of Chinese reform have kept actors from engaging in it. This feature is prominent across all of China. Hence, while Beijing, Shanghai, and the PRD each opted for a different interpretation of reforms and implemented quite different policies—two conditions that have had a lasting influence on the development of their regional IT industries—in all three regions, incentives have been high against undertaking significant novel-product R&D.

The second feature of the Chinese political-economic system leading to structured uncertainty is the organization of the bureaucracy. The Chinese bureaucracy is not only vast and complex but also pervaded by numerous cross-allegiances and competing lines of authority. These exist across domains, such as telecommunication technology; within the same agency; between the national, regional, and local layers of bureaucracy; and between the local and central branches of the same bureaucratic organization. Not surprisingly, it is unclear which organization has final authority over specific domains, and it is not even clear who is in charge of whom at each level of the bureaucratic structure. This unwieldy construction is then further muddled by the CCP's infusion into every nook and cranny of both the bureaucratic system and industry.[4] An example of this is offered by Lieberthal in his classic text on governance in China (2004, 187–188):

> A hypothetical energy department under the Zhongshan county government would be subordinate to *both* the Zhongshan county government *and* the energy bureau under the Guangdong provincial government. At the same time, the Zhongshan county government must answer to both the Zhongshan county Communist party

committee and the Guangdong provincial government. In addition, the organization department of the Zhongshan county Communist party committee will strongly affect the career opportunities of the leaders of the Zhongshan county energy department, who must also obey party discipline as members of the party committee of the energy department.

In the case of China's IT industry, the situation is even more complex because of the multiplicity of state and nonstate actors involved. For example, in telecommunications, the interaction of policy, party, research, and economic actors forms a multifarious, integrated, and overlapping structure.[5] Using Beijing as an example, figure 2.1 shows how national policy bodies directly and indirectly affect the operations of a telecommunications provider, as do municipal-level bodies and research groups. The NDRC formulates telecommunications-rollout and universal-access targets that require research, input, and support from the Beijing government, MOST, the State-Owned Assets Supervision and Administration Commission (SASAC), and the MII. The plans of the NDRC are filtered and fine-tuned by its municipal-level bureau in Beijing, which also responds to the interests of the Beijing government itself. To conduct its mission, the Beijing-level development and reform commission requires the services of the Beijing Science and Technology Commission, which answers to the Beijing government and directly acts upon the telecom munications provider. SASAC, as the owner of the telecommunications company, attempts to make its operations as profitable as possible, which may or may not correspond with the goals of the Beijing government, the NDRC, or the MII.

The MII controls the legal actions the company can take. In addition, through its policy and technology-research groups, like the Chinese Academy of Telecommunications Research (CATR), the MII can influence the types of services the company will be able to offer. In this example, the MII's spin-off —Datang —supplies Time Division–Synchronous Code Division Multiple Access (TD-SCDMA) 3G equipment to China Mobile, which must purchase this equipment, although not necessarily from Datang, since the MII licensed only China Mobile to operate a TD-SCDMA 3G network. Finally, MOST provides financing to research groups and companies conducting research in next-generation telecommunications and services. It can directly influence the Beijing government, and through its local branch, it is in charge of certifying high-technology enterprises and, hence, holds power over the industry. This entire structure is overlaid with the institutions of the CCP at all levels. Party committees have their own interests as well as responsibilities to their superiors in both the formal institutional hierarchy and the party structure.

The result of this complicated structure is that it must allow for a degree of procedural ambiguity in order for any action to take place. Leeway must be given to actors on each level so that they can advance what they see as the manifold goals that will satisfy their multiple superiors without angering any of them. Each level of the various bureaucracies is responsible to its superior and to other units at the same level. Each level also depends upon the actions of other responsible groups and is therefore influenced by their interests.

This complicated structure instills structured uncertainty in two ways. First, any action or policy implementation must satisfy multiple superiors who often have contradictory roles and preferences. Second, it is impossible for any of the entities involved to know in advance whether a specific action they take will be looked upon favorably by any or all the bureaucratic agencies that might (or might not) view it as falling under their jurisdiction. As a result, economic actors avoid taking on long-term high-risk endeavors, preferring actions that lead to immediate, secure, positive material results, which can then be touted as a tangible proof that the measures taken were in accordance with the correct interpretation of policy. Another related outcome of this structure, to be detailed later, is that virtually all high-technology enterprises in China seek what Adam Segal (2003) terms "a bureaucratic mother in-law" by becoming an affiliate of a state agent, be it a ministry, local government, SOE, university, or research institution.

The third feature of the Chinese political-economic system leading to structured uncertainty is the configuration of power within the complex bureaucracy. Power in modern China resides more in individual actors and their network of reciprocal relations than in a given office or rank. Because of this complex web of interpersonal connections operating within a shadow world of actual authority, an actor's formal location or contact point with the state apparatus does not necessarily ensure desired outcomes. There are two aspects that determine the possession of and use of power in China: the relationship between the de facto and de jure power in any political unit, and *guanxi*.

Power within Chinese politics is often wielded in ways not suggested by formal organizational charts. For example, constitutionally and organizationally, the government of China considers the National People's Congress (NPC) to be the organ with the greatest amount of power, since it is the national law-making body.[6] However, in practice, laws and policies that come before the NPC have already been approved and endorsed by the CCP apparatus—which

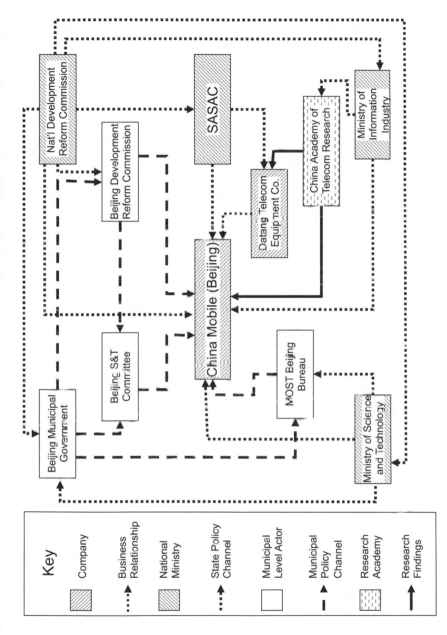

Figure 2.1—Policy and Influence Channels in Telecommunications in China

Key

Company	
Business Relationship	
National Ministry	
State Policy Channel	
Municipal Level Actor	
Municipal Policy Channel	
Research Academy	
Research Findings	

Nat'l Development Reform Commission

SASAC

Ministry of Information Industry

Beijing Development Reform Commission

China Academy of Telecom Research

Datang Telecom Equipment Co.

China Mobile (Beijing)

Beijing Municipal Government

Beijing S&T Committee

MOST Beijing Bureau

Ministry of Science and Technology

also exerts considerable influence through the vetting of candidates for people's congresses—and the executive branch of the government (Chao 2003;
O'Brien 1988, 1990, 1994).[7] Although votes against laws and policies are occasionally cast—and not infrequently, a dissenting representative will opt to ab-
stain rather than vote—issues that come before the NPC are nearly always
passed by overwhelming margins (Baum 1994; Lieberthal 2004).

A parallel structure of power exists in all organizations in China. Under Mao,
the party secretary clearly exercised formal authority over any given unit, dic-
tating practice and wielding an absolute veto over the formal manager.[8] Since
the 1980s, the relationship has become far more nuanced (Walder 1989). One
interviewee explained the power relations in his own institution, one of the
premier research universities in China: "Although there are administrative institutions with clearly defined responsibilities, even in this elite university, those
who want power and promotion should still do well to belong to, and focus
their energies on, the party structure. Those who do so tend to become full
professors or are invited to become academicians quicker and more often than
those who just do great research, even if many times these people are not successful researchers themselves" (authors' interview).

Since the centers of actual authority often remain invisible, it is difficult to
ascertain who wields true decision-making authority. This forces actors to hedge
their bets and appeal to multiple authorities in hopes of pleasing the right person. The actions of the de facto authorities in any given unit are not fully bound
by rules or restrictions and therefore can be unpredictable.

Adding to the complexity of de facto and de jure authority relations is the
oil that lubricates and sustains China's polity and economy: guanxi (关系).
Literally translated as "connections" or "relationship," guanxi's meaning in Chinese discourse ranges from a complex web of reciprocal relationships to implications of corruption and official protection for illegal activities (authors' interviews; Feng 1995; Gold 1985; Gold et al. 2002; Tsai 2002; Wank 1996; Yang
1989, 1994). The practice of seeking connections and using relationships as a
primary means of conducting business or securing access to scarce resources
and services is ancient, but its importance increased markedly during the chaos
of the Cultural Revolution (Bian 1994).

In much early research on business practices in China and East Asia, scholars noted that a reliance on guanxi was necessary for those seeking to secure investment permits, open a business, build a factory, secure components, or generally conduct business. Scholars of China's economic reform in the 1980s and
1990s noticed that extreme deinstitutionalization discouraged entrepreneur-

ship and forced the use of tightly knit communities based on guanxi (Gold 1985; Guthrie 1998; Hsing 1996; Yeung and Tung 1996). China has greatly advanced the rule of law and the orderly process of business since the 1980s, so today there is evidence, albeit hotly debated, that the importance of guanxi has decreased (Gold et al. 2002; Yang 2002). In many interviews, it was noted that whereas passing out cartons of cigarettes or buying liquor during the Spring Festival was still important for currying official favor, the absolute need to wine and dine officials in order to secure basic operating licenses or avoid arbitrary fees has ended.[9] Whereas calling on high-level connections could formerly guarantee support for an investment proposal or a policy initiative, all large companies and powerful individuals now have high-level connections. As a result, while guanxi may help secure a meeting with powerful officials, proposals are increasingly weighed on their merits rather than the status of their supporters (Kennedy 2005, 2007a, 2007b, 2009).

Although diminished in importance, guanxi remains a fact of life for those doing business in China, one that any entrepreneur must address daily. The strength of one's guanxi is determined by an understanding of where authority is actually wielded and how to access it through one's support network. Within a government unit, guanxi networks link officials in different offices to one another, to their superiors, and to the CCP apparatus. A guanxi nodal point—a person with strong connections to other well-connected or influential persons—will be a powerful force in a given unit of Chinese society. The cultivating of relations with such well-connected officials, regardless of title, is an art form in China. In many interviews, it was noted that entrepreneurs, particularly in political hotbeds such as Beijing, find themselves spending more time courting well-connected officials in order to secure protection and access to rents than they do pursuing their business.

A guanxi network enables businesses or officials, to varying degrees, to see that their policy preferences are enacted and properly enforced. Such networks are necessary, since the multiple cross-allegiances and overlapping lines of authority in formal bureaucracies almost ensure that some people—those who view a proposed policy as harmful to the interests of their group—will do their best to block it. The stronger one's guanxi network, whatever one's title or rank, the more power and influence one wields.

Guanxi networks themselves are nonetheless fraught with weaknesses and uncertainties. Ties easily break when a well-connected person does not see it as being in his or her interest to assist a weaker partner. Similarly, entire networks are susceptible to collapse if a few key players fall. Guanxi cultivation also increases risk, since all members of a network can be held responsible for the malfeasance of others in the group. Hence, while necessary for ensuring the realization of a desired outcome, guanxi increases uncertainty and risk for participants and, hence, systemic structured uncertainty.

The fourth feature of the Chinese political-economic system that leads to structured uncertainty is the ambiguous and ever-changing nature of the overarching goal of reforms. In most countries, economic reforms are conducted within a system infused with consensus about both the overarching goal of economic reforms—typically, sustained growth—and the principles of the reforming system itself, that is, the basic tenets of state-society relations. In China, there is no such consensus. Thanks to the socialist state structure created after 1949, economic reforms are a redefinition of both the overarching goals of the system and the basic tenets of state-society relations. For these reasons, the early reforms never specified the aims or the overall sphere of the reforms. The actual final goals have not been officially determined since, nor, we argue, will they be decided in the near or midterm future. Currently, the official goals of the CCP and its ongoing reforms are "scientific development" and the creation of a "harmonious society."[10] However, the exact definition of these goals is uncertain; interpretations range from simple social stability to comprehensive redistributive justice. It is not a surprise that the reformers themselves have described the entire process as "groping for stones to cross the river"—a route of extreme uncertainty without defined goals and means. This is especially true in the case of S&T and innovation, since both are intimately connected with security and national power and, therefore, with China's self-image and conception of its role in the international system.

This inability to define goals and means infuses the system with a high degree of uncertainty and a tolerance for contradictions. These, in turn, lead the vast multitude of formal institutions in the Chinese system to interpret goals and the proper mechanisms for achieving them in their own way and in accordance with their parochial interests. The result is policies and actions that are simultaneously baffling and seemingly contradictory to the outside observer. A widely publicized example is the effort, since the 1990s, to reduce the absolute number of SOEs and spur more private entrepreneurship. However, even as they promulgated this goal, China's central authorities enshrined the state-owned and state-planned economy as the core of China's economy. Accordingly, SOEs were backed with funds that were denied to private entrepreneurs. The amended wording in the Chinese constitution, adopted at the

Eighth National People's Congress in 1993, declared: "The state-owned economy, namely, the socialist economy under ownership by the whole people, *is the leading force in the national economy.* The state ensures the consolidation and growth of the state-owned economy" (PRC 1993; emphasis added).

A recent example of conflicting goals in the realm of innovation policy is the technology-standards policy. Analyzed as a coherent strategy for upgrading national technological and innovational capabilities, it seems to have many features that are both counterproductive and contradictory. However, as we shall delineate later in this chapter, the logic becomes clear if the standards policy is analyzed as a group of procedures developed by a multitude of agencies and organizations, each interpreting the procedures differently in an attempt to advance its own power, goals, or perception of the national interest. Indeed, when seen through this lens, the proliferation of Chinese technological standards is quite logical.

What makes sense for political dynamics creates another layer of uncertainty for economic actors. This uncertainty, again, incentivizes enterprises and individuals to prefer short-term economic growth above all else and to shy away from long-term high-risk activities. Consequently, at least as important to the behavior of economic actors are the processes of policy debates rather than their often long-delayed final outcomes. It is therefore imperative to understand the various kinds of uncertainties and the areas in which they operate and to trace how they shaped the development trajectory of the Chinese IT industry, especially with regard to R&D and innovation.

In the next sections, we analyze how the persistence of structured uncertainty, interacting with other key elements of the Chinese system, led the IT industry to adopt "run of the Red Queen" logic, which then became its modus operandi, even for types of growth and enterprises that vary significantly between regions. We examine two critical domains that are primarily under the control of national-level actors: telecommunications and domestic technology standards. Looking at these domains allows us to describe the various actors and to analyze their dynamic interactions in policy making. We then follow with an analysis of two additional domains—science parks and the founding and sustaining of "nongovernmental" technological start-ups (minying enterprises) —which exemplify what happens when the center delegates entrepreneurial policy making to the regions without giving them full control over basic economic institutions.

POLICY MAKING AT THE CENTER

As discussed above, the structure of China's bureaucracy and the somewhat amorphous nature of power relations within it increase structured uncertainty. To gain a full appreciation of how these power relations function in practice, we must understand how policy is made in China and which aspects of policy are centrally versus locally controlled. A core component of our argument is that the particular process of reform in China—in which the most extensive experimentation has been delegated to the provincial and local levels while the center has remained far more cautious—led to two sets of institutional systems affecting the behavior of the Chinese IT industry. The first system is the set of national practices, institutions, and organizations that govern the economy, specifically those presiding over the transition to China's current semi-market economy. These have largely been far less oriented toward market-based reforms than have institutions and organizations operating at the level of the provincial or municipal governments. Crucial among these national institutions are those that regulate property rights and other rights, as well as those that oversee finance, education, and the S&T-research infrastructure. It is these institutions and organizations that create the national framework within which China's local economies operate. Partly because of the influence of structured uncertainty and partly because of their own internal dynamics these national institutions reduce long-term risk taking in both large and small companies. Consequently, national policies channel firms toward process, organizational, and incremental innovation, limiting the development of novel technologies.

The second institutional system comprises the organizations and institutions that have effectively separated China into a series of regional economic fiefdoms, which both compete fiercely and cooperate with one another and the center. This dynamic, wherein each region develops its own unique strengths, has facilitated China's rise to global supremacy in many stages of production while deterring businesses and entrepreneurs from engaging in cutting-edge novel-technology and novel-product development. Thus, the dual-track nature of reforms and the deeply ingrained structured uncertainty at every level of the political-economic system have significantly influenced the particular development trajectory of the IT industries. To elaborate on this argument and show its dynamics, we focus on two crucial domains in the development of the IT industry—telecommunications and domestic technology standards—explaining how the political conflicts around them were solved at the national level and presenting the dynamics of the policy process and the far-reaching impacts of structured uncertainty in action. Doing so also allows us to analyze the various organizations in China that play a role in S&T and in innovation policy making and implementation: MOST, the MII, the national academies and universities, the NDRC, the CCP, and SASAC. This analysis allows us to inquire into the extensive matrix structure of the Chinese bureaucracy, the major differences between formal and real power, and the impact of these on the growth trajectory of the Chinese IT industry as a whole. We contend that the constellation of power at the center allows for regional policy entrepreneurship and a plurality of actions with regard to the IT industry, but within significant limits. These limits and, especially, the ever-present encompassing uncertainty unleash the impressive Chinese capabilities for many forms of innovation while simultaneously inhibiting the development of novel-product-innovation activities.

We start with the domain at the heart of the IT revolution—telecommunications. We then move to look at the development and internal logic of what most observers view as the current uniquely Chinese national R&D and innovation policy—Chinese domestic technology standards.

I JUST CALLED TO SAY I ~~LOVE~~ OWN YOU:
THE HEAVY AND CONFUSED HAND OF
CENTRAL GOVERNMENT CONTROL IN
THE TELECOMMUNICATIONS MARKET

The telecommunications sector in China provides a clear example of a tangled policy environment beset by structured uncertainty and hemmed in by limits on free-market-based behavior. The central government, with its conflicting ministerial and organizational interests, regional governments seeking to promote the best services and most rapid expansion of access, and enterprises seeking profits all compete fiercely for dominance. This section shows how much arbitrary control the central state wields over this critical IT sector, how enterprises cope with uncertainty from above, and how technological changes, innovation, and growth affect government behavior toward these sectors.

The telecommunications industry and services sector has been officially reformed, and now features competing operators overseen by a separate regulatory agency, a significant change from 1994, when telecommunications operation was an integral duty of the MPT.[11] However, the continual policy shifts, changes in management, and direct interference by many different, and sometimes competing, national political actors have discouraged novel-product R&D activities. Thanks to the central importance of telecommunications to the IT industry, this instability causes significant ripple effects throughout the industry as a whole. Nonetheless, even with these limits, state action has also been positive, since it has facilitated the development of the telecommunications industry and provided a platform on which telecommunications-enabled businesses can develop.

For these reasons, the telecommunications sector perfectly illustrates our arguments concerning structured uncertainty, the strong hand of the central state in critical areas of the IT industry, and the impact of central-government policies on the kinds of R&D and innovation activities in which the industry engages. Through the development and reform of the telecommunications industry, one can easily trace the impacts of central conservatism and intervention in critical high-technology sectors, the lack of institutionalization in policy making and execution, and the impacts of the pervasive climate of structured uncertainty.

Telecommunications is one of the largest and most concentrated sectors of the Chinese economy. In 2006, telecommunications accounted for as much as 7% of the output of the entire Chinese economy, standing at 1.477 trillion RMB.[12] The sector also remains one of the key strategic economic sectors controlled by SOEs (Low 2005; I. Wu 2009).[13] State-owned telecommunications operators account for one-sixth of all assets directly controlled by the central government through SASAC. These firms bring in 20% of SASAC's corporate profits (C. Li 2006). Despite China's accession to the World Trade Organization (WTO), telecommunications network operation remains almost exclusively a Chinese state domain.[14] China's telecommunications industry has undergone extensive reform, restructuring, and re-restructuring since the introduction of limited competition in 1994. Telecommunications remains a politically controlled domain imbued with competing interests from the SOEs, their owners, the national regulator, and several other ministries, all of which are part of the state structure, as well as from equipment suppliers, many of which are also partly or fully owned by various state agencies.[15] This mixed structure, which, as we note below, also frequently involves the movement of high-level personnel from industry to government to regulator and back again, points to a far from fully competitive market in which both the providers and the regulator do not enjoy independence from political, as opposed to professional, concerns (I. Wu 2005).

Until 1994, telecommunications operation was an MPT monopoly. The sector operated similarly to most Western national telecommunications operators until they were widely deregulated and privatized in the 1980s and 1990s.[16] The MPT was formed in 1950 as part of the initial Soviet-style reorganization of the Chinese government. The MPT handled operation of postal and telecommunications services, while the Ministry of Electronic Industry (MEI) was responsible for the development and production of hardware for the sector (Chung 2002). During the 1950s, beneath the MPT, six dedicated Posts and Telecommunications universities—*youdian daxue* (邮电大学), known collectively as the "yous"—were established to train cadres for ministerial or industry roles in posts and telecommunications.[17] The telecommunications sector thus recruited its cadres and professionals from within its own educational system, especially from the Beijing University of Posts and Telecommunications (Beiyou), the hegemon of the yous. As recently as 2006, three of the top seven directors of China's telecommunications operators were graduates of Beiyou (C. Li 2006). This system remained unchanged until 1998, when MPT control over the yous formally ended and the universities joined China's general higher education bureaucracy (Xia 2007a).

The 1994 reform had two goals: to adapt the sector to the structural changes in the quasi market economy and to meet the MEI's demands for a second operator so that it could compete with the MPT, which increasingly encroached on the MEI's economic territory—equipment manufacture. However, the reform effort was extremely limited. Although China Unicom, an MEI enterprise, received both wireless and landline licenses, the capital costs for landline precluded its extensive development. The MPT (through its operator, China Telecom) frequently refused interconnection, making Unicom's service highly unreliable. China Unicom remained a small player through 1998, a significant delay in light of the sweeping technological changes occurring in the industry. The impact this huge delay had on the development of the IT industry and the whole of China's economy, which relies on affordable and dependable telecommunications, can only be imagined. The MPT's resistance to further deregulation hampered development of modern telecommunications even as the information revolution began to take hold.

In 1998, China Telecom ranked as the eleventh-largest telecommunications operator in the world, with $24.061 billion in revenue (ITU 2007; J. Wang 2001).[18] China Telecom's sole competitor, China Unicom, had only a 5% market share. Even in 2005, China Mobile's profits of 53.6 billion RMB were nearly ten times those of China Unicom (C. Li 2006). This monopoly market structure led to predictable results—even the most minimal of services were unavailable. For example, in the mid-1990s, installation of a new residential phone line cost 5,000 RMB ($610) in Beijing with an average waiting period of six months (DeWoskin 2001).[19] In the early 1990s, mobile telephone service was so high priced—China Telecom levied a 28,000 RMB ($3,500) fee when users purchased a new phone—that even businesses found the cost prohibitive (Y. Lin 2004; Xia 2007a).[20]

It is not surprising, then, that by 1998 the growing gap between China and the West in telecommunications development moved the central government to take steps to break up the MPT's monopoly. Nonetheless, this was done in a classic Chinese way: the MEI, which led the 1994 pro-deregulation group, was merged with the MPT to become the MII (Chung 2002).[21] Mixing the two antagonists was effective in neutralizing opposition and forcing some change. It did, however, reduce the urge for extensive restructuring. China Telecom (and its later divisions, China Mobile and China Netcom) continues to dominate Chinese telecommunications.[22]

Since 1998, the sector has been best viewed as a quasi-competitive semimarket. Political reforms in 1999 limited the MII's role to being solely the industry regulator. Paging services became the responsibility of a separate entity —the China Paging Group—and China Telecom was formally established. Ownership over China Telecom was transferred from the MII to SASAC. In 2000, China Telecom was divided again when its mobile division became the China Mobile Communications Group. In 2002, China Telecom split into two landline only operators—China Telecom and China Netcom. China's final landline operator, China Tietong (formerly China Railcom), developed with the backing of the Ministry of Railways, separately from the MII. Its landline and Internet network mostly followed the right-of-ways along railroad tracks. This system of five operators—two in mobile, three in landline— lasted six years. In May 2008, the five companies were reorganized into three consolidated and integrated mobile-landline-Internet service providers, all still state owned.[23]

These oligopolistic industry structures remain tightly controlled and under the frequently unpredictable influence of the central state; as a result, the companies have limited ability to innovate. While formally separate commercial entities, these corporations are tightly bound together, not only through final ownership—by SASAC and the State Council—but also by being managed by a closely knit group whose members tend to rotate between the companies and the MII.[24] The CEOs, presidents, and board members of the telecommunications companies are all appointed by the State Council through SASAC. The promotion, transfer, and demotion of top managers in these SOEs remain political decisions: all suggested appointments are officially nominated and approved by the CCP Organization Department (Xia 2006).[25] This ensures that political concerns take precedence in the management of these "commercial enterprises."[26] Political meddling in management includes the shuffling of boards, CEOs, and chairmen from companies to their erstwhile competitors. In addition, most managers spend long spells in government before being given their first management roles. The truth that government supervisors, and not shareholders, retain final authority over management can be seen in a selection of 2004 and 2008 management transfers among telecommunications operators (see figure 2.2).

Political control is used in ways that further dilute incentives for true competition and innovation. Because management shake-ups routinely involve the transfer of top managers from or to their former rivals, managers are careful not to fully destroy what might very well be their next job. The situation was aptly described by one of our interviewees: "Generally speaking, entrepreneurship in the Chinese telecommunications sector is yet to be established. Even telecommunications company heads are basically government technocrats promoted and demoted according to a political logic, and not businessmen" (authors' interview).

The politicization of management and the transfer of top managers to their former competitors illustrate the principle of structured uncertainty. Specifically, these changes show how the configuration of power among the party, the government, and the enterprises matters even more than formal bureaucracy. As stated before, telecommunications companies have become market-oriented state-owned corporations separated from their former ministerial and political masters. Although this structure, as applied to boards, investors, and the search for profits, is the formal structure, the final decision-making authority in this case remains the top-level State Council masters.

The transfer of managers ensures that the companies remain under the influence of political masters and are motivated by the State Council's perceived goals for structuring the industry and accomplishing national informationalization. Reforms and changes have less to do with the established institutional setting than with political deals between individuals and their power factions, made in a sphere at least once removed from the sector itself. The power center, while not fully visible, exerts direct influence over the behavior of the sector, regardless of the interests of the companies or the market. Thus, it is never fully clear to companies and their managers what the appropriate behavior is or what their interests and goals should be. This uncertainty, as detailed below,

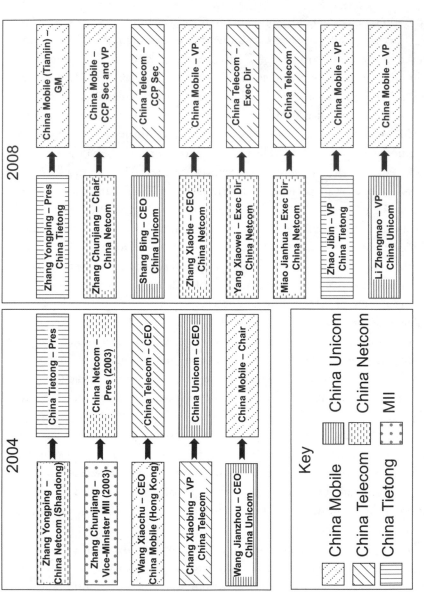

Figure 2.2—Management Transfers among Telecommunications Operators, 2004–2008

Source: China Mobile 2008; China Telecom 2010; China Unicom 2006, 2008a, 2008b; C. Li 2006; Ming 2008; Ye 2008

directly affects the development trajectory of innovation capabilities, R&D, and the structure of the telecommunications market in China.

In addition to the uncertainty stemming from the method and frequency of promotion and transfer of high-level managers, the actual lines of authority, interest, and loyalty in Chinese telecommunications are similarly opaque. Ownership rights are formally exercised by SASAC, whose stated goal is to ensure the profitable and stable restructuring of SOEs (SASAC 2003). Officially, the MII serves as the impartial industry regulator and governs the telecommunications industry but does not make telecommunications policy. Responsibility for making and enforcing policy lies with the State Council itself.[27] The NDRC sets social and developmental goals for the industry, such as universal service obligations. Thus, it can be seen that even in this idealized, institutionalized, and functionally differentiated setting, various state actors—owner, regulator, and social policy planner—all set their own, frequently contradictory goals for the companies.

Despite having defined roles, the reality of political action in the telecommunications sector is even more ambiguous. For example, the MII suffers from a split personality that affects its behavior in the market. Supposedly, its sole role is that of regulator, yet many MII officials still view it as the rightful operator. Not surprisingly, MII regulation has strongly protected the profits and interests of the incumbents and controlled their competitors' actions (Wu 2009). Furthermore, while the regulator officially has no market interests, its national telecommunications research institution, the Chinese Academy of Telecommunications Technology (CATT), is the owner of the Datang Group, the largest producer of equipment for the homegrown TD-SCDMA 3G mobile standard (L. Chen 2005; Xia 2007a, 2007b; Xia and Lu 2008).

These dynamics clearly influenced the development of the landline and mobile telephony markets after 1998. After the breakup of the incumbent MPT monopoly in 1998, the bulk of the landline and Internet services became the property of China Telecom. In landline telephony, competitors included China Netcom (after 2002) and China Tietong. The incumbent operator, China Netcom, and China Tietong were explicitly barred from participating in the mobile telephony market. Mobile licenses were initially granted only to China Unicom and China Mobile.[28] Tight market restrictions and extremely high barriers to entry—all the companies are SOEs, licenses are only granted to incumbents, and no foreign participation is allowed—do not suggest the existence of a truly competitive market. Regulatory limitations and the occasional shuffling of top-level managers suggest that the government sanctions only controlled competition (Xia 2006, 2007a, 2007b). Indeed, managerial switches by SASAC are designed to encourage cultural convergence among the actors as well as to prevent "malicious competition" among them (Xia 2007a).

For example, as part of this "gentlemen's" competition from 2002 to 2008, an informal agreement divided China into specific geographic domains and, in so doing, created de facto regional monopolies for the dominant landline operators. China Telecom dominated China south of the Yellow River, while China Netcom dominated northern China. The two operators were formally urged to compete nationwide but effectively enjoy regional monopolies, which they inherited as a result of the 2002 administrative division of China Telecom along geographic lines (Xia 2006).[29]

What does this degree of central control and interference mean for innovation? The lack of full market competition effectively shields China's telecommunications companies from the need to compete on the basis of novel-product innovation.[30] Incremental improvements to, and enlargement of, their networks are more than sufficient to ensure handsome profits. Moreover, since top managers are very much aware that if all goes well and they do not make any grave mistakes, they will likely be promoted and transferred to one of their rivals within a couple of years, they have little incentive for extensive investment in novel-technology, which, although it might give their current company an edge or even propel it to market dominance, carries high personal risk. Adding to the uncertainty is the fact that although duties are defined, the actual authority or ability to enforce telecommunications laws—particularly against the MII-backed incumbent—is questionable.[31] This raises uncertainty about the future viability of different players as well as concerns about the willingness of incumbents to bend or break rules in order to preserve their market positions. Uncertainty over enforcement also serves to direct the innovation activities of operators away from novel-product innovation, since there is little guarantee of the legal protection of profits, property, or technology if the licensing regime changes or enforcement becomes strict.

Mobile telephony illustrates the dynamic of insufficient regulatory authority and unpredictable outcomes against the powerful operators. Until 2008, China strictly regulated telecommunications operators, limiting them to either landline or mobile telephony. While officially restricted by its MII license to offer only landline services, China Telecom was unable to resist the fruits of a growing mobile market, and the MII proved too tied to the company to prevent it from entering that sector.[32] Starting in 1998, China Telecom began to overtly disregard national regulations by offering a personal handy-phone system (PHS) of locally enabled mobile phones called *xiaolingtong* (XLT) (Yuan et al. 2006).[33] XLT handsets operate solely within a specific urban market—for example, Shanghai—and so China Telecom justified the service by arguing that the service was not a competing mobile service. Proving the tolerance given to multiple and oft-times contradictory interpretations of policy, the MII decided to allow this creative interpretation of landline and mobile voice-telephony regulations.[34]

The choice of XLT was significant in shaping the trajectory of mobile telephony technology in China—a concern that was part of the initial MII opposition to the technology. From the point of view that novel-product innovation is the key to national prosperity and strength, XLT was a major inhibitor of the technological upgrading of China. The success of XLT ensured there has been no incentive for China Telecom to push any of the more advanced technologies. Moreover, until recently it was administratively prevented from entering the mobile market outside XLT. With no ability to profit from innovation or new mobile technologies, and despite the fact that mobile telephony will continue to dominate China, China Telecom preferred to use off-the-shelf, incrementally improved, low-cost technology XLT is considered a mature technology with little room for further innovation. It has limited data-transfer capacity (128 megabits per second), is prone to signal interruption because of low transmission strength and frequent transmitter changes, and cannot—by MII regulation and the microcell structure of its transmission technology—provide intercity roaming. This should limit its market to those with limited mobility and low data-transfer demands (Yuan et al. 2006). In addition, rather than contribute to novel-product innovation within China Telecom and China Netcom, the XLT market is ripe for cross-subsidization, which would allow the two to gain market share on the basis of cost rather than service or any technological innovation arising from their traditional landline sectors, whose revenues are protected by their regional monopolies (Xia 2006).

With more than ninety-one million subscribers in 2006, XLT had gained 16.5% of the mobile telephony market, and the rise of XLT contributed to skewing competition in mobile telephony away from technology toward price (as the two mobile operators, China Mobile and Unicom, were quick to point out). By successfully employing XLT solutions, China Telecom lowered the incentive of mobile operators to invest in expensive new technologies but raised their incentive to expand service and drive down costs at a given level of technology. It also focused the attention of many equipment manufacturers on older technology, again narrowing the scope for novel-product innovation.

Nonetheless, from the broader perspective of innovation and economic growth, the same story looks very different. XLT has allowed millions of Chinese, particularly those with limited disposable income and personal mobility, to gain access to mobile technology (Yuan et al. 2006).[35] Furthermore, XLT technology forced the two mobile operators to lower prices and concentrate on affordability. This ensured that the penetration of other mobile technologies was more rapid than it would have been otherwise and lowered the cost of voice-telephony access across all levels.

Since the benefits of mobile telephony to economic growth are widely known, it might well be that given the particularities of telecommunications in China, XLT should be considered the best thing that could have happened to mobile telephony; not least, it provides strong support for telecommunications-equipment manufacturers such as ZTE (Q. Lin 2003; Yuan et al. 2006). Furthermore, while probably lowering the chances that a Chinese company would be the first to come up with the equivalent of the iPhone, XLT technology did usher in significant innovation in low-cost mobile telephony. As stated by a PHS handset general engineer at ZTE: "PHS was born in Japan but grows up in China" (Q. Lin 2003). As the less developed world becomes the new frontier of the industry, it would be ironic if Chinese companies, by specializing in a somewhat "lower" technology, find themselves with a significant competitive advantage thanks to their XLT experience.

The notion that XLT should be seen as a positive development for innovation and economic growth is further strengthened by an analysis of the mobile telephony sector in China. Indeed, the sector itself is another area in which central regulation stifles innovation and increases uncertainty. Set up as an effective duopoly and protected by restrictive regulations and licensing, two dominant companies—China Mobile and China Unicom—had little incentive to compete on innovation and technology development.[36] This was especially true because state action ensured that China Unicom did not become a true competitor of China Mobile. Created in 1994 as an SOE to compete with the then-monopolistic China Telecom, China Unicom was forced in 2000 to offer services based on two competing technologies: the Global System for Mobile Communications (GSM) and code division multiple access (CDMA).[37] De-Woskin (2001) notes that the decision to adopt CDMA was largely a political one with little commercial justification. This duplication of technologies added cost and complexity, since each system requires a separate and expensive transmission infrastructure. As a result, since China Unicom's heyday in 2001, when it offered only GSM services and controlled approximately one-third of China's mobile market, its market share has sharply declined, and just when mobile telephony uptake was at its peak. By 2007, China Unicom had reached its post-1990s nadir, one-fifth market share, and was saddled with a huge investment (100 billion RMB) in the CDMA network infrastructure (EEO 2008).

China Mobile, split from China Telecom in 2000, not only started with a significantly larger market share than China Unicom, but was also allowed to operate a solely GSM system, ensuring its de facto quasi-monopolistic stranglehold on the market. Therefore, direct state interference in the management of China Unicom left China with a duopoly overwhelmingly dominated by one company—China Mobile. Because no other entrants were allowed into the market, both players had a strong incentive to preserve the status quo. They did not need to upgrade their transmission technologies, since continued rollout at a given level of technology remained highly profitable (Q. Lin 2003). Moreover, with continued delays in the licensing of 3G technology (more of which in the discussion of domestic technology standards below), there was little incentive to invest in 3G-transmission technologies. China was one of the last mobile markets in the world to implement commercial 3G in any format (Lemon 2008a).[38] The delay has been costly for the advancement of China's capabilities as a telecommunications leader, yet it has not inhibited the rapid growth and penetration of mobile technology, albeit at lower levels of technological sophistication.

As an extremely critical and sensitive technology area, telecommunications remains the target of policy and market intervention by all levels of the state. In May 2008, the MII, the NDRC, and the Ministry of Finance announced another major restructuring of the telecommunications market, this time in the direction of consolidation. The proposal, "Announcement on Deepening the Reform of the Structure of the Telecommunications Sector," rendered existing regulations defining mobile, broadband, and landline telephony obsolete. The reform's declared goal was to increase competition, penetration, and service quality; however, it amounted to further consolidation of the oligopoly. China Unicom and China Netcom merged, and China Telecom purchased China Unicom's CDMA business. China Mobile merged with the landline and asymmetric digital subscriber line (ADSL) broadband services of China Tietong. In this way, the MII hoped to create three large, fully integrated telecommunications companies, each offering landline and mobile telephony services. As in the past, a major personnel swap among the leading telecommunications players accompanied the restructuring. Once consolidation of the operators into three integrated companies was completed, each was issued a 3G license that gives

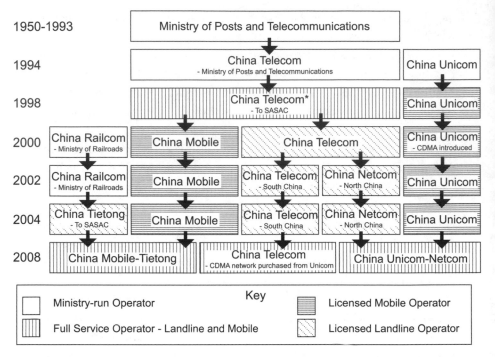

Figure 2.3—Evolution of China's Telecommunications Oligopoly
* Paging services and satellite telephony were also split from China Telecom in the late 1990s, but these are not significant market players.

them—at least theoretically—an equal basis for next-generation mobile services (see figure 2.3 for a schematic history of the major restructuring of the telecommunications market in China, to date).

To conclude, the telecommunications industry in China clearly reflects the conservative and interventionist hand of the central state in the IT industry. Telecommunications is the basis of all IT businesses—and is especially important to services. For historical, institutional, and political reasons, this critical sector remains the domain of the state, not the market. Uncertainty reigns: managers are transferred by political whim, and policies are implemented—or not—with only limited adherence to the declarations or intentions of the nominally controlling bureaucracies. Market actors continue to be constrained by regulations designed to restrict or channel competition.

This reality has not changed despite the radical shifts in China's economy through the 1990s and 2000s. The impact of the latest restructuring will likely depend partly on the fate of China's indigenously developed TD-SCDMA 3G standard. Likewise, the interests of China's telecommunications-hardware manufacturers and their international businesses will be strongly shaped by the ongoing fractious debate on whether the country should go it alone in telecommunications. The current situation makes it even more difficult for companies to undertake long-term strategic planning or major R&D, and there is the added risk that a wave of the State Council's hand could make an expensive investment legally unusable. Furthermore, as the next section shows, politics and structured uncertainty also rule the contested domain of the domestically developed technological standards.

THE MAD HATTER'S RIDDLE:
TECHNOLOGY STANDARDS IN CHINA

China's central authorities make frequent use of technology standards as a policy tool for promoting the development of certain industries. However, as we will reveal, structured uncertainty also dominates this policy region. Most importantly, the Chinese government does not have a single coordinating body like Japan's Ministry of International Trade and Industry (MITI). Different government and economic actors speak with different voices and pull standards policies in different directions. As a result, measures get adopted without full debate or consideration, and are then either abandoned or promoted at great expense, in many cases only to be quietly forgotten. Technology standards in China are a hotly debated topic in political, academic, and business circles—foreign and domestic alike. Perspectives range from support of domestic proprietary standards as a necessary tool for developing brands and novel technology in China's IT industry, to strict opposition to domestic standards; some view standards as simply a cynical new trade-policy tool (Kennedy 2006).[39] The actual rationale for, and impact of, technology standards policies lies between these extremes but there is an element of truth to all sides (Kennedy 2006). The fact that so many perspectives from China's own authorities coexist and compete shows that there is no overarching coordination or planning.

To understand the forms of innovation in China and the approach of economic actors to risk and novel-product development, it is important to understand the role of technology standards. Technology standards serve a useful purpose: they encourage investment in R&D and help IT companies upgrade their technological and innovational capacities. However, the nationalistic and purely political aspects of standards—as trade weapons or as patronage for favored firms—increase uncertainty for Chinese companies whose chosen technology may be excluded once a national standard has been adopted. Thus, technology standards shape the Red Queen run by encouraging innovation and development while, at the same time, discouraging firms' novel-product innovation by increasing uncertainty and the fear of being excluded by restrictive and arbitrarily imposed standards.

We must emphasize that although the supposed goal of Chinese technology standards is to create indigenous novel technologies and even set global trends, the fact remains that technology standards themselves adhere to the logic of the Red Queen run. China's technology standards are political creations adopted in sectors for which the system or product in question is already defined. Hence, even if adopted, they in no shape or form embody novel-product (or technology) innovation (Stevenson-Yang and DeWoskin 2005). In addition, the process of setting domestic Chinese standards discourages Chinese enterprises and research groups from conducting independent or novel-product research, since they fear that if exclusive national standards are adopted, their time and resources could end up having been wasted. Accordingly, they avoid cutting-edge R&D.

Nonetheless, there are two significant benefits to the Chinese domestic standards: they do encourage some form of R&D in enterprises otherwise disinclined to invest in such a high-risk activity; and they have proved to be a powerful tool for forcing foreign standard bearers to lower license fees for Chinese companies. By lowering the licensing costs, they enhance the profitability of Chinese companies employing business models that follow the logic of the Red Queen run.

Why does China seek proprietary, or unique, technology standards? Technology standards were first created, and are still used, to make technologies and equipment compatible across companies and regions. Standardization enables the development of applications and products by many companies around a given technology. A common platform facilitates faster innovation and diffusion, which results, all else being equal, in faster economic growth and development.[40] Standards provide a degree of certainty that encourages innovation because there is a guaranteed open and secure platform—with a large potential market—on which to develop new ideas and services. Technology standards fall into two types: de facto and de jure (Besen and Farrell 1994; Linden 2004). De facto standards are those decided in the marketplace; an example is the standards war for video players that was fought between Betamax and Video Home System (VHS) (Cusumano et al. 1992).[41] Once a standard wins out and rival technologies are squeezed out of the market—for example, in the recent battle between HD-DVD and Blu-ray technology, most content providers in the entertainment industry and many big retailers, such as Wal-Mart, opted for Blu-ray—all manufacturers who wish to stay in that niche must adopt the standard. In such cases, the companies that developed the standard, or the component technologies upon which the standard was built, are able to secure another revenue stream by demanding royalties on the use of their technology.

De jure standards are determined by governments, usually acting upon the decisions made by international standards bodies such as the International Organization for Standardization (ISO) or the International Telecommunications Union (ITU), which deals with telecommunications-specific standards.[42] Before making a decision, the standards bodies examine each proposed technology, down to the level of components and source code.[43] If approved, the standard is officially listed by the ISO or ITU as the standard that all countries and product manufacturers should adopt for a given technology. For some technologies, there is only a single international standard; for others, such as 3G mobile telephony, there are multiple competing, internationally accepted standards.[44]

For defining a new standard, the ISO and ITU set several conditions for potential applicants. First, the standards must be open, with technology and products made available to all (Kushida 2008; Kushida and Zysman 2009). Second, for a technology to become a standard, its developer must show that the proposed standard is superior in technology, use, and application across the industry to which it is to be applied. Failure to meet these two terms may result in rejection of the standard.[45] If the proposed standards are based on proprietary technology, the review committee must have access to all technical data during the approval stage. Proprietary standards that are approved authorize the payment of royalties by users to the developer. The logic behind royalty payments is to provide economic incentives for private actors to develop the most cutting-edge technology and make it widely accessible.

In China, the decision to seek domestic technology standards comes from multiple sources and accords with different political logics, with institutional and economic backers for each. In the 1990s, as China emerged as a major player in the global electronics and telecommunications industries, the government ministries responsible for these sectors (the MII and MOST in particular) began pushing for indigenous standards (Linden 2004). Such a policy builds on the historical PRC preference for limiting the country's reliance on foreign technology. An overly simplistic view of technology standards would suggest that government actors are uniformly in favor of domestic standards, for nationalistic reasons, while industry is more reticent about unique standards, for market reasons. However, we contend that a given actor's institutional affiliation does not predetermine his or her perspective on domestic standards. There are actors in the technology bureaucracy who are opposed to shutting out foreign competition through domestic proprietary standards, and there are industry actors fully in favor of developing exclusive Chinese standards.

The debate revolves around three key issues: nationalism, economic development, and bureaucratic politics. Since the 1980s, Chinese government policy has pursued the rapid dissemination of information technology at the lowest possible cost (Kroeber 2007). This has led to a general disregard for intellectual property rights (IPR)—foreign and domestic—and great disdain for paying royalty fees to foreign companies, especially in order to compete in standardized industries (Stevenson-Yang and DeWoskin 2005). Nationalistic opposition to paying foreigners for the right to use a standard is strong in the bureaucracy, academia, and even within the IT industry. Foreign standards dominate China's IT industry, and having to pay to use them cuts into already slim profit margins and is seen as leading to "overwhelmingly cruel competition" (Suttmeier et al. 2006; Zhong 2004). While the different actors, public and private, disagree on the proper path that should be followed to rectify this situation, they all agree that Chinese companies should not have to pay for the right to use a technology that every economic actor is required to use.

Second, economic concerns dictate the approach of certain actors to domestic standards. Occasionally, economic growth concerns overlap with nationalistic ones. Given that proprietary standards exist, China's IT manufacturers must pay foreign consortia for the right to use certain technologies. In industries with already low profit margins because of commoditization, such expenses are seen as retarding China's growth and the development of indigenous technology (Powell 2006; Suttmeier et al. 2006). Lower profits, so the argument goes, mean insufficient funds to reinvest in technology R&D. This holds back China's companies, which find themselves trapped as the lowest-value-added final-stage assemblers for finished IT goods. Actors who support domestic standards for China believe they will alleviate the burden of fees for foreign proprietary standards. Furthermore, proponents of strong domestic standards policies argue that foreign companies would then be forced to conform to Chinese standards in order to access the coveted Chinese market. This would serve the dual purpose of bringing royalty fees into China and giving Chinese manufacturers access to foreign core technologies when the foreign and Chinese partners collaborate on making technologies compatible (Kroeber 2007; McDonald 2006; *People's Daily* 2004).

Finally, traditional bureaucratic politics also plays a role in the standards debate in China. Standards development brings in grant money and increased recognition from government units. Increased recognition helps open more doors to cooperation and financing, which in turn serves the interests of many actors in the Chinese Academy of Sciences, national research institutes, and universities. Therefore, the proliferation of uniquely Chinese standards strongly serves their parochial interests (authors' interviews). For companies with less than stellar success in selling to international markets, the incentive to participate in standards development may even be greater, given the potential that a proprietary Chinese standard could emerge, shutting off foreign competition and leaving the company in a domestic monopoly position.[46]

Taken together, these three perspectives shed light on the development of Chinese domestic standards—arguably one of the strongest national-level influences on the behavior of the Chinese IT industry. The creation of standards policy is a classic example of structured uncertainty and the conflicting, and at times confused, relations between China's central state ministries and industry, which frame the economic climate in which regional policies and business models develop. The types of standards implemented and the decision to issue or withhold licenses increase uncertainty about the future of any given technology. Fighting for influence within the government shapes the emergence of different standards, often without concern for the industries that would be most affected by such a change. Because of this, the development of standards policy provides a revealing look at the relationship between China's central government and the industries for which it sets general policies and guidelines. At times, the central state acts on behalf of and in accordance with the interests of industry, as in the case of trying to negotiate lower rates for core-technology licenses in DVD players or 2G mobile telephony. At other times, the central state has acted on behalf of patron enterprises, with little concern for the overall market situation or the industry's growth. As will be shown later, it is local governments, operating within the limitations of the central state and its policies and regulations, that have attempted to support industries in more effective, market-conforming ways. Their actions have enabled incomplete or even wholly absent central-government policies and economic legal reforms to bear fruit in economic growth.

To illustrate these dynamics at work and show how they constrain novel-product R&D while unleashing innovations across a broad spectrum of the industry, we turn to two cases of domestic technology standards development in China: DVD encryption and the TD-SCDMA standard for 3G mobile. These illustrate how standards both encourage and constrain innovation in China and how fighting within the government prevents coherent policy making, thus increasing the uncertainty under which economic actors must compete.

In the late 1990s, Chinese manufacturers began to assemble a then-new and relatively high-technology consumer electronic system—the DVD player.[47] As had happened with other IT industries in China, rapid market entrance by multitudes of similar, nondifferentiated firms ensued. This contributed to an extremely rapid decrease in the cost of DVD players. Falling prices increased their popularity in foreign, and eventually domestic, markets, which only encouraged further production.[48] Just as with video compact disc (VCD) players, while Chinese manufacturers successfully pushed for the expansion of domestic component production, the highest-value-added components—the video decoder and optical pickup chips—remained the proprietary technology of foreign firms (Kennedy 2005).

Throughout this period, many Chinese DVD-player companies barely managed to earn profits on their operations. Companies attributed their extremely low profits to excessive licensing and royalty fees levied by foreign IPR-holders on key DVD components.[49] China's government adopted two simultaneous policies to address the difficulties faced by their manufacturers. Facing increased scrutiny and the enforcement of licensing fees as a result of WTO accession, the central government renegotiated required royalty fees for domestic manufacturers from more than $20 per unit to $13.80 for technologies from Toshiba, Matsushita, JVC, Mitsubishi, Hitachi, Time Warner, Philips, Sony, and Pioneer (Linden 2004; People's Daily 2004). While this helped reduce costs, many Chinese manufacturers still perceived as unfair the need to pay royalties and reduce already thin profits (Clendenin 2006). While the central government sought lower royalty payments, an assortment of government research institutes and DVD manufacturers collaborated under the auspices of the MII to form an industry alliance: Beijing E-World Technology. This industry alliance committed itself to developing China's own DVD-style technology standards for use both as a bargaining chip with foreign companies and as a technological-upgrading vehicle for member companies (Clendenin 2006; People's Daily 2003; Smith 2003). In 1999, the MII and the State Trade and Economic Commission provided $1.2 million to begin development of Chinese digital video technology (Smith 2003). Two years later, Beijing E-World produced the Advanced High Density Disc System (AVD). For the next several years, the MII would promote AVD as China's national standard, adopting it in 2005 (Powell 2006).

However, the rapidly increasing popularity of standard DVD players in China's domestic market had largely removed the market incentive for a competing standard. Nonetheless, Beijing E-World paired the AVD system, which was seemingly stillborn, with a "basically compatible" Taiwanese system called Enhanced Versatile Disc (EVD). The Taiwanese partners, for reasons never fully disclosed, backed out of the arrangement shortly thereafter. Despite the much lower royalty fees paid for the domestically developed AVD system, the popularity and relatively low cost of standard DVD players meant that AVD never managed to gain any market share. Furthermore, although AVD was able to generate higher-quality images, the low quality of most Chinese TV screens meant the improvement was unnoticeable—and therefore of little interest to the consumer. The technology and standard had been successfully developed, but without consideration for market realities or its appropriateness for Chinese consumers.

In April 2004, nineteen IT consumer-electronics manufacturers, including Skyworth, Changhong, and TCL (also members of Beijing E-World), announced the creation of another industry alliance to promote yet another competing standard—High-Clearness Video Disc (HVD) (CTN 2004a). Also in 2004, the Beijing K-City High Definition Electronic Technology Company formed an alliance to promote its own homegrown high-definition DVD standard—High Definition Video (HDV) (AsiaInfo 2004). Hedging their bets in response to uncertainty over which standard would be viable, Skyworth, Changhong, and TCL joined this alliance as well. Both standards added to the confusion among Chinese consumers.

In 2004, the HVD and HDV alliances cooperated to prevent the central government from anointing AVD-EVD as the national standard (CTN 2004b). The technology advantage of AVD-EVD was further eroded by the arrival of the High-Definition Digital Video Disc (HD-DVD) and Blu-ray high-definition formats. As early as 2006, it was clear that AVD-EVD was unsuccessful, since sales remained in the hundreds of thousands of units per year rather than the millions predicted (Clendenin 2006). By 2008, all three Chinese formats, AVD-EVD, HDV, and HVD, had proved to be market failures. The MII had succeeded neither in creating a protected and proprietary national standard nor in helping China free itself from a foreign technology.

From a purely economic perspective, government and industry invest-ment in alternative DVD technologies has had a largely negative result. Large amounts of resources were channeled into the development of alternative tech-nologies, which—at least in retrospect—were clearly not market viable from the beginning. While the effort marshaled the resources of many Chinese man-ufacturers and brought them together for a common purpose, the existence of similar competing standards, often developed by companies participating in multiple alliances in order to hedge their bets, starkly revealed the lack of long-term planning and organizational capacity by the central state. The failure to develop a DVD technology standard once again reveals that China's central government is not at all an all-powerful coordinator or industrial organizer in the vein of a traditional East Asian developmental state (Johnson 1982; Wade 1990; Woo-Cumings 1999; Zysman 1983).

The AVD-EVD standard also failed to break China's dependence on for-eign proprietary-technology standards. The AVD-EVD system still relied on codecs, the VP5 and VP6 video codecs, that were developed and owned by a U.S. company, On2 (CTN 2003; Yoshida 2003). (A codec—from "coder-de-coder"—is a device that encodes a digital stream for transmission and decodes it for playback.) In addition, the decoder for AVD-EVD was developed with foreign assistance, in this case in cooperation between the U.S. company LSI Logic, and Beijing Homaa Microelectronics Technology and Beijing E-World (Frauenheim 2004). Moreover, the AVD-EVD system itself was not path-breaking or novel, since it was simply a Chinese modification and incremen-tal improvement on existing technology (McDonald 2006; Powell 2006).

We must emphasize, however, that the lack of novelty does not discredit the value of the AVD-EVD experiment for China's IT industry. The experience with developing a unique standard showed, perhaps for the first time, that China's commoditized manufacturers could create a differentiated product and invest coherently in R&D. China's manufacturers revealed that they possessed the ability, both with and without (in the case of HVD and HDV) central state support, to develop new products and move up the value chain (*People's Daily* 2004). In this sense, many companies institutionalized meaningful and rou-tinized R&D for the first time. Such a lesson in technology and skill upgrad-ing, even if the final product was a failure, is valuable for institutional learning.

Additionally, within the wider context of China's political economy, Chi-nese DVD standards were quite successful. If, as some of our interviewees ar-gued, the domestic DVD standards were never intended to serve as a viable market alternative but rather to provide Chinese trade negotiators with another tool when discussing licensing and royalty fees on technology, then the DVD standards were very successful. The standards development and the threat to close the Chinese market to foreign-standards-based digital optical electronics forced foreign companies—the standards holders—to lower their royalty fees. Such is the essence of the power of the Red Queen. Although China does not own and did not develop the standards it uses, it exerts significant power to influence the practices of technology innovators because of its critical position in the global IT-industry chain (and the powerful attraction of its potentially vast internal market). Last, the Chinese DVD-standard case remains a clear indication of the prevalence of structured uncertainty in China's IT industry. While the standards appear to have passed into obscurity, China's government and research institutions actually incorporated these technologies into their wider Digital Home initiative (authors' interviews). So at least in this subsector, the possibility, however remote, of China closing itself off in favor of technical autarky remains alive. The technology remains a potential tool the state can wield if a faction decides that technological autonomy or autarky in this sector is desirable.

A much greater economic, political, and technological question rests on the future of 3G mobile telephony in China. The outcome of the 3G standardization and licensing fight will have a great impact on the global viability of China's telecommunications-equipment manufacturers (C. Li 2006). This battle also reveals the degree to which China's central state continues to pursue technology independence, but not novelty, in critical sectors—even at the expense of market efficiency.

Three-G mobile telephony is a qualitative and quantitative advance over 2G.[50] Third-generation transmissions are designed to handle high levels of data transfer, enabling voice, audio, video, and Internet data to be easily accessed from a mobile handset. Originally, the ITU intended to have a single international standard for 3G, one based on CDMA technology—a propriety technology developed by the U.S. company Qualcomm.[51] However, since the 1990s, three distinct competing standards for 3G mobile telephony have emerged. In North America, principally in the United States, the CDMA2000 standard is the most popular. In Europe, a locally developed standard, W-CDMA, is the preferred option. In May 2000, China succeeded in having its own indigenous 3G standard, TD-SCDMA internationally certified by the ITU as a viable 3G standard (Suttmeier et al. 2006). Each standard competes for market share and for the manufacturing capacity of telecommunications-equipment providers. With the global proliferation of 3G, the potential profits arising from firms upgrading entire mobile phone networks make the control of the standards and mastery of the technology necessary for their transmission a very attractive prospect.

In the 1990s, the MII began sponsoring R&D efforts for the creation of a domestic 3G standard to compete with foreign standards.[52] The ITU certified the TD-SCMDA standard, making this case qualitatively different from that of other Chinese standards, which were not international certified. As early as 2000, the developers of the TD-SCDMA technology completed development to the satisfaction of the ITU. However, difficulties, delays, and setbacks plagued the development of commercially viable transmission equipment.[53] According to an interview we conducted in June 2008, the situation was quite stark, even in the final months before licenses were issued: "Bluntly speaking, the TD-SDCMA standard is not as mature as CDMA2000 or WCDMA. It takes time. It needs support. It needs a market. If we lose this standard, and run a pilot project using the WCDMA or the CDMA2000, then the whole Chinese market has no chance for the TD-SCDMA. We will be swamped and lose our standard."

Knowing that the granting of 3G licenses before its own technology became commercially viable would virtually assure the dominance of foreign standards in the Chinese market, the MII simply refused to grant operating licenses (Rottenberg 2007).[54] Since the MII opposed allowing the buildup of any 3G network that used different standards as long as TD-SCDMA was not fully operational, these difficulties held back China's implementation of 3G networks. Although commercial 3G networks had appeared in developed countries as early as 2001, the MII did not issue 3G licenses until December 31, 2008, when the three reorganized operators each received a license (CNN 2002; Loney 2001; D. Zhang 2008).[55] The result has been a continued lack of technological advancement, incremental improvement, and applications work in 3G technology in China. So while many countries are already preparing to launch fourth-generation (4G) networks, China remains trapped.[56] Currently, it is not at all clear whether TD-SCDMA will, after all these efforts, prove to be a viable 3G technology. Even the *China Daily* reports that test runs of TD-SCDMA networks since the early 2000s have been "disappointing" (W. Li 2005). As a result, manufacturers of telecommunications hardware, such as Huawei and ZTE, have long since switched to researching, developing, and manufacturing foreign-standard 3G equipment, even if there is currently no domestic market for them (Bishop 2007; Fan 2006; Kroeber 2007; X. Liu 2006). Although all three standards have been licensed for use, the MII continues to exhibit behaviors typical of an institution caught in structured uncertainty. In January 2009, the MII announced further support for the TD-SCDMA standard, including a preference for TD-SCDMA networks in government procurement, preferential access to R&D funds, and priority network-access licenses (D. Zhang 2009).

The potential advantages of relying on a domestic 3G standard are obvious to certain industry actors. Equipment manufacturers would have the largest mobile market in the world as a captive market (Suttmeier et al. 2006). Indeed, during the long delay in 3G licensing, MII-owned Datang has developed its TD-SCDMA transmission technology. The prospect of TD-SCDMA becoming China's domestic 3G standard (and a potentially huge market for a first mover) encouraged Philips and Samsung to enter into joint ventures with Datang for chip sets and reference designs for TD handsets, although the ventures failed to turn a profit through 2008 (Business Wire 2003; Linden 2004). However, since its market is entirely domestic, Datang, unlike the two Chinese wireless communication giants Huawei and ZTE, does not concern itself with foreign reactions to a uniquely Chinese standard. This is a glaring difference between the companies' behavior, since even ZTE, which is not only state owned but also still predominantly domestic market oriented, has expressed serious reservations about the licensing of TD-SCDMA, especially about the prospect of its adoption as the sole Chinese 3G standard. While Huawei and ZTE produce equipment for China's TD-SCDMA standard, both hope to continue to aggressively expand their international businesses and thus fear that if they focus resources on a technology with very dim prospects of ever being used abroad, they will diminish their ability to compete in the global market (Kroeber 2007; C. Li 2006). As stated in an interview we conducted with a former vice president of a leading Chinese technological university: "The decision to support TD-SCDMA or another standard is related to the size of the market. If most of the Chinese company's market is worldwide, then the company's leaders, like the CEO, will think about the global market. If the company's market is just the domestic market, then they pay great attention to the local. If the company wants to export products, the leaders want to use international standards so that the company can do OEM or support foreign markets."

TD-SCDMA is an example of how political concerns and intentions can interfere with the operation of China's market. Standards such as TD-SCDMA are at the heart of China's drive for technological independence. These standards serve the goal of enhancing national pride by helping the country break free of its dependence on foreign technology and by having indigenous technology certified by the ITU as a viable global technology standard (X. Liu 2006; *People's Daily* 2007). More cynically, however, the development of TD-SCDMA provides support for well-connected companies such as Datang and Xinwei, both owned by the MII's CATT research institute.[57] The standard has also served as an effective weapon against the payment of royalties for foreign proprietary technology in 3G (Fan 2006). Finally, it is clear that political concerns can, at times, supersede market or technological ones, given the continued support for TD-SCDMA and the preference for it as a national standard, even though China's most successful telecommunications-equipment providers are lukewarm toward the technology.

TD-SCDMA has also provided a continual level of high uncertainty in China's telecommunications industry. The state's protracted unwillingness to license a 3G network for the operators and its clear preference for TD-SCDMA have, we argue, discouraged long-term investment, since Chinese manufacturers of telecommunications equipment did not know which technology for the domestic market they would need to support. Hence, the long-running TD-SCDMA saga did not merely encourage the Red Queen run but in fact compelled it, because firms will not invest in long-term novel-product innovation in a climate of uncertainty where certification or uniform adoption of a standard can render expensive long-term investments obsolete. It is ironic that the declared idea behind the standard was to foster indigenous cutting-edge innovation, because many Chinese companies, faced with the uncertainty surrounding TD-SCDMA, preferred to concentrate their efforts on the mature 2G technologies and overseas markets. Consequently, the central government's aggressive move to achieve technology independence ended up discouraging the development of China's indigenous novel-product innovation in mobile telecommunications.

To conclude, China's technology standards, despite their official intent of encouraging novel innovation in China, serve only to accelerate the Red Queen run. The standards themselves are only improvements or extensions of existing and defined technologies, the exact types of R&D in which China excels. The constant standards battles discourage enterprises and researchers from blazing their own paths, since they fear that a political shift could render their efforts moot. However, the standards, even if not novel, do encourage domestic enterprises to engage in research that might otherwise be ignored or underfunded. By involving industry, standards policy encourages, finances, and facilitates routinized, meaningful R&D and improves the endurance of second-generation innovative companies and producers in China. Technology standards reflect two critical points: there is no effective central coordinating body in China's high-technology industries, and the decision whether to adopt a proprietary Chinese standard has great influence on the behavior of enterprises, typically constraining their long-term R&D efforts.

REGIONAL (SEMI) EMANCIPATION:
THE DYNAMICS (AND LIMITS) OF
REGIONAL POLICY ENTREPRENEURSHIP

The systems of institutions that have molded the development trajectory of the IT industry in different regions developed in a coevolutionary process influenced by the legacy of local planning from the Mao era, the piecemeal and ambiguous nature of reforms since Deng Xiaoping's era, and the fact that the central government has been unable to impose its will at the local level.[58] Starting in the final years of the Mao era, the role of local economic officials in economic policy has gradually expanded, albeit in fits and starts. By 1980, only the largest enterprises remained under direct central control, and the vast majority of the industrial economy was locally planned and managed.

An important aspect of this reform process, one that has attracted little interest in the literature, is that while regions have been effectively transformed into the loci of dynamic economic policy making, they have never been given control over many policy domains with significant influence over final outcomes. These domains control fundamental concerns affecting the profitability and practicability of novel-product R&D, such as property rights and the financial system.[59] As a consequence, this dichotomy of authority tended to ensure that even when developing very different policy paths, all regions followed the logic of the Red Queen run. This logic then became the dominant policy principle, thanks to the other main characteristic of the reforms—their inherent structured uncertainty.

As we described earlier, all national reforms that delegated responsibility for policy entrepreneurship to the regions were deliberately ambiguous, open ended, and ever changing, which meant that, on the one hand, it was never clear how much leeway was being given to local officials to interpret the "true" wishes of the center. On the other hand, it was patently obvious that rapid and continual economic growth continued to be the sole reliable approval benchmark. This led local officials to prefer lower-risk activities with a high potential for producing short-term, rapid economic growth. Since this was a tendency that local officials already preferred for personal and career-advancement reasons, long-term high-risk activities, especially in market niches that had not already proved profitable, were shunned. This has been true even in cases of policy actions whose declared aim has been to spur the development of industries based on novel-product R&D—like IT.

To show these dynamics in action, and to explore both the positive and negative effects on the IT industry of making the regions the loci of policy entrepreneurship, we investigate two central industrial S&T and innovation policies that were delegated to the provinces: science-based industrial parks and nongovernmental enterprise formation. This focus allows us to analyze the national institutions and regulations—such as those affecting property rights, incorporation rights, and IPR—that sharpen the ability of different regions to shape the development of their IT industries.

We begin with the domain at the core of the national industrial-innovation policy—science-based parks—and then look at the development and internal logic of what most researchers view as a crucial part of any novel-product, innovation-based high-technology industry—nonstate and private enterprise formation. The science-based industrial parks are a critical policy instrument by which local and regional governments can push their economic development while honoring, at least on the surface, national plans for high-technology industries. In fact, these parks have created the basis for much of the initial growth in the IT industry, although they have done so in ways not envisioned by central authorities. Similarly, while reform-era central-government pronouncements encouraged the development of market-based enterprises, the lack of clarity on ownership reform meant that for new market enterprises to survive, the local authorities needed to invent wholly new systems of ownership without running afoul of central plans.

THE CHESHIRE CAT OF PROPERTY RIGHTS: SCIENCE PARKS AND HIGH-TECH MINYING COMPANIES

Within a few years after the initiation of economic reforms in 1978, the central government became acutely aware of the huge economic-growth potential of the IT industry and the role that nonstate enterprises could play in its development. However, this realization immediately led to two policy dilemmas. The first was how to allow for market-based "private" industry actors and property rights within a supposedly socialist planned economy that forbade private enterprise. The second dilemma was how to make needed resources, especially finance, available to these enterprises.

The first policy initiative directed at the provinces took the form of national programs to spur the creation of the high-tech industry by turning over management to the provinces. The second approach was to create a new, undefined, yet legal form of enterprise: nongovernmental people-run enterprises, better known by their somewhat ambiguous Chinese name: *minying qiye* (民营企业).[60] The science-based park initiative commenced in 1988 with the Torch Program, which followed in the footsteps of the 863 Program; it aimed to address at least some of the problems perceived as arising from the over-centralization of the 863 Program (Segal 2003). At the heart of the Torch Program has been the establishment of science-based high-technology parks (henceforth referred to as high-technology development zones—HTDZs) in which funding, special tax treatment, and other resources were to be channeled into nongovernmental high-technology enterprises (China Torch 2008). Control over the establishment and management of these zones was given to local governments. Furthermore, central funding for the Torch Program was limited, and most of the funds came from other sources, mainly local governments and foreign direct investment (FDI). The precise definition of a science park, its aims, and the definition of the high-technology minying that are supposed to populate them have been left purposely ambiguous.

However, rapid economic development was clearly defined as a priority for the Torch Program. The program differed from its state-sponsored predecessors in that its official mission was the industrialization and dissemination of technology to generate economic growth. All proposals to be given support under the program were to involve already-mature and advanced technologies. The conditions or plans for batch production had to be already available, and proposals had to have a predicted output value that would exceed investment by a ratio of five to one within less than three years (China Development Gateway 2004; Pei 2005; Segal 2003, 32). Hence, although touted within and outside China as promoter of high technology, the Torch Program, as a careful analysis of its investment criteria reveals, focused on proven technologies as a way to jump-start local production and supply a large number of manufacturing jobs.

Regional officials have taken up the task of establishing numerous science parks. Indeed, there are currently fifty-four national-level zones—many founded explicitly under the Torch Program—and hundreds of provincial, municipal, district, or university-run HTDZs in China, each of which operates in its own way.[61]

Five parks are considered national leaders, among them Beijing Zhongguancun (北京中关村科技园区), Shanghai Zhangjiang (上海张江高科技园区) and Shenzhen High-Tech Industrial Park (深圳市高新技术产业园). These three parks account for 29.8% of the total profits of the fifty-four national-level HTDZs (MOST 2008b). The central government holds up these zones as national leaders, especially Zhongguancun, to be emulated for their model policies and their practices for attracting investment, conducting and commercializing research, and developing novel technologies (Cao 2004). However, even these leading HTDZs are locally administered and managed through development companies owned by the local municipal government.

The HTDZs in China differ somewhat from the classical image of a science-based industrial park or a high-technology zone in developed countries. The zones all supposedly mimic Silicon Valley; HTDZ planners uphold this model, which, it is commonly held, unites science, industry, education, and services, as the ideal structure for a science park. Zhongguancun is frequently referred to as Beijing's (or China's) Silicon Valley, although even less well-known parks frequently make similar claims for themselves. For example, the Suzhou Industrial Park outside Shanghai advertises itself as the "New Silicon Valley" (SIP 2007). Nonetheless, aspirations and rhetoric aside, China's HTDZs are more akin to export-processing zones, free-trade zones, or foreign-invested industrial parks than to highly integrated zones of innovation. While certainly hoping to become centers of technological innovation, even the best HTDZs function primarily to spur local economic growth, taking whichever route provides the fastest growth, regardless of whether their projects involve high technology.

Most HTDZs developed by using local financing. They adopted different incentive packages to encourage enterprises to invest in one park or another. Preferential policies are often geared toward accomplishing local goals of rapid export or employment creation, and not necessarily the national goal of encouraging cutting-edge R&D. National policies set by the Torch Program and others are supposed to govern things like the educational composition of the workforce, investment in R&D, and the percentage of a firm's income to be derived from a required high-technology source, but are often quietly neglected at the local level (authors' interviews; Cao 2004; S. Wang et al. 1998).[62] The result is that thanks to local support, IT enterprises that are not high tech (as defined by the central government and so perhaps not qualified to receive national benefits) are able to thrive in market niches better suited to China's actual level of development. Therefore, rather than becoming vehicles for novel-product innovation, the HTDZs have become an institutional component enabling the "run of the Red Queen" development path.

The HTDZs represent the primacy of local over national politics and priorities. As the HTDZs became increasingly local organs, the Red Queen run emerged. Parks competed fiercely for investment and sought rapid returns, which was the least risky way to expand the local economic and industrial base and ensure the greatest potential returns. Enterprises attracted by economic, although not necessarily technological, incentives flocked to the zones, creating clusters of suppliers, consumers, exporters, and supporting businesses. Because of the HTDZs' focus on local economic growth, their development priorities also included questionably high-technology sectors, such as paper and packaging in the case of Zhongshan or Coca-Cola in Shanghai. However, as the more successful parks attracted diverse companies to themselves and their environs, they gave rise to true industrial clusters, in what the literature terms "the North Italian Mode" (Piore and Sabel 1984). In Chapter Five, we will elaborate on this point by analyzing the growth of the uninterruptible power supply (UPS) industrial cluster in Dongguan.

Each region in our study has taken a slightly different approach to the management and use of their HTDZs. In Beijing, national proclamation and local preference have made Zhongguancun into the flagship park of the country. Zhongguancun's success and operation are, therefore, of great interest to political actors in the central and Beijing governments who are looking to burnish their image as enablers of economic growth based on high-technology industries. To that end, Zhongguancun is the only park in China where administrative rules carry the force of law (authors' interviews). In other HTDZs, administrative policies are not contractually or legally binding. Second, the direct administrative hand of the Beijing government can be felt in the movement of specific enterprises into particular subparks within the overall HTDZ. The administrative goal is to force the clustering of related enterprises—the most obvious in IT being the Zhongguancun Software Park in the Shangdi area of the Haidian District—and to foster the innovation benefits of clustering. The development of production capacity, at least in the Haidian portion of Zhongguancun, is discouraged.

In Shanghai, the approach to the flagship park—Zhangjiang—is somewhat less directly activist. Although the local government has launched a "Focus on Zhangjiang" development program that aims to make the park a leading force in Shanghai's economic development, there is little evidence of administrative picking and choosing. The park itself, like others in the Pudong New Area, is heavily dominated by large foreign enterprises, many of which combine production facilities with their R&D facilities. Shanghai encourages the development of a hub-and-spoke type of industrial cluster with various degrees of embeddedness (Markusen 1996; Walcott 2002). The preference for large enterprises encourages the formation of joint ventures with large state-owned conglomerates. Beyond large formal collaborations, however, the actual pattern of farming out activities to smaller enterprises and start-ups appears to be of little concern to the Shanghai government. When it comes to guiding the market and industrial structure, however, the fostering of large-scale investment—especially prestige investment such as the Semiconductor Manufacturing International Corporation's (SMIC's) pureplay semiconductor foundry—is very important to Shanghai's leadership. This is especially evident in the HTDZs outside the city proper, which tend to be industrial parks with little or no high-technology focus or interfirm collaboration, despite official titles and pronouncements.

Finally, in the Pearl River Delta, regional authorities at the provincial, municipal, and township levels take a highly activist approach to their HTDZs, but less in an attempt to pick winners than to streamline procedures and provide complete value and production chains or infrastructure in order to encourage value-added manufacturing. In the PRD, the HTDZs are meant to be engines of growth by encouraging the upgrading and increased development of supporting industries throughout the PRD and further afield (authors' interviews).[63] Lower-value-added activities—frequently highly polluting—are priced out or denied investment permits for the HTDZs, but other venues in industrial parks at the city, district, and even village level are provided. This ensures the completion of an industrial chain within the region. Such a complete chain, along with intensive investment by the regional authorities in infrastructure (telecommunications, highways, rail, seaports, and airports), enables the PRD to continue to attract IT industries with embedded manufacturing, despite rising costs. Keeping advanced manufacturing in the PRD is a priority, and the HTDZs are designed to spearhead that effort. In sum, the development of HTDZs in China's IT industrial regions has come about as the local implementation of a national high-technology-development initiative. By creatively interpreting the meaning of "high technology" and building upon the chosen image of an ideal local industrial structure, the parks have built the industrial base for China's run of the Red Queen. Thus, policy entrepreneurship by provincial governments transformed a central-government directive, which was ostensibly aimed at the stimulation of novel-product activities, into one of the main pillars of the "Red Queen run" industrial-development model.

The second prong of China's industrial innovation policy—the creation of a new class of companies—minying enterprises—is another exemplary case of the positive influence of refusing to define objectives and key policy concepts. Developed concurrently with the Torch Program, the high-tech minying policy has been intimately tied to the special science-based economic zones, since enterprises that are recognized as high-tech minying are the companies to which the special funds and tax benefits of the zones are supposed to be given.[64] However, as Adam Segal (2003) has extensively detailed, not only has the minying concept been left purposely undefined, but the limits of this "un-definition" have also been constantly changing. During our own interviews with IT companies, we found that this confusion still exists. Many companies still prefer to register multiple firms, each with a different legal status.

High-tech minying has been defined in many ways: as any kind of high-tech company that is not an outright SOE; as any high-tech company, including an SOE, where management is free from direct bureaucratic control; or, most vaguely, as a desirable outcome of the reforms to direct the Chinese innovation system toward market-oriented enterprises. Furthermore, central officials have repeatedly stressed that "minying" does not necessarily mean "private," and that the concept does not have any relation to property rights. This should not come as a surprise, since the definition of property rights and private enterprises goes to the heart of the definition of China itself and contradicts traditional interpretations of the communist ideology that is still formally espoused by the CCP.[65]

Local officials were given full control over the operational definition of minying and were motivated to develop their own interpretation and policy implementation. Adam Segal recounts how one of his interviewees recalled that central officials were quite aware of the fact that the minying concept has never been defined, and when asked by one local official, a representative from the State Science and Technology Commission (SSTC, the predecessor of MOST) answered: "If we clarify what it means to be *minying*, we are going to have problems. You keep doing what you want, and then we can see what works best" (2003, 41).

This uncertainty with regard not only to property rights but also to lines of authority and jurisdiction has motivated IT companies to seek refuge by affiliating themselves with specific supervisory agencies such as the local government, the Chinese Academy of Sciences, a university, or a ministry. Interviewees throughout China repeatedly stressed that such an affiliation is necessary to provide security against bureaucratic interference. Without an affiliation, uncertainty over ownership and permitted activities allows other agencies that are so inclined to interfere in the daily operations of businesses by claiming that the business or its activities falls under their jurisdiction.[66] Hence, entrepreneurs find themselves devoting a large amount of time to cultivating the correct relationships with various bureaucracies just so that they can run their businesses with minimal interference.[67] Even when an enterprise is in an "encouraged sector" and is within a supported park or incubator, negotiating the bureaucratic labyrinth can take many months (ZhuLu 2008).

Finding similar dynamics, Adam Segal (2003, 12–15) has termed this process the search for a good mother-in-law. The search for bureaucratic protection creates uncertainty and directs some of IT companies' key resources, such as management time and attention, away from business development and R&D. Furthermore, by increasing both uncertainty and transaction costs, it further strengthens the tendency of entrepreneurs to gravitate toward short-term and proven technologies. This is reinforced by the fact that almost all the Chinese bureaucratic "mothers-in-law" value economic growth above all else for both financial (personal and organizational) and career-advancement reasons.

The political battles around the definition and control of high-technology minying continue to the present day. After two decades in which the central government's main aim was to allow the regions as much leeway as possible, the latest political maneuver regarding high-technology enterprises, effective in 2008, once again shows the vast extent of structured uncertainty in China. The policy, the National Indigenous Innovation Certification Management Method (国家自主创新产品认定管理办法), throws the definition of high-tech enterprises back into question. Significantly, the new law makes it impossible to know who, local or central officials, has the authority to certify enterprises as high tech.[68] Formally, the new law is now in force, and all enterprises, established or new, are required to register or reregister in order to be approved as high-tech enterprises. However, it is not yet clear with which agency they should register or what the criteria are for recognition. In theory, the power to designate enterprises as high tech has now (once again) been taken away from local or regional officials and given back to national-level committees operating under the auspices of MOST, the Ministry of Finance, and the NDRC. However, how exactly the entire, already-certified high-tech IT industry (and other high-technology industries) will be recertified and its applications confirmed remains an unanswered question. What is clear is that the sheer number of enterprises involved means that these committees, even if they are formed, will not have the resources or expertise to handle all the applications, and thus power, in some form or another, will devolve back to regional authorities (authors' interviews). Tellingly, according to the Public Policy Division of MOST, certification will be done through the provincial-level offices of MOST. However, as discussed above, this structure will reactivate the same region-centric influences and interests that the centralization of certification was designed to prevent.

On the one hand, the ambiguity in China allows each region, and sometimes even townships and villages, to quickly start operations within the IT industry. Such vagueness helped not only low-level operations but also those at higher levels of sophistication. The mere fact that minying was now a legal entity allowed various deals to be cut between entrepreneurs and state agencies or between researchers and their home institutions. These deals permitted companies to be formed, enjoy official (and formal) investment, quickly expand, and come out of the shadows. On the other hand, such ambiguity also meant that uncertainty remained very high and that property rights, especially IPR, remained ill defined. This limited the amount of risk taking, but also, more rarely, endangered enterprises that became so successful that the wealth they generated became crucial to their institutional mothers-in-law. The agencies then used the ambiguities surrounding ownership as a way to gain full control over the companies.[69] Needless to say, the result has been that while the initiation of minying enterprises has allowed the IT industry to flourish, their inherent ambiguity, constant redefinition, and high level of structured uncertainty have diminished the ability of entrepreneurs to undertake long-term high-risk novel-product-innovation R&D activities.

CONCLUSION

In this chapter, we have explained how politics are crucial for an understanding of China's run of the Red Queen. Economic activities in high-risk longterm activities such as R&D are highly dependent on the institutional system in which they are embedded. For this reason, we have chosen to analyze the particularities of the Chinese system and the mechanisms by which they translate to specific behaviors of the IT industry. As the Chinese system has passed through systematic transformations since 1978, it has been constantly molded by political battles that have determined the speed and nature of reforms. Understanding how these contestations were and continue to be settled is crucial to understanding the trajectory path taken by the Chinese IT industry.

We further argue that two prominent features of the Chinese political economy, in comparison with other rapidly growing emerging economies, are its very low level of institutionalization and its high level of structured uncertainty. Thus, we contend, to understand the development of the IT industry in China, we must not only recognize the formal and informal institutional environment or the ways in which political battles around policy are settled, but also become cognizant of the spheres of uninstitutionalization and the encompassing impact of structured uncertainty.

A third central feature of Chinese reforms that has received considerable attention in the literature is the fact that China's central government has been delegating large amounts of responsibility for the actual interpretation and implementation of reforms to the regions, allowing each to implement (or not implement) these reforms as it sees fit. However, a dimension of this feature that has received little if any attention is the fact that while responsibility has been delegated to the provinces, decision-making authority and control over major institutional features crucial to the development of the high-technology industry remain firmly at the center. Thus, to understand the trajectory path of the Chinese IT industry, either nationally or within a particular region, we need to acknowledge these tensions and analyze their influences. These tensions, we argue, are one of the reasons why the Chinese IT industry, while it has developed unique regional models, always adheres to "run of the Red Queen" logic. We need to emphasize that although it retained much authority in certain critical legal, policy, and technological areas, the central government itself had very little capability for constructive action and lacked the "coordinated developmental state" capacity of countries such as Japan and South Korea.

With a macro view, we have elaborated on the impact and causes of structured uncertainty. Taking a systemic view, we have shown that structured uncertainty is a result of the need to start reforms in the face of a strong conservative center and a ruling ideology of communism; the organization of the bureaucracy; the configuration of power within the Chinese political-economic system; and the ambiguous and ever-changing overarching goal of the reforms themselves. These high levels of structured uncertainty are one of the main causes for the prevalence of "run of the Red Queen" logic in China, leading economic actors to avoid taking on long-term high-risk endeavors. Instead, economic agents in China prefer actions that secure immediate positive material results, which are safer investments and can be presented as tangible proof that the actions taken were in accordance with the correct interpretation of policy.

This chapter also looked at the tensions between the center and the regions in two ways. First, we analyzed policy making at the center and its impact on the development path of the Chinese IT industry. To do so, we utilized two policy arenas crucial to the IT industry—telecommunications and the development of indigenous technology standards. Analyzing both, we showed how action by the center has led the Chinese IT industry to develop impressive innovation capabilities in many spheres, but not novel-product innovation. We also elaborated on why this has probably yielded an extremely positive result from the point of view of rapid and widespread economic growth. We then looked at how the delegation of control over reforms to the provinces while crucial domains were kept fully under the control of the center again led companies away from novel-product innovation.

To fully understand the development of the Chinese IT industry and its multiple runs of the Red Queen, we must also analyze it at the micro level. Such an analysis will enable us to show how politics and its regional variances within China's political economy influence particular actions taken by businesses at the micro level. The next three chapters take up this task by examining the impact of national and local political factors on the behavior of research actors and enterprises in Beijing, Shanghai, and the Pearl River Delta.

Chapter 3 Beijing

Beijing is a great center for innovation and entrepreneurship. There are many, many small firms but no cooperation. Even when cooperation occurs, it tends to break down.
—*University professor, Beijing*

To the eyes of a first-time visitor, Beijing is the ideal showcase for the rise of China's rapid-innovation-based industry and unceasing improvement in R&D capabilities. Touring the IT parks of Haidian District, the visitor is bombarded with statistics celebrating the sheer volume of R&D-based start-ups, R&D centers of leading MNCs, research labs within China's major universities, central-government research units, and emerging Chinese technology giants. The cultivated image is one of large corporations, foreign and domestic, competing with exciting start-ups to lure the best graduates of China's premier schools to work in R&D-intensive operations. There certainly is some truth to this image.

It is true that Beijing is home to many IT companies' most advanced Chinese R&D centers. Domestic leaders such as Lenovo and

Aigo are busy developing and selling their own branded products. Foreign MNCs, such as Microsoft and Google, have high-profile research centers in Beijing, capitalizing on the rich talent pool. Google's Beijing headquarters is purposefully located in a facility owned and managed by Tsinghua University and situated adjacent to its campus. Microsoft Research Asia's elite scientific publication record is on par with those of the world's most advanced university or industry labs. Further enhancing Beijing's claim to the vaunted title of "China's Silicon Valley" is the dense concentration of SMEs throughout Haidian District and the whole of the Zhongguancun Science Park. According to the Zhongguancun Administrative Committee, there are more than 20,399 certified high-technology enterprises in the park, out of 26,704 total enterprises. Of these, some 3,600 are start-ups founded by returning overseas students (BSB 2008; ZGU Park 2008).

In addition, on the policy side, Beijing's developmental agencies have formed a web of formal organizations and programs to encourage the growth of the SME sector. Educational institutions such as Peking University's School of Software and Microelectronics created "innovation and entrepreneurship" programs designed to encourage graduate students to launch their own start-ups. Policy makers spurred the creation of dozens of enterprise-incubation facilities run by universities, science parks, and even SOEs. Each of these incubators claims a different business, investment, or enterprise focus.[1] In addition, the Beijing Municipal Science and Technology Association created an affiliated institution, the Beijing Startup Incubator Association, to ensure collective interaction and learning among the enterprise incubators (BJKW 2008). The municipal government even provides a special "Green Pass" program for entrepreneurs in order to facilitate their access to loans from state banks.

The wide variety of formal organizations and programs designed to support the development of high-technology SMEs makes it appear that Beijing has successfully created physical and social infrastructure mirroring that of successful technology-innovation zones in developed countries.[2] Upon deeper analysis, however, the actual research-and-innovation output paints a rather different picture. Leading Beijing IT companies devote almost all of their research either to second-generation innovation or to filling domestic market niches. Aigo's leading products are Chinese-market-oriented low-cost versions of products first developed and successfully marketed by Western, Japanese, and South Korean companies.[3] Lenovo, known outside China mostly for its acquisition of IBM's PC division, is known within China as a Chinese imitator of Samsung that develops and sells simplified electronic products. A case in point is Lenovo's mobile phone division, which earned a particularly bad reputation with regard to quality (authors' interviews).[4] A different type of second-generation R&D-intensive model is exemplified by one of Beijing's most technologically sophisticated and successful mobile telephony companies, Techfaith Wireless. The company, founded by former managers of Motorola's research division in China, specializes in original design product (ODP) mobile phone handsets for foreign and domestic brands.[5] By specializing in improving the applications software and the design of mobile phones, Techfaith has become very successful. Founded in 2002, it went public on NASDAQ in 2005 and has more than 1,300 employees.

In the pure software sector, the gap between reality and Beijing's novel-product-innovation image is particularly pronounced. The most famous software-product-based company is Baidu, a company that defines itself as the "Chinese Google," since its business model is a direct copy of the U.S. original and it has localized technology and ideas originally developed elsewhere. Similarly, Sina.com, another leading Beijing Internet-software giant, fills a market niche occupied by Yahoo in the West. Furthermore, a current goal of Beijing's municipal policy makers is to ensure that the local software industry follows the footsteps of the Indian software industry, and so they promote the creation of software-outsourcing-services companies—a far cry from novel-product-innovation.[6]

Despite Beijing's failure to live up to its reputation and projected image, the IT industry there is thriving and continually growing. The city fills a vital node in China's IT industry. A systematic analysis reveals three central characteristics that define the place of the Beijing IT industry in China's run of the Red Queen:

- There is minimal local manufacturing and extensive sourcing of production to other regions in China, either in-house or via outsourcing arrangements. This trend is enforced by local officials intent on deindustrializing Beijing and retaining only R&D and high-end service activities within the city.
- R&D activities focus on the localization of IT technology, not on the creation of new technologies and products. Beijing's enterprises of all sizes tend to concentrate their R&D, design, and marketing efforts on second-generation innovation in established niches or on tailoring foreign technology, ideas, and products to local needs and tastes.
- Successful Beijing enterprises use R&D-intensive business models that rely on the continual local supply of a highly educated yet comparatively inexpensive workforce.

When viewed through the lens of economic development and job creation, Beijing's approach to the IT industry and innovation has been highly successful, even if enterprises' technologies and products lack true novelty. The city is a major hub within the Chinese IT industry, as indicated by the annual statistical report showcasing the region's success in high-technology-based economic development. In 2007, Beijing's economy grew at a year-on-year rate of 12.3% (BSB 2008). The report noted that information transmission, computer services, and software all grew at above-average rates. These service industries are now the core of the municipal push toward value-added services. Beijing's high-technology exports are primarily in IT hardware, specifically communications equipment, computers, and other electronic equipment; together these three account for 74.2% of Beijing's total industrial exports. The Haidian District, the core of Beijing's IT industry, attained a total output value of 394.1 billion RMB. By comparison, Shanghai's showcase Pudong New Area attained a total output of 275.076 billion RMB. Even from its larger base, Haidian grew 23.6% year-on-year in 2007, while Pudong grew 14.4% (HSB 2008; Shanghai SB 2008).

Beijing's research institutions and enterprises boast of their innovation capabilities. Although, somewhat surprisingly, the total output of patents (both applications and patents granted) is lower than that of Shenzhen (not to mention the whole of the PRD). Nevertheless, the number of invention patents is the highest in China, with some five thousand granted in 2007 (BSB 2008). Beijing's R&D spending is also the most intense in China. It accounted for 14.4% of China's total R&D investment in 2006, compared with 10.4% for Guangdong province, and 8.6% for Shanghai (NSBPRC 2007).

Located in the home of the central government, Beijing's enterprises, particularly large or foreign, enjoy access to central-government services and the institutions directly under its purview, especially education and science policy. Beijing hosts the majority of national research institutions and has the highest concentration of universities, which creates the city's greatest strength—a highly educated workforce. Local government policies, specifically the push for deindustrialization, force enterprises to outsource their production, almost always within China. This outsourcing in turn enables other Chinese regions to specialize in different stages of production, strengthens the regional division of labor, and assists China as a whole in its continued domination of multiple stages of the global IT production network. Beijing concentrates on higher R&D (even if not novel-product R&D) and design activities at the top end of the "Red Queen run" model. Other regions focus on perfecting production technologies, assembly, and logistics. As a center for foreign R&D centers and foreign venture capitalists, Beijing acts as a bridge, infusing the latest global technology trends into the Chinese market and, hence, keeping the Chinese IT industry on the cusp of the global frontier.[7]

Through trial and error, Beijing's local government has developed mechanisms to encourage the growth of high-technology industries. Accordingly, Beijing's IT industry has shown that state intervention can greatly benefit the development of rapid-innovation-based industries, even if that development does not follow the trajectory envisioned by the state agencies devising the policies. A few questions thus arise: How did the Beijing model evolve? What are the mechanisms that allow it to prosper? And how does the local political-economic model affect the behavior of Beijing companies and their relationships with the Chinese IT industry as a whole?

This chapter will answer these questions by analyzing the development of the IT industry in the region. To do so, we first present a historical introduction of the development of local and national policy from the prerevolutionary period to the present and its impact on Beijing's enterprises. We then turn to evidence from field research to examine in detail how Beijing's leading enterprises fit within the national and global IT industry, analyzing how their particular innovational capabilities affect the whole of the Chinese IT industry and economy.

THE INSTITUTIONAL HERITAGE OF BEIJING'S IT INDUSTRY

Beijing lies on the Bohai Gulf coastal plain at the foot of mountain ranges separating China's heartland from the grasslands and deserts of Inner Mongolia. South of the mountains, the flat terrain is ideal for construction. The region, however, receives little rainfall and relies on an increasingly depleted aquifer to supply industry and personal needs. The mountains also frequently trap pollution over the city, a condition that, by the 1990s, forced city leaders to reverse Mao's push to concentrate industrial manufacturing within the city proper. Thus, the city now actively encourages manufacturers to relocate outside the city and restricts the growth of new factories. These efforts culminated in a rapid deindustrializing push before the 2008 Summer Olympics.

Beijing's comparative advantage as an education center emerged during the late Qing dynasty (1644–1911) and the Republican era (1912–1949). Faced with severe existential threats from foreign encroachment and China's profound backwardness, the Qing court initiated belated educational changes. In 1898, Beijing Imperial University, today's Peking University, also known as Beijing University, was established as one of the first modern universities in China. Beijing's higher-educational development expanded greatly during the republican era. Tsinghua University, China's top university (often called "China's MIT"), was established in 1911 with assistance from the United States, which supplied funds from the Boxer indemnity paid by the Qing government. Through 1949, four more top universities—Renmin University, the Beijing Institute of Technology, Beijing Agricultural University, and Beijing Jiaotong University—opened their gates. While many faculty and administrators fled to Taiwan after collapse of the Kuomintang (KMT) government, the university infrastructure became integral to PRC development plans (Andreas 2009). Currently, fifteen of China's top hundred schools are in Beijing (Wu et al. 2008).

In 1928, scholars in Nanjing under Cai Yuanpei created the Academia Sinica (中央研究院), the forerunner to the Chinese Academies of Science and Engineering. As the KMT's Nanjing government collapsed, the Academia Sinica was renamed the Chinese Academy of Sciences (中国科学院) and moved to Beijing in September 1949. The CAS was the critical research body for scientific and strategic research until the 1980s.

Beijing's modern research and educational infrastructure was radically reorganized after 1949. In 1950, Mao and Stalin signed the Sino-Soviet Treaty of Alliance and Friendship. In accordance with the treaty, Soviet bloc advisors restructured China's government along Soviet lines.[8] Sweeping nationalizations and turnkey heavy-industrial projects from the Soviet bloc enabled the Chinese government to implement an ambitious, even if somewhat coarse, system of comprehensive economic planning and heavy industrialization (Lieberthal 2004; Naughton 2007). In Beijing, planners created or expanded existing steel, machinery, weapons, electronics, and chemical industries with factories often located within the city itself.

The Soviet advisors also helped restructure the scientific-research infrastructure. In March 1954, the CAS officially became the central organ of a national push for scientific development in cooperation with universities and the research bodies of leading industries. The CAS became "the national center for scientific research." In the vertical orientation common to Soviet institutions, the CAS was to focus "on the scientific research within its own institutions." However, it was also to "keep a close contact with the scientific researchers around the country, and help coordinate the scientific research of various sectors" (CAS 2008).[9] CAS institutes proliferated in Beijing. In 2007, there were

213 CAS and Chinese Academy of Engineering (CAE) research institutes in the capital. Beijing accounts for 37% of the total number of academicians in China.[10]

In addition, Soviet advisors worked with the central government to reorganize Beijing's university system. The reformers separated and reassigned university faculties of engineering, sciences, humanities, and social sciences into specialized universities. Eight more leading national institutions opened in Beijing from 1952 to 1960. The reformers also clustered universities together in the Haidian District, relocating many of them from other districts of Beijing (see map 3.1). This heavy concentration is apparent today: thirty-nine universities are located within Haidian (Q. Zhang 2005). Shanghai followed an opposing strategy. The top universities were located away from the city and away from one another, which, as we elaborate in Chapter Four, has created specific obstacles to Shanghai's attempt to become a high-technology center. The 1952–1960 reforms also cemented Beijing's dominance in higher education.

China's first S&T development plan took shape in 1956 and 1957. The initial, twelve-year plan laid out the top-priority research areas, mostly related to national security. Targets included nuclear weapons, ballistic missiles, and satellites.[11] In 1958, S&T developments culminated in the State Council's creation of the State Science and Technology Commission (SSTC). The SSTC planned, administered, and directed the R&D activities in critical scientific disciplines. Today's MOST, the successor to the commission, continues to formulate five-year S&T development plans.[12] Through the 1960s and 1970s, research in all units of the CAS conformed only to the directives in the S&T plans. CAS labs produced research and developed equipment necessary for specifically delineated national "construction" tasks.[13] Funding for research and the salaries of researchers and university academics was set by the central government's Ministry of Education. While not highly paid, researchers had access to the subsidized privileges of Beijing's urban economy.[14]

During the Mao years, Beijing's technologists lived and died under the *danwei,* or work-unit, system. The system became known as the "Iron Rice Bowl." Housing, education, medical care, pensions, and employment were fixed by an individual's danwei.[15] Since a danwei was responsible for all aspects of an urban resident's life, including the provision of rationed goods and services, danwei became exceedingly insular in Beijing and other large cities. In Beijing, the danwei system gave rise to structures that came to resemble industrial city-states. Walled complexes, many blocks long, enclosed a segregated world with

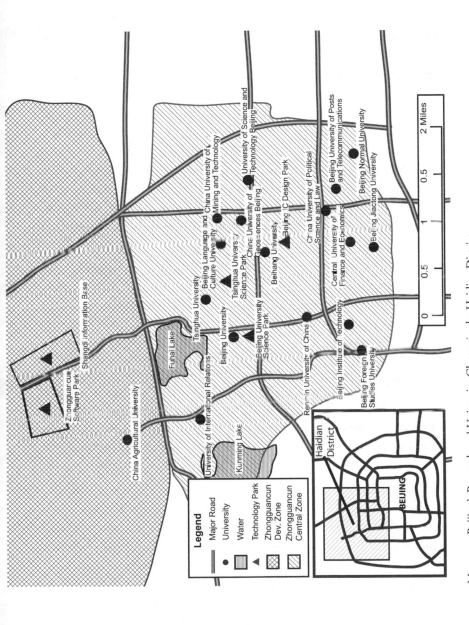

Map 3.1—Beijing's Research and University Cluster in the Haidian District.

Source: Chuang et al. 1990; Cn18dao.com 2010; Sohu.com 2009; TeleAtlas and Google.com 2009

a central factory, apartments, medical clinics, community centers, and even schools (authors' interviews; Naughton 2007).

The structure of the planned economy enhanced isolation between Beijing's danwei. A research unit looked to the planning apparatus for direction and inputs. There were few, if any, horizontal linkages among units. This insular system created a mindset called "unitism" (单位主义; literally, danwei-ism) among Beijing residents and leaders. Today, the legacy of unitism, in which one's loyalty to the work unit is absolute and linkages to outsiders are limited, still inhibits cooperation. During an interview we conducted, the director of an innovation-and-entrepreneurship program at a leading Beijing university was particularly explicit in explaining how the danwei system still influences patterns of behavior in Beijing:

> We don't cooperate in Beijing because of our societal structure. In the old days, the structure was that when you were born, you belonged to a *danwei*. It's almost like a tribe in the Middle East. Your life is associated with the tribe. The danwei was responsible for you from kindergarten all the way to marriage and career. So the system is all-inclusive, and for leaders, all about guarding turf. People have loyalty to their own clan and not to the country, because the clan, the danwei, gives them everything. The people are very ingrained in this system. Today, people usually look into creating a new single legal entity that has complete authority. The first thing they do in business is to try to grab as much as they can and then encircle it. That is the way you build your power base. You build your power base by bullying other people and then build this intense loyalty to yourself and your unit. Cooperation with other units therefore is treated with great suspicion. (authors' interview)

An extreme example of the detrimental impact of the unitist mindset was noted by the manager of one of the incubators we visited in Beijing. He reflected that the incubator offers a wide range of shared office and technical-support services to their enterprises in order to help them to focus solely on their research and the completion of their products. However, to his bewilderment, many start-ups refuse any types of assistance, even when help is offered free of charge. He found that Beijing's enterprises still tend not to trust those outside the danwei (in this case, their own company) and prefer to avoid connections with other enterprises or entities (authors' interviews).

In the 1980s, fiscal reforms reduced the central government's income, which led to sharp budgetary cuts, most notably in the military, education, and scientific research. In Beijing, these cuts brought the CAS and the university system to the brink of crisis. Additionally, since Beijing residents who engaged in commerce had become comparatively prosperous, many researchers began to question their safe but low pay. To cope with declining funding, research institutions started to develop alternative sources of income, and many opted to establish commercial ventures. Some CAS units went as far as to open shops and send pushcarts out to sell light-industrial consumer goods (Ling 2005). Whether the commercial activities related to the work or core competency of the CAS unit or university parent was largely immaterial.

Many of these small commercial start-ups clustered in the Haidian District and formed what became known as "Electronics Street" (Cao 2004; J. Wang and J. Wang 1998; Wu and Sha 2008; Q. Zhang 2005). Enterprises sold electronics hardware (especially color televisions), imported computers, and components for the most part, but also IT services.[16] While these companies included private or "collective" businesses, the most successful ones were sponsored by governmental units or universities. These market enterprises used, and were used by, their bureaucratic in-laws. For example Lenovo, a CAS commercial venture, enjoyed free access to discoveries made by the CAS Institute of Computing Technology (ICT) and had the exclusive right to develop and sell these products, making the ICT Lenovo's R&D center in all but name.[17]

The rapid pace of market development in Beijing outstripped the city's institutional and legal capacities. There were no laws that made the operation of a private business explicitly legal, nor were there property rights, patent protections, or financial regulations. To cope with this ambiguity, technologists frequently registered their businesses as collectives (a fully legal form of ownership) or simply hung on to their original units as commercial units affiliated with the parent, regardless of ownership or management in practice. The institutional parents provided legal cover, financing, access to foreign currency, market access, and protection from bureaucratic interference. Nonetheless, the need to seek formal institutional affiliation complicated business plans and left businesses open to political interference by their masters. Indeed, the success of the Founder Group (方正集团) led Beijing University to take full control of the company and force out the company's founders (Segal 2003; see also Chapter Two, note 69).

As the number and variety of market-based enterprises affiliated to research institutions increased, CAS units and universities established holding companies to manage their enterprises.[18] By the 1990s, Beijing's university-sponsored holding companies grew to include finance, real estate, manufacturing, sales, services, and research.[19]

The business model—now the quintessential Beijing model—of focusing

R&D on the localization of existing foreign products or concepts became paradigmatic in the mid-1980s with the commercial success of the Stone Group's word-processing and printing hardware, Lenovo's Chinese-language card, and Founder's Chinese-language publishing equipment. High tariff barriers and a vast underserved market meant that these companies were able to charge a premium on their products, achieve high profit margins, and keep R&D investments very low. While their products were novel in China and often quite innovative in adapting foreign technologies to work with the Chinese language, the concepts for these technologies—hardware-based language adapters—already existed.

The modern history of Beijing significantly influenced the development of the IT industry in China. The university legacy created a platform for human resources, facilities for technology development, and, most importantly, clustered these activities within the city in the Haidian District. The danwei system created an insular corporate culture of self-reliance that discourages cooperation among enterprises, universities, and labs. Reforms in the 1980s opened the door for entrepreneurs but forced many of them either to affiliate with state agencies such as universities or the CAS, or to create a complex ownership structure in order to avoid interference from rent-seeking or overzealous government officials. This business environment also led entrepreneurs to abandon the pursuit of new products or technology development in favor of localizing R&D efforts or turning to original equipment manufacturing (OEM) and original design manufacturing (ODM) activities. Having set out this historical background, we now turn to an analysis of the current situation of Beijing's IT industry.

THE TALENT ADVANTAGE: MUNICIPAL POLICIES AND INSTITUTIONS UNDERLYING BEIJING'S IT INDUSTRY

While China's central leaders have been striving to create an industry based on novel-product innovation, Beijing's IT industry has quietly attained success and strength through market and political mechanisms that are outside the scope of this central plan. As discussed in Chapter Two, it is the regional governments that enable economic growth and the development of the myriad capabilities of the Chinese IT industry. Beijing's municipal government, having recognized several of its local comparative advantages, encourages the development of enterprises even if they do not engage in cutting-edge research.

Beijing has developed policies that define and encourage the development of the IT industry while simultaneously pushing for deindustrialization. The central focus of the developmental plans is the Zhongguancun Science Park (ZGC). Unlike Chinese cities that have multiple competing parks run by different national-, provincial-, municipal-, or district-level administrations, Beijing has one overall science park—Zhongguancun—and it is firmly under the authority and policy direction of the Beijing municipal government.

Beijing's general plan, as stated by a government official responsible for local environmental planning, is for the city to be deindustrialized and to seek only the highest-end manufacturing or services: "Our current economic plan is to promote the high-technology-based third industry, services, which comparatively consumes less energy than the second industry [manufacturing]. Our plan is against large-scale construction and energy-consuming industries. We have already reduced energy consumption in Haidian and will continue to do so by promoting high-technology sectors" (authors' interview).

To accomplish the dual goals of developing Zhongguancun while deindustrializing the city, Beijing keeps close control over migration to the capital, particularly in comparison with migrant-friendly cities like Shenzhen. This policy, combined with the rising cost of land, has resulted in a limited supply of low-cost industrial labor and increased costs for labor-intensive manufacturing. High costs skew new investments toward service industries and toward automation and precision "modern" manufacturing in the remaining production facilities.

Adhering to their vision of a new Beijing, municipal officials currently accept only those manufacturing investments with proven results or that offer very significant economic or prestige benefits. If a high-end venture proves successful or has been endowed with high status in another region, Beijing may then grant permission for and even actively pursue the construction of a new production facility. Beijing's IC-foundry experience provides the most recent example. In 2000, Richard Chang, a Taiwanese businessman, sought to open a pureplay foundry in China. The company, the Semiconductor Manufacturing International Corporation (SMIC), sought to supply chips for the domestic market. Before deciding on a location, Chang made overtures to several cities. Beijing's government was interested in Chang's proposal. However, it tried to force Chang to make concessions and placed heavy demands on him in exchange for the necessary permits for the foundry. Shanghai's municipal authorities, on the other hand, were much more amenable to investments in large-scale manufacturing and strongly encouraged the project. Not surprisingly, Chang established his first foundry in Shanghai.[20] Once SMIC proved successful in Shanghai, and was deemed to bring the region prestige as well as profits, Beijing changed its original position and offered SMIC significant incentives, including subsidized land and water, to open a foundry in Beijing (authors' interviews). In 2004, SMIC opened its twelve-inch fabrication facility in Beijing ("twelve-inch" refers to the diameter of the computer chips, or wafers, produced). The facility also serves SMIC's interests by securing political capital with Beijing and the central government, both of which will likely prove beneficial in future expansion.[21]

While manufacturing is curtailed by the city government, the development of other IT enterprises is strongly encouraged throughout Beijing. In ZGC, the city's stated goal is to create clusters of related high-technology service and research enterprises. To do so, Beijing's government has taken an interventionist role in the allocation of land. In many interviews we conducted in Beijing, representatives of large foreign and domestic enterprises stated that a desire to adhere to local development plans dictated their selection of location. By investing where the city desires them to invest, firms are able to secure access to favorable government treatment, even if the clustering enterprises adhere to a unitist mindset and have no intention of collaborating with their neighbors or utilizing the services of the cluster. In one particularly frank interview, the director of an IC design company fully admitted the firm chose its location in order to receive government support made available only to IC enterprises that established their offices in one designated building. Since the promotion of officials is strongly related to their success in both finding new occupants for the park and helping current occupants prosper, administrative committees have an economic incentive to lobby on behalf of enterprises in their zones. Thus, investing according to government plans benefits companies in the long term as well as the short.

Within the overall Zhongguancun system, the development of the Zhongguancun Software Park illustrates the impact of local planning and land-allocation policies that aim at creating spatial concentrations. Opened in 2001, the software park is located in the Haidian District, to the northwest of the main university cluster (see map 3.1). By the end of 2007, it was home to 172 foreign and domestic enterprises employing some fifteen thousand software engineers (authors' interviews). The success of the original 343-acre park in creating such a concentration of software firms led its administrative committee to submit plans in 2006 to Beijing's government to develop a second phase, and the city transferred land-management rights for 395 acres adjacent to the current park to the park's administrative committee.

It is clear, then, that municipal land allocation is a primary tool that political actors use to attempt to shape the IT industry. But units in ZGC also seek to create clusters of high-technology IT businesses through other policy incentives. These incentives more generally seek to encourage investment and increase revenues and occupancy rates for different Zhongguancun units. Individual park administrations allot rent subsidies to specific investments in targeted sectors, such as IC design or software-service outsourcing.[22] Enterprises can also receive grants from the municipal government to help them train workers in the specialized skills necessary for an industry cluster to thrive. For example, a company can receive a grant of four thousand RMB for each worker trained in outsourced software programming (authors' interviews).[23]

Collectively, local plans for promoting deindustrialization and an increase in services have proven successful in encouraging the establishment and development of new enterprises. However, the greatest lures of Beijing are its human resources and the business models developed by private enterprises—not ordered government fiat or industrial policy—that profitably utilize them within the Chinese political-economic system.

While preferential policies and subsidies are always welcomed by businesses, they are not critical in determining the types of activities conducted in Beijing. Thanks to its comparative advantage within China in terms of highly skilled labor, Beijing has become a locus for R&D investments.[24] With its annual output of graduates from many of the best universities in China—192,000 in 2007—the city has become the country's richest source for engineers and scientists (BSB 2008).[25] Representatives of more than 78% of the large enterprises, and 53% of the small enterprises, we interviewed in Beijing listed access to human resources as their first or second reason for choosing to invest in Beijing (authors' interviews). Human resources also rely on the infrastructure that creates them. Start-ups, university companies, and overseas-returnee enterprises all noted that proximity to their home institution determined not only whether to establish themselves in Beijing but also their location within the city.

The development of Beijing's host of leading universities has been actively promoted since the 1990s by the national government. In 1998, answering President Jiang Zemin's call to develop world-class universities, the Ministry of Education launched Project 985 to upgrade thirty-four Chinese universities in an effort to make them leading global institutions. Two schools in Beijing, Tsinghua University and Peking University, were the first ones selected for this program. The central government increased direct subsidies to the two universities to 600 million RMB a year. The universities were encouraged to modernize their research, teaching, and course structures. Project 985 university labs still need to compete for central-government R&D funding, but they enjoy privileged access to it (authors' interviews).

For the development of R&D capabilities in the IT industry, the proximity of Beijing's universities to one another is Beijing's single greatest asset. In Shanghai or the Pearl River Delta, universities are dispersed across geographically distant campuses and are more often than not remote from business or industry centers. By comparison, Beijing's universities are typically housed within a single campus and closely clustered together in the Haidian District, surrounded by thousands of companies. This provides enterprises with access to students, faculty members, and technology-transfer offices. Beijing's human-resources advantage goes beyond mere access; many interviewees noted that student quality continues to improve. They rated the quality of talent in Beijing as the best and Shanghai and the Yangtze Delta generally a distant second; they only periodically mentioned Shenzhen or the PRD.

The human-resources pool is not without weaknesses. Beijing's enterprises admittedly consider the quality of university research, administration, and even professors to still be inferior to these in other countries or even within the greater China region. A professor at one of Beijing's top universities described the gradual improvement of Beijing's universities in this way: "In the last few years, undergraduate students at Tsinghua and Peking University have become in no way inferior to those at MIT. However, graduate students are of a lower caliber, faculty is lower still, and the research is even worse. Finally, the quality of administration is much worse than in the West" (authors' interview).

Foreign-enterprise managers note that while technologically skillful, university graduates in China lack the ability to work independently, especially on projects that require workers to be creative. This makes them significantly less productive than their peers in the United States or even in Taiwan. For example, the Greater China chief technical officer (CTO) of a major MNC noted: "While I would hire a Stanford graduate over a Chinese graduate any day, local graduates are technologically brilliant. Culturally, they are fiercely dedicated to their work. However, their initiative and passion for their work is below the average for our company, globally. Their dedication is amazing but is more about working because of cultural expectations and peer pressure rather than love of work. Thus, while technically, on average, the Chinese graduate is better than, let us say, Taiwan, the Taiwanese graduates are more effective in R&D" (authors' interview).

However, in all our interviews, managers repeatedly stated that Chinese graduates excel when supervised, structured, and given clearly defined developmental tasks. This may be attributed to the still-fundamental weaknesses in university research in China, and not only in Beijing. A director of a major foreign MNC's research lab described the situation bluntly:

> For the past five years, every time when I talk with a Chinese university professor, I come away believing they cannot perform world-class research. In my generation, my peers went overseas twenty or more years ago and were trained there through their PhDs. Some came back to China and some stayed overseas. After twenty years, those who came back to China became professors and later universities' presidents. However, their research level is far below the world level. A marked difference from what happened to those that stayed in the West. Those who returned focused on the Chinese government's requirements, while our overseas friends kept researching, and now they really are world leaders. The environment in which a researcher operated has had significant influence on his or her development. (authors' interview)

Thus, the already-strong national tendency to avoid cutting-edge high-risk R&D, such as novel-product innovation, is further enhanced by the perceived quality of research training available to graduate students in Beijing. Beijing's IT companies address these difficulties in two ways. Some opt to hire top local talent, slowly train them to address deficiencies in research skills, and target the level of their R&D efforts in China accordingly. For example, a manager of a MNC lab in Beijing reflected on his tenure: "As you know, Beijing is still full of talent, so it is not a problem to hire researchers. The only headache is to find research leaders. Team leaders are not easy to find. So for the last five years, we have struggled to train them and build leaders. As a result, we have tried to conduct meaningful research that is close to the market but still not limited to China" (authors' interview).

Other companies opt to hire returning overseas students or even foreigners to direct research teams. However, this preference has created a sense that there is a glass ceiling in Beijing. Many Chinese-educated candidates believe that in enterprises that hire foreign-educated researchers, only the foreign-educated can rise to the top. An interviewee at a leading MNC lab described the risks of trying to quickly resolve the difficulty in procuring effective research managers by hiring foreigners: "Microsoft hired foreign-trained Chinese or foreigners to lead their research when they started. Their top director told me they had a big debate about how to proceed. By hiring foreign, high-level, experienced researchers, the main problem is it may have negative effects on local people, because it looks like a local researcher has no chance to rise to the top, even if educated at the best Chinese universities. But on the other hand, hiring outsiders can be a quick start, and the lab's research level can quickly reach the world level" (authors' interview).

To sum up, the university system in Beijing provides the R&D workforce with high skills but limited capabilities in team management and in conducting in-depth long-term R&D. These limitations, coupled with an institutional environment infused with structured uncertainty and already tilted against taking on long-term high-risk projects, further dampen businesses' appetite to conduct novel-product-innovation R&D activities. However, the ready supply of large numbers of highly skilled graduates allows IT companies in Beijing to conduct sophisticated second-generation, localization, and components R&D. Thus, the university system in Beijing is critical to the success of both the industry and its development around business models that rely on second-generation innovation and the localization or indigenization of foreign technologies, concepts, and IT services.

Nonetheless, while the development of the higher-education infrastructure significantly increases the supply of highly educated labor, Beijing's regulations, increasingly strict since 2003, for the local household-registration system, hukou, and its attendant benefits, have complicated the picture. In the past, most large IT companies received a generous annual hukou quota from the Beijing government. Furthermore, graduates from Beijing universities could remain in the city while searching for work. To restrict Beijing's population growth, the former provisions have been rescinded. While most university graduates who find employment in Beijing can obtain work permits, true hukou are scarce. Since non-hukou holders find it more difficult to stay in Beijing, the pool of educated labor, even of graduates of Beijing universities, is more limited than it would appear on the surface.

In Beijing, more than in other cities, there are distinct advantages to having a hukou. For families, a true Beijing hukou provides a better chance for higher education, particularly with regard to admission to one of the top universities. In China's education system, university admission is based on a student's score on the *gaokao* university entrance exams.[26] Beijing hukou holders, however, are able to enter Beijing universities with a lower score than nonresidents. This provides a strong incentive for family-oriented young people considering a position to find out whether an employer can or will help them obtain a Beijing hukou.

An unintended result from the tightening hukou regulations has been the increased desirability of large enterprises in Beijing, at the expense of SMEs and start-ups. Young applicants hoping to remain in Beijing target enterprises that will most likely lead to their receiving a hukou in the near future. If they cannot secure a promise of a hukou from their employer, or if the employer is unable to provide one, employees tend to leave their posts after a short stay in favor of larger enterprises, thus increasing the turnover in SMEs and reducing workforce stability. An MNC director explained how the hukou still plays a role when candidates weigh potential employers: "About 50% of employees still will not take a job unless a hukou is promised by their employer. While this is more old thinking and pressure from their parents, who feel that if the company cannot give the hukou the job is not safe, it is still a concern" (authors' interview).

Since the hukou remains important, enterprises and industrial-park officials work with and around the hukou system. Preferred enterprises in Beijing's promoted economic sectors, such as software and IC design, can more easily circumvent hukou restrictions. Large enterprises are able to apply directly for a hukou quota with the Beijing municipal government. Local industrial-park or incubator administrations can, and do, introduce companies to officials within Beijing's Human Resources Bureau in order to open the door for guanxi. Well-connected enterprises are able to secure larger hukou quotas than those that depend solely on the open process. One major foreign MNC director explained: "We got every hukou we wanted because I personally know the person in charge of issuing Beijing hukou. He knows we are a trustworthy company and will only bring in the best talent to Beijing, so he convinced the responsible group to grant us as many hukou as we needed" (authors' interview).

Consequently, the tightening of hukou policies has also led to the increased importance of Beijing's government in the IT industry. Maintaining good relations with city officials is high on the agenda of representatives of many of the IT companies we interviewed. But even as enterprises with good state relations can enjoy greater access to the hukou, this comes at the expense of hewing closer to the state with, as discussed in Chapter Two, its attendant risks. In this way, in addition to simple uncertainty about access to talent or the ability to retain it, the hukou system increases the structured uncertainty under which Beijing's IT companies work. The behavior of IT enterprises within this system of local incentives, difficulties, and highly educated personnel is the subject of the following sections.

MNCS IN BEIJING

Foreign IT MNCs play a major role in Beijing's IT industry. As elsewhere in China, local authorities strongly promote investment by MNCs. Beijing has the highest concentration of foreign R&D centers in China (Shanghai is second). Looking at the behavior of MNCs gives us an angle from which to see how the particularities of the human resources available, coupled with the regional and national political economy, shape the ways in which MNCs structure their R&D activities. At the same time, it also reveals how MNC R&D activities, in turn, shape the capabilities and opportunity structure of the Beijing IT industry.

Our findings suggest that there are two primary considerations for MNCs when they decide which activities to locate in Beijing. The first, which was much more salient in the past, is political—that is, the need to be near to the nexus of political power in the capital. The second and currently more important consideration is the availability of highly skilled researchers. However, the limits of this talent pool, as well as the specific political-economic environment, shape how MNCs structure the R&D they conduct in Beijing. In addition, the two considerations, proximity to political power and the availability of a highly educated workforce, have been changing in their importance to MNCs as institutional and policy shifts continue to breed uncertainty and drive firms to limit their risk.

Foreign MNCs first began investing in Beijing during the 1980s. In 1984, the municipal government created the Haidian Economic and Technological Development Zone, Beijing's first industrial park devoted to attracting FDI. Despite the official welcome, local and national officials in the 1980s were still highly suspicious of foreign businesses. Officials subjected foreign enterprises to arbitrary fees and regulations, making business operations difficult. During the 1980s, the levels of taxation and arbitrary levies imposed on foreign-invested enterprises made Beijing one of the most expensive locations in the world for foreign businesses, negating any low-cost benefits that Beijing might have offered at the time (Garver 1993). Nonetheless, the environment during the first decade of reform, when regulations were opaque and policy changes rapid, led many MNCs to locate their Chinese headquarters close to China's center of power.[27]

This political motive is still prominent today. Interviewees stated that the Beijing-based investments made by Microsoft and Motorola were made with a strong political motivation. For Microsoft, it was an attempt to earn the central government's good will (Saxenian 2003). For Motorola, the reorganization of its existing local and regional R&D infrastructure and the rebranding of them as a "research institute" in 1999 earned the company national and local government support (authors' interviews). Political calculations were apparent during many of our interviews, as when a director of a major foreign MNC explained the company's strategy: "In the 1980s, the economic rules were very unclear, so it was important to be close to power. This meant investing in Beijing. Today, we only locate offices in Beijing when we need the high-level political connections, such as when we want to deal with government regulations or programs" (author's interview).

During the 1990s, China broadly opened itself to foreign investment. Today, other cities, especially Shanghai, offer similar, even better, incentives and benefits than Beijing, particularly for production activities or R&D in politically nonsensitive sectors. This led several foreign enterprises to move their headquarters from Beijing to other cities. One such move, in 2001, came when General Electric decided to move its Chinese headquarters and R&D center to Shanghai. Nonetheless, many enterprises still believe that having a presence in the capital is important, as stated by an MNC lab director:

> Outside Beijing, businesses probably have more flexibility in terms of policy, but in Beijing, since you are close to the central government, sometimes you can do bigger business or make bigger decisions. Once investors get strong support from the central government, central authorities will help persuade stubborn local officials or help solve local problems. Whether it's good or bad is hard to say, but this is why a lot of foreign multinational companies still set up their headquarters in Beijing. In China, the government still has strong influence on business and industry. If you want to do something big, then you have to get the support from the government, especially from the central government, so you still want to court Beijing. (authors' interview)

The political logic that drew early MNCs to Beijing remains strong in some sectors seen as politically sensitive: IC chip design, telecommunications, media, and online content. The political atmosphere in Beijing also provides space for enterprises to bend the rules. One interviewee with more than a decade of experience in Beijing and Shanghai remarked on the difference in government-enterprise relations in each city: "It's easier to get around [regulations] in Beijing. There's a lot more gray area, even though you're close to the government, closer to the emperor. In Shanghai, authorities behave more by the book. For Beijing, political maneuvering is more of a consideration. So a big difference between Beijing and Shanghai, regardless of the business that you are going to set up, is the degree to which you think you will need to bend or manipulate the rules" (authors' interview).

While establishing an R&D center in Beijing served the political interests of many MNCs, their investments were not universally welcomed. Central authorities tried to prevent what they saw as a crowding-out effect caused by the MNCs hiring the best graduates and offering salaries higher than those that local companies could afford. A local researcher recounted: "As recently as 2000, weekly articles in all the dailies said that talent who went to work for MNCs were traitors. In those days MNCs had to recruit last and pay back full tuition to the universities whose graduates they took. The central government tried to protect the interests of CAS and Chinese companies against leading MNCs" (authors' interview).

Such obstacles limited the development of MNC-based R&D centers in Beijing. As late as 1999, there were only 30 major R&D centers (Xue and Liang 2005). Over time, however, the more conservative central-government ministries have lessened their resistance, and R&D centers have proliferated in response. By 2004, their number had grown to 82, and in 2006, Beijing claimed 189 MNC R&D centers (*China Daily* 2006).

MNCs' investments are not purely political, however. The single greatest reason, by far, for MNCs to invest in Beijing is to have access to China's best college graduates. A leading MNC director explained: "If we were to go to a second-tier city, we could get free rent or even better promotions. However, for us, getting talented engineers and scientists was more important than saving money, so we came to Beijing and Shanghai, even though they are expensive" (authors' interview).

Our interviewees bluntly stated that to conduct R&D, they have to locate in Beijing or, to a lesser degree, Shanghai.[28] However, the presence of rich human resources and the interest of foreign MNCs in conducting R&D in Beijing have not led to novel-product innovation. Outside a few leading MNC labs, such as those of Microsoft and Google, most interviewees stated that foreign MNCs conduct only developmental work in China. In interviews with managers of MNCs' labs, three reasons were given for the focus on development at the expense of research. The first, and most frequently cited, reason is that intellectual property rights (IPR) are not well protected in China. Therefore, to protect their IP, leading MNCs choose one of four strategies: limiting their R&D by concentrating more on development than research; breaking down their R&D into components and ensuring that the components developed in China have very little commercial value without integration (which is usually done in the home country) or concentrating on Greater China localization of their products; or opting for pure research that is so far removed from the market that the IPR would have little commercial value for would-be pirates.[29]

The second reason cited for focusing on development more than research in

China was the already-discussed fact that the Chinese-educated researchers, while perceived as technically capable, are also considered by the R&D managers not to be on par with their R&D workers who were educated outside China. Last—and in our view, at least as important a reason as the other two—is the fact that many of these MNCs need to devote a considerable amount of their R&D to making their products both compatible and appealing to the Chinese market. Hence, focusing their China R&D center on the localization of their products is an optimal, and necessary, solution.

Nonetheless, even if most MNCs do not conduct cutting-edge research in their Beijing R&D centers, the work they do is vital for bringing new technology into China and improving the skills of local researchers. Because of the impact of innovation on local economic growth, this developmental research is a highly desirable outcome for China and further enhances the specialization of Beijing around second-generation innovation R&D. Examples of such developmental work abound. Motorola set up its first array of research centers in Beijing in order to synchronize its products with China's telecommunications network. China's mobile-telephony regulations and particular transmission infrastructure meant Motorola needed to do major localization and market adjustment of its products. The complex customization necessary for Motorola phones to function in China forced the company to set up a research lab in the country. Later, in 2002 and 2003, Motorola aggressively moved into China, transferring development, entire production lines, and even chip production to a network of facilities in Beijing and Tianjin. It also began outsourcing much of its intermediate developmental work and incremental improvement work to Huawei, which helped build up Huawei's technological capabilities. And graduates of Motorola's R&D center have left to open their own companies in the mobile telephony market, Techfaith Wireless being one of the most successful.

In a similar fashion, Google's Beijing R&D center directs the company's activities for the Chinese-language world. Unlike a simple translation of interfaces, which Google outsources to domestic Chinese enterprises, the layering structure in a Chinese-language search algorithm is different from the same process in English. This requires in-depth software design and development in China. As a result, Google generates wholly new software systems as well as localized content in Beijing. The location of Google's R&D center also illustrates the interests of MNCs and Beijing's political actors and the desire to access top-quality talent and tenants. Its facility is located adjacent to Tsinghua University in the Tsinghua University Science Park. Tsinghua University's president was deeply involved in the negotiations between the park and Google.

He visited Google's CEO, Eric Schmidt, to personally request that Google set up its facility in the Tsinghua University Science Park, hoping to cement a long-term relationship between the company and the university (authors' interviews). Google secured access to graduates of China's top university and Tsinghua gained both a prestigious anchor tenant and a leading software lab, with which it cooperates on research and training. The Google-Tsinghua cooperation has matured. Most recently, Tsinghua became the first Chinese university involved in Google's global "cloud computing" project (W. Zhou 2008).

Investment patterns by MNCs in Beijing illustrate the region's strengths in the IT industry. Today, Beijing's greatest attraction is its human resources. These become the R&D basis for MNCs' operations in China, which direct the activities of subsidiaries and sourcing partners throughout the country. Thus, because of a political move, Beijing has become the innovation and research center for China's foreign MNCs—a development that parallels the evolution of Beijing's domestic IT companies over the last two decades.

LARGE CHINESE IT ENTERPRISES IN BEIJING

Beijing's large-scale IT enterprises emerged from diverse sources, but the most successful have been those started by entrepreneurs and not by government fiat. Analyzing the stories of companies that managed to sustain growth and comparing them with the stories of those that declined or failed to grow reveals a few patterns. First, all the Beijing IT firms that became large companies or conglomerates began their rapid growth only after each started to follow a very similar business model. The first leg of this model is a strategy aimed at the domestic market, which involves extensive R&D to localize products and solutions already well developed abroad, such as word processing, consumer electronics, or Chinese-character output. At the same time, these enterprises embedded themselves in global production networks through OEM, ODM, or distribution contracts with foreign MNCs—at least during their developmental phases.[30]

A second part of the model has been the need to control diversification. All large Beijing IT companies have been prone to considerable diversification; however, those that managed to contain their diversification largely within the IT industry sustained their growth, even if, in all cases, many of the diversification efforts proved to be costly or wasteful detours. The problem of overdiversification might be related to another attribute separating successful companies from their peers: the ability to transform their core business in tandem with changes in the global market and its relation to China's domestic market, which ensures they will sustain their growth.

These thriving firms perfectly executed, in two ways, the run of the Red Queen where the Chinese market is concerned. First, in their developmental phases, they offered new localized products. As Western MNCs began to offer Chinese versions of their original products and destroyed the Chinese companies' original market niches, successful Chinese firms continued to incrementally innovate and to develop competencies in new areas where they could secure a lasting local advantage over MNCs. These competencies built upon the skills learned through the companies' earlier stages of OEM-ODM and distribution work for MNCs. Second, successful large Chinese companies offered other, more sophisticated OEM-ODM services to MNC clients. Companies that lost their focus, such as the Stone Group, which moved into such unrelated markets as running a taxi company and a chocolate factory, could not keep pace with the Red Queen run and ended up being marginalized.

The last part of the successful business model has been the ability to manage the company's relationship with the state. It is here that the structured uncertainty of China's political economy is most clearly revealed. There are two ways in which an IT company's relationship with the state can be detrimental to its growth. First, the state will actively prosecute a company when it is caught on the wrong side of changing policies, specifically with regard to politics. The Stone Group's fall from grace provides an example. In 1989, the then-dominant company came under fire for its management's involvement in the Tiananmen protests and the creation of a pro-constitutional-reform think tank in 1988, the Stone Social Development Institute. During the crackdown, its president and cofounder, Wan Rennan, fled to France, and the company's headquarters were occupied by a detachment of the People's Liberation Army (Kennedy 1997). The company survived but never regained its former preeminence.

The second way the state can inhibit the growth of a company is the exact opposite—full capture. As we shall describe in more detail below, using the cases of Red Flag Linux and Xinwei Telecom, there are two main reasons why becoming the national champion of an R&D effort leads to market marginalization. First, the Chinese state is large and complex, with many units advancing competing goals. Hence, having MOST or the MII designate a company as the official champion of a given technology or project does not mean that other state organs, including some formally under the auspices of the same ministries, will follow their guidelines, even with regard to procurement. As discussed in Chapter Two, guanxi with a powerful sponsor potentially holds great promise but also profoundly increases the risks and uncertainty for a given industry actor. This inhibits their R&D efforts and ability to conduct long-term planning. Second, the Chinese state itself has many goals in its pursuit of indigenous innovation, including securing access to or improving terms concerning the use of foreign technology. Therefore, market success might not even be on the state's agenda. Without success in the market, however, even SOEs stagnate. While the central government has taken a direct interest in IT companies throughout China, their prominence in Beijing is significantly higher, since the city is both the capital and the location of China's highest concentration of research institutes.

It can therefore be concluded that successful Beijing companies have been those that exploit the comparative advantage of the region, in particular the highly educated workforce, control their diversification, and manage their interaction with the state to avoid either prosecution or capture. Operating in this environment is difficult, given its high structured uncertainty and less than efficient markets as well as the various shifts of local and central policy.

To elaborate on these issues, this section considers the experiences of two sets of companies. First, we analyze the experiences of two exemplarily successful large Beijing IT firms: Lenovo and Aigo. Each company represents a different approach to the IT industry in Beijing: different ownership structures, interactions with the state, and strategies. We then analyze two companies established by the central government in order to create independent Chinese technologies in what were deemed critical domains: Red Flag Linux in software operating systems, and Xinwei Telecom in mobile telecommunications.

Two of the most renowned Beijing IT companies that successfully employed the strategy of plugging into the fragmented global IT industry, controlling diversification, and managing relations with the state are Lenovo and Aigo. Both began as resale businesses with only slight value added, but over time they plowed revenues into developing their own quality, branded products for the local market. However, neither has seriously attempted to control the core technologies that underlie its consumer business.

Initially known as the New Technology Developer Inc., Lenovo was established in 1984 as the commercial arm of the CAS Institute of Computing Technology. All of Lenovo's eleven founders were employees of the ICT (Lenovo 2008).[31] Between 1984 and 1990, Lenovo imported and distributed foreign personal computers for IBM and Hewlett-Packard, among others. Its transformative moment occurred in 1987 with the launch of its first branded product, a Chinese-character input card for use in PCs.[32] In 1989, Lenovo opened its own manufacturing facilities, and the following year it created its first branded PC. As both global and domestic markets changed, Lenovo concentrated more and more of its efforts on its computing division, expanding it to include servers in 1995 and adding its own branded laptops in 1996. By 1997, its efforts to secure its own brand name domestically were crowned with success when Lenovo became the largest computer company by market share in China and displaced then-dominant foreign brands (Lenovo 2008). In 2004, Lenovo achieved global fame when it purchased IBM's PC division. The acquisition made Lenovo the third-largest personal computer manufacturer in the world. By then, the PC market had long since ceased to be a novel-product-innovation business. Indeed, the fear of commoditization and the perception that its high-level R&D competencies no longer granted it any advantage were precisely the reasons why IBM decided to exit the PC market.

Feng Jun, a graduate of Tsinghua University, established Aigo in 1993 as the Huaqi Information Digital Technology Co., Ltd. His initial business involved the purchase and resale of keyboards and other computer peripherals (authors' interviews; Xinhua 2006). Feng reinvested the revenues, and in 1996, the company began to produce OEM computer peripherals. The same year, the company began to sell products in China under the trade name Aigo—designing and selling digital consumer devices that were essentially Chinese versions of Western, Japanese, and South Korean products.[33] In 2001, Aigo reached a breakthrough with the development of its first digital memory products. The following year, the company began producing what would become its core business: MP3 players. Since 2002, Aigo has diversified into a range of digital consumer goods and is now the largest producer of digital memory devices in China and is becoming a leader in the lucrative market for MP3 players and portable digital devices. Since 2005, Aigo has concentrated on manufacturing higher-quality, more expensive (but still affordable by Chinese standards) digital devices in order to escape the intense competition between OEM-surplus and lower-end Chinese-brand competitors such as Neuman (3mt 2006). Currently, Aigo concentrates solely on its own brand and has fully exited the OEM market.

In their developmental phases, both Lenovo and Aigo linked themselves with the global IT industry and performed their own versions of OEM-ODM work. From operations in resale and the value-added sale of foreign products, both companies built their technological capabilities on the basis of their relationships with MNCs and focused on the domestic market. Unlike firms following the classic OEM model of producing goods for export, Lenovo and Aigo produced or resold foreign brands in the domestic market. Lenovo and Aigo succeeded by connecting their businesses with global and local suppliers and production networks rather than attempting to build in-house capabilities in all areas. Lenovo sources its components and production capacity both internally (within Lenovo factories) and from external providers, either globally or in other regions of China. Indeed, in its quest for the highest-quality production, Lenovo has been noted for outsourcing laptop production to Taiwan for machines that will be sold in China (Ernst and Naughton 2007). Similarly, it continues R&D on its IBM-descended products at former IBM facilities (or in nearby ones built since the acquisition) in the United States (Zimmer 2006). Lenovo's business model is one of low-cost logistical and brand innovation rather than technology leadership. As explained by an interviewee in the CAS: "Lenovo's true strategic genius has been to try to sell computers to Chinese peasants. In the long term, the strategy is not really to compete on technology with the likes of HP. They acquired IBM's notebook division mostly for the market share and technology-acquisition benefits. The goal was never to lead the market in new innovations, only to be able to quickly follow the leaders" (authors' interview).

Lenovo utilizes the advantage of Beijing and its connections with the CAS in order to conduct second-generation and incremental R&D in the city, while it has moved production and assembly to other regions of China.

In a slightly different manner, Aigo has leveraged the advantages offered by Beijing and the rest of China to facilitate its rise through the Chinese market (McDonald 2008). Aigo concentrates fully on design and sources all of its production in southern China. All of its design and R&D work is done in Beijing. The majority of the employees are recruited locally, either directly from university or, especially since 2000, by poaching experienced researchers from other Zhongguancun enterprises (authors' interviews). By outsourcing production and focusing on the utilization of proven technologies and products, mainly for the Chinese market, Aigo, like Lenovo, holds costs down and minimizes risk, both financial and technological.

Both companies controlled their diversification by two methods. Lenovo divested itself of many of its unrelated business activities and relegated responsibility for their management and losses to its state-controlled parent, Legend Holdings. Thus, Lenovo could concentrate on personal-computing and business-computing hardware. Aigo has opted to compete only in the areas in which its technology has an advantage: digital consumer electronics or those using a comparable flash-memory chip set.

With regard to the central government, Lenovo and Aigo have skillfully managed their relationships with it and avoided being captured by the state. Nonetheless, the support of the state, especially in the case of Lenovo, has been crucial. In its earliest years, Lenovo's access to foreign exchange and import licenses were acquired at minimal cost from its patron and owner, the CAS. In the early 1990s, the China Torch Program certified Lenovo's products as high-technology goods, earning the company tax breaks and other central-government incentives. However, perhaps the most important factor for the development of the company has been its privileged access to finance. One of our interviewees went so far as to argue that "Lenovo would have gone bankrupt ten times over if it did not have access to state bank loans" (authors' interview). Its access to cheap sources of capital has also helped cushion the blow from frequent failed or distracting ventures (such as FM365.com and Lenovo Mobile).[34] In addition, since its status is still that of an SOE, Lenovo continues to enjoy a very lucrative business supplying supercomputers for use by various government actors.

Aigo manages its relations to the state differently. Having never been state owned, the company enjoys an extra buffer from bureaucratic interference. Instead, its interaction with the state is largely limited to selective clientelistic assistance from interested central-government actors. Interviewees mentioned that Aigo received help with brand development and market penetration in emerging markets in Latin America and the Caribbean through central-government travel and exhibition subsidies. While these are not key markets for Aigo, building its presence there serves the interests of the central state by building the Chinese presence in markets either underserved or neglected by established MNCs.

The rather different fate of companies too close to the state serves as a warning about the necessity of ambiguity for successful business operations in China. In 1995, MOST, the MPT, and the NDRC (then the State Planning Commission) made development of a CDMA-based 3G mobile standard a key project of the Ninth Five-Year Plan (T. Zhou 2004). At the same time, a group of Chinese nationals in the United States founded Cwill Telecommunication with the intention of developing their synchronous code-division multiple-access (SCDMA)–based "smart antenna" into a commercially viable product. Since their transmission standard, SCDMA, was closely related to the emergent Chinese TD-SCDMA standard, the founders contacted senior scientists at

MPT and inquired about opportunities for cooperation in developing transmission devices and other complementary technologies for the new standard. In November 1995, the MPT's Chinese Academy of Telecommunication Technology and Cwill jointly established Xinwei Telecom, a Beijing-based company, to develop these technologies (Agilent 2006). By 1997, the entire company had relocated to China and closed down its U.S. operations.

Xinwei has since grown into an SOE that is 45% state owned; its R&D operations are in Beijing, and its equipment manufacturing, including IC fabrication, occurs in subsidiary facilities in Chongqing (Xinwei 2008).[35] The company employs five hundred researchers in Beijing and more than one thousand workers at its IC foundry and production facility. In addition, Xinwei has a special relationship with state-owned production firms such as Putian (a state-owned telecommunications-hardware company), which produces antennas and receiving equipment under the Xinwei brand. Moreover, as part of China's state-sponsored TD-SCDMA alliance, the company has access to the research and cooperative resources of more than fifty partner firms in developing TD-SCDMA products and services. Xinwei has developed products for several facets of telephony, including local loops, private networks, rural connectivity, and low-cost urban mobile phones (authors' interviews). It would thus appear that Xinwei, as a research-intensive, government-connected enterprise that is rapidly growing, expanding into new activities, and employing an ever-larger number of engineers, is a great success.

However, Xinwei's fortunes are tied to those of the TD-SCDMA standard. As discussed in Chapter Two, the standard languished for years. Furthermore, Xinwei's intimate connection to the central state limits the company. Although, on the one hand, the company's state connections have granted it access to capital and partners, on the other hand, its long-term fortune is completely dependent on political decisions regarding the Chinese domestic telecommunication market.[36] Furthermore, even though Xinwei has access to what amounts to unlimited capital resources and is armed with a central-government designation as a new mobile-telephony-equipment champion of China, the company has yet to develop any novel products, but instead mimics or upgrades already mature products. Finally, Xinwei's relationship with the state has meant that it need not test its ideas and products in the marketplace. Hence, even assuming that a market for TD-SCDMA and its related technologies will develop in the future and that the central state will not decide that TD-SCDMA has outlived its strategic utility, it remains an open question whether any of Xinwei's products will appeal to consumers.

While Xinwei began as the opportunistic merger of a private foreign enterprise and central-government units, other firms began life entirely within the state structure. In the late 1990s, the MII launched a high-profile attempt to create a proprietary computer-operating system to compete with Microsoft's Windows. In 2000, with the MII's direct support, the CAS established the Red Flag Software Technology Co., Ltd. Red Flag was established as a Linux-based company that would cooperate with the CAS to develop a commercially competitive Chinese operating system based on open-source software (OSS). Red Flag's envisioned role was to commercialize the OSS work done by CAS and MII researchers. The company was given significant funds and privileged access to the government procurement market.

In 2001, Red Flag Linux secured its first state software contract, supplying operating systems to the Beijing municipal government. However, while government procurement gave the company a valuable boost, all the Chinese OSS companies together held only 1.6% of China's rapidly growing operating-systems market that year (Saxenian 2003). Even with its technology support from the MII and the CAS and its assured government-procurement deals, Red Flag Linux succeeded in earning only a minor position even within the government-procurement market. Government units across China do not, as described in Chapter Two, adhere to a single policy direction or chain of command, and many of them preferred to use Microsoft Windows. As with Xinwei, Red Flag Linux discovered that even when central support is strong, human resources are readily available, and government clients are supposedly secured, there are structural impediments to advancing by relying on the state, as well as uncertainties with regard to even supposedly assured procurement orders.

Nonetheless, from the national point of view, the two companies serve a useful though rather expensive function, which might be the true aim of the central government and the reason why both companies are located in Beijing. For example, shortly after the central government committed to promoting Red Flag Linux, Microsoft agreed to lower its prices on both the Windows and Office software packages sold in China and, in 2003, also granted several Chinese actors access to portions of the Windows source code (Microsoft 2003).

IT SMES IN BEIJING

A tour of Beijing's Haidian District leaves the visitor convinced that Beijing has developed an entrepreneurial culture. Students and professors launch new companies from their research groups' prototypes and preliminary findings. Workers in large enterprises see opportunities for striking out on their own. Indeed, many of our interviewees sounded as if they have reached the entrepreneurial promised land: "Why did I start my company? After working for several major companies abroad, I felt bored. Being an employee in a big company was just dull. So I decided to find some friends and former colleagues, and we opened a company ourselves" (authors' interview).

And Beijing's entrepreneurial pull has become international. The most promising start-ups have been those founded by returning Chinese, and Beijing boasts more than 3,200 such firms. Sixty percent of these companies are estimated to be involved in the IT industry (authors' interviews). The sheer number of start-ups, the annual rates of new-enterprise formation, and the growing technical sophistication of Beijing's new IT companies led Segal (2003) and Walcott (2003) to declare Beijing's efforts to become an innovation zone successful. While we agree that Beijing has developed a thriving ecosystem of new, small IT companies, our findings suggest that if Segal and Walcott are referring to novel-product innovation or the creation of new technologies, then Beijing is a failure. If, however, one uses the broader definition of innovation that we argue is the essence of the Red Queen run, then Beijing's IT SMEs are indeed an unqualified success.

Beijing's universities and large numbers of research institutions provide a fertile ground for spin-off enterprises. Nonetheless, unlike their foreign counterparts, Beijing enterprises tend to remain tied to their universities instead of being fully spun off. For example, nearly half the nonstate budget of both Tsinghua University and Peking University comes from their partially or wholly owned enterprises. Universities and CAS institutions in China have taken a commanding role in the lives of their supposedly spun-off enterprises (Sunami 2002). In the 1980s, a university administrator would take charge of investment in, and oversight of, university enterprises. During the 1990s, the Ministry of Education initiated reforms designed to separate university administrators, who officially should concern themselves only with education and research, from the administration of university enterprises. As a result, many universities established holding companies to manage the large and rapidly growing collection of firms they owned and operated. Beijing's university holding companies usually provide capital injections in exchange for an equity stake. Holding companies also place board members and executives in companies under their control. An executive of a university holding company explained the extent of their involvement: "We send administrators, including legal deputies, chairmen of the board, and CEOs into the company" (authors' interview). Needless to say, while such strong involvement helps alleviate many of the problems associated with the founding and running of a new IT company in China, financial and legal problems in particular, it is fraught with peril as well, especially if the company is highly profitable. The creation of holding companies under universities is an example of political entrepreneurship by the schools. Central policies concerning spin-off enterprises changed, and the universities responded by changing what they called such enterprises and how they managed them, but not by ending their control of them or giving up the streams of revenue they generate. Such flexibility in the face of uncertainty has made Beijing's spin-off climate even more successful.

The second major source of new IT companies in Beijing is the returning overseas Chinese, the so-called Sea Turtles. Within the political economy of China, returning technological entrepreneurs face a radically different, and somewhat easier, environment for financing and regulation than local spin-offs. Because Sea Turtles are seen as bringing with them a wealth of experience in industrial R&D, management, and marketing practices, numerous programs were created to fund, assist, and spur Sea Turtles to open IT start-ups. Some of the positive perception of Sea Turtles is certainly correct. In his study of IT start-ups, Douglas Fuller (2005b) found that the Sea Turtles' firms are the most technologically sophisticated and best managed in China in general and in Beijing in particular.

However, being a returnee carries with it a degree of risk and uncertainty also, as expressed by an incubator manager who targets Sea Turtles: "The overseas students who start these enterprises have never started an enterprise in China. So when they get here, we teach them how it is done more efficiently. For example, we inform them about where to go for this or that business permit. After they arrive, we help them solve the registration and legal problems they will face, the financial problems, and their management issues. We help them understand the complex affairs of starting a business in Beijing" (authors' interview).

Even though Sea Turtles enjoy such support and are, on average, more technologically sophisticated than native Beijingers, their companies still follow the logic of the Red Queen run. Like other Beijing IT firms, they tend to focus on exploiting gaps and openings in China's domestic market for which reliable and less than cutting-edge technologies are sufficient. Typically, a venture established by a Sea Turtle aims to introduce a foreign technology or business idea with which the founder is familiar and to utilize the available human resources in Beijing to localize it. Thus, these businesses enrich the IT products and services available in the city, even if they are not pushing China to the technological frontier.

Both types of enterprises—university spin-offs and those started by Sea Turtles—as well as start-ups founded by local entrepreneurs, exhibit three common traits. First, they rely on incubators to provide a variety of services necessary to launch a technology business. Second, they all face common difficulties in accessing the capital needed to finance R&D or expansion. Third, whatever the education and skills, or even intentions, of their founders, Beijing's SMEs tend to follow in the footsteps of large enterprises by specializing in second-generation innovation, concentrating their R&D activities in Beijing and outsourcing production to the south.

It might be the particularities of the Chinese political economy that make it especially challenging to start and fund a new IT business. To address this difficulty, many IT start-ups seek support in the abundance of incubation centers in Beijing. Within the context of the high structured uncertainty in China, well-placed business incubators provide a wide variety of services to their enterprises. All offer subsidized utilities and occasionally improved telecommunications services.[37] Several, such as Tsinghua Science Park's incubator, offer access to the university's labs, which are some of the best facilities available in China (authors' interviews). Other parks provide access to libraries and advanced mainframes or supercomputers for the benefit of their enterprises' research. Most incubators offer lectures on business law and administrative practices to interested entrepreneurs.

Nonetheless, while the quality of these services has improved over time, the managers of many incubators admit that their ability to help turn scientists into businessmen remains limited. Thus, one reason why so many of Beijing's start-ups still opt for an incubator as their first location is simply the availability of discounted lab or office space, the terms of which are negotiable. Furthermore, as part of their attraction to prospective enterprise tenants, all incubators offer lower rent than that available to similarly well-located offices in Beijing. While most incubators wish for enterprises to graduate within eighteen to thirty-six months, many of our interviewees flatly stated that they never plan to leave the subsidized rent and facilities of their incubator unless the incubator management forcefully evicts them.

Another important reason that IT start-ups choose to work with incubators is that, in Beijing, the incubators are frequently run by highly connected officials, who are useful in serving as links to the state. In addition, while incubators are usually not sources of capital in themselves, they are one of the main matchmakers for either government grants or private investors. As such, the incubators serve as a first screening mechanism. An analysis of our interviews suggests that this matchmaking capability is the main differentiator among incubators. For example, the Tsinghua Science Park is known for its particularly strong connections to venture capitalists. Other parks, such as those operated by CAS units, serve primarily as technology-transfer mechanisms for their own members (authors' interviews).

Beijing's incubators play a particularly significant role in the run of the Red Queen. Since most of them are state actors managed by the municipal government or a university, their policies reflect the interests of local authorities and not those of the central state. Typically, incubator managers are judged by their impact on economic growth and job creation, not on whether their enterprises develop novel technologies.

One of the greatest difficulties still faced by Beijing's IT start-ups is access to capital. The question of financing remains one that the local and national governments in Beijing have not yet been able to address, especially for start-ups that aim to conduct novel product R&D and, hence, are deemed riskier. The response of most small enterprises to these financial constraints is, not surprisingly, to refrain from novel-product innovation and, in fact, to minimize the length and scope of their R&D activities.

For its part, the VC industry in Beijing operates differently from the U.S. VC industry. One of our interviewees put it succinctly: "In China, you see most VCs invest in agriculture, hotels, or other nontechnology businesses. Even in information technology, they invest mostly in copycat Chinese companies. Only a small percentage of VCs want to invest in high-risk novel-technology companies, because there is a lot of low-risk investment elsewhere. They justify this by stating that there are no prior stories of success in new-products development, so they say 'Why not invest instead where the money is easy and the risks are low?'" (authors' interview).

In general, investment patterns in Beijing are similar to those in Taiwan (Breznitz 2007b). VC firms invest in businesses with proven models, such as IT services, whose revenues and potential viability have already been demonstrated in foreign markets. The professional backgrounds of Beijing's venture capitalists account for some of their behavior. The majority of venture capitalists in Beijing come out of finance, banking, or party officialdom and the SOEs. These would-be venture capitalists lack the set of skills a professional American VC is assumed to have.

VC partnerships in Beijing tend to invest in later-growth-stage companies —those that have already proved themselves. Here are two typical answers we received from our interviewees when we referred to this pattern:

> Novel technologies are high risk and maybe high return. However, we have now shifted away because the risk is high and may bring no return. We now focus on having a good business model like IT services.

> We have changed our strategy with experience. In 2000, we did a lot of seed investment, and our emphasis was twofold: make money and get technology and experience for the parent corporation. But since 2008, we have changed. Now we concentrate on making money through investing in growth-stage firms that will list soon. (authors' interviews)

In addition, during our interviews it became apparent that the investment time frame for most Beijing venture capitalists is less than three years. Many venture capitalists referred to this fact when they explained why they prefer to avoid new start-ups or those who need to develop their own technologies: "We generally avoid big projects because we cannot handle long-term commitments" (authors' interview). At an extreme, in 2007–2008, a number of VC firms began to delve into stock market investment management as a diversification strategy.

The reasons that Beijing's venture capitalists prefer shorter-term investments are primarily political. Regulations concerning investments, management, property rights, and, in particular, exit strategies are vaguely defined. For example, it is uncertain whether (or when) using stocks to pay for M&As is allowed. It is also uncertain when Beijing's high-technology small enterprises will be able to easily list publicly. These uncertainties mean that the traditional financial exits—M&As and IPOs—are not always available, even if the company is successful.[38] Even government administrators who pointed to the presence of a Beijing VC industry as a sign of the city's maturity as an innovation zone fully admitted that VC funds are limited and generally open only to enterprises that have already established themselves. One high official described the situation: "China's VCs are not mature, so most enterprises in the park rely on themselves in the earlier period. When they are profitable, we can help find VC funds for them" (authors' interview).

The lack of venture financing is especially acute because banks, in particular Beijing's state-owned banks, refuse to serve small, private IT companies. Our interviewees repeatedly said the only acceptable collateral for a loan is physical property. However, most entrepreneurs (Sea Turtles in particular) do not have enough property to back up loans. As a result, they are cut off from China's largest single source of capital. Kellee Tsai argues that the problem is structural, since loan officers know they will be forgiven for authorizing a loan that turned out to be bad for an SOE, but punished for a bad loan given to a private company. This leads them to avoid granting loans to most private companies, especially smaller ones (Tsai 2002).

To overcome this resistance, Beijing SMEs turn to the local government. Incubators and branches of the city government select promising enterprises and act as the guarantor for the loan. Banks will lend to start ups if the government guarantees the loan. One entrepreneur explained his experience with receiving loans:

> Basically we have continuous communication with the government and incubators, so they know us very well. They then recommended us to the banks. But the banks need collateral, and we don't have any collateral. I told them, 'I don't have anything,' to which they responded, 'Well, if you don't have anything, then we can't lend you money.' The government then stepped in and said, 'We'll use our access to the banks in your name to provide the collateral, if it's okay with you.' And then the bank said, 'Well, we don't care whose collateral it is; if it's money, it's fine.' And they gave us the loan. (authors' interview)

With IT SMEs' continued difficulties in accessing both venture capitalists and banks, the direct support of the Beijing government becomes even more important. For example, an incubator official explained: "When an enterprise reaches a certain stage, low-interest loans will be provided by Zhongguancun Administrative Committee. We also run our own loan guarantor company for them" (authors' interview). Government loan guarantees often take the form of the "green pass" system, in which certified companies receive guarantees from the state, which in turn enable them to secure bank loans. This need for government approval and certification also points up the importance of SMEs having the right bureaucratic mother-in-law. Consequently, many entrepreneurs spend much of their time managing their relationships with various officials.

Even with growing state support, many enterprises are unable to access capital, instead relying solely on their revenues and other internal sources of financing. As pointed out by Fuller (2005b), this lack of growth capital inhibits the development of many promising start-up enterprises, forcing them to adopt less R&D-intensive business strategies. In his research, Fuller found that many new enterprises start out by offering OEM or ODM services as a way to secure a revenue stream. A firm's need to secure revenues while still developing its first product often diverts resources and attention away from novel-product R&D. Many of the entrepreneurs we encountered were highly aware of these risks, but they explained that such is the reality in Beijing: "We need to rely on ourselves for financing. We have felt a capital shortage, and this will limit our development speed. Even though we have a good product and a good market response, without capital, it is hard to expand our company, and so we get stuck in this loop of securing other revenue streams that lead us to divert our attention from our main market" (authors' interview).

Thus, the structural capital shortage is another reason why so many of Beijing's SMEs adjust their focus and move away from long-term R&D. The relative scarcity of venture financing strengthens the allure of employing a "Red Queen run" business model, even for the most promising start-ups.

This tendency is further strengthened by the need to secure government support. To set up in municipal incubators and receive benefits, including access to capital, enterprises must be clearly within one of five government-determined high-technology sectors (authors' interviews). And so incubators evaluate their technology and business models by seeing how they align with local state-developmental plans. If a company's models do not appear to match the plan, it will be denied support. Proven business models tend to get approved and novel ones do not. Consequently, at their inception, start-ups are steered away from novel-product innovation.

Once Beijing's IT SMEs manage to reach profitability, their behavior starts to resemble that of the larger, more established enterprises. For example, SMEs deeply involved in hardware will often source their production elsewhere and sometimes relocate their center of activities to southern China (Walcott 2003; W. Zhou 2008). One incubator manager explained the typical pathway for nonsoftware enterprises in his incubator:

> In China, there are places willing to be a development center. Some places choose to specialize in production. Production sites specialize in cell phones or other goods such as MP3 or MP4 players, especially in the area around Guangzhou, Shenzhen, and Fuzhou. Their production abilities are quite developed. So for our enterprises, after they complete their product, they generally move to areas with better production abilities. They generally go to these production bases to develop their goods for market. But that isn't to say they leave Zhongguancun altogether. Because high-technology products have rapid turnover, they still keep their research and development activities here in Zhongguancun. (authors' interview)

In addition, the strategic need for access to capital from the state and for rapid returns on investment in an uncertain market leads many of Beijing's SMEs to follow in the footsteps of their more established peers by focusing their attention on the domestic market. The representative of an IC design company was especially candid on these issues: "Just about all of our chips are consumed domestically. We do not need to export. If we target China's market and can meet China's requirements, which are a lot lower than, let us say, the U.S., then we will already be huge. Furthermore, we don't need to produce overseas, since the home market is so large. If we want to go into the international market, we must invest a lot, and we do not have the capital for that" (authors' interview).

The result is that the conditions and behaviors proven successful by market leaders such as Lenovo and Aigo are being repeated in the next generation of companies. These enterprises do not engage in novel-product innovation but do fill valuable domestic market niches and fit foreign technologies and concepts to the realities of China.

The national impact of this developmental pattern is similar to that made by large enterprises. By enhancing the drive of each region toward greater specialization, this business development path significantly augments each region's productivity and enhances the development of particular innovative capabilities and capacities that are rarely, if ever, found outside China. This, in turn, broadens the potential areas in which Beijing start-ups can operate. Knowing that once they reach the prototype phase, they can easily tap the developmental and production services of southern companies, entrepreneurs can work in areas like Beijing that otherwise would be too capital- or labor-intensive for small, cash-strapped enterprises. The availability of a technologically educated workforce coupled with outsourced production networks makes Beijing an attractive site within China for new-enterprise development.

CONCLUSION

In this chapter, we used the theoretical and empirical understandings developed in the first two chapters to analyze the development of the IT industry in Beijing. Inquiring into our four themes—the particularities of regional history, center-local tensions, the impacts of structured uncertainty, and the local implications of the global fragmentation of production—we followed the co-evolution of industry and state in the Chinese capital. By building on an institutional heritage of strong universities and S&T institutions, Beijing has come to possess the highest-educated human resources in China. However, the impact of this legacy is somewhat blunted by the effects of the unitist mindset, which significantly limits cooperation across organizational boundaries, and a restrictive hukou system.

Center-local tensions are apparent in Beijing, where companies need to navigate between a local government that aims to maximize high-technology activities, even if not novel-product R&D, while forcing deindustrialization, and a powerful central government that officially encourages novel-product innovation even as it pursues a wide range of competing strategic goals through the IT industry. Consequently, successful domestic IT companies have converged around a particular business model. In its R&D focus, the ideal Beijing business model calls for a firm to use proven technologies to develop China-centric products and also to be plugged into global production networks through OEM-ODM and local distribution arrangements. Mastering these two features allows Beijing companies to be tied into the latest developments in the global IT industry and to use their impressive R&D skills to translate innovations developed elsewhere into products that cater to the tastes and needs of the Chinese market. In their domestic location decisions, Beijing IT enterprises keep their R&D facilities in the capital and source (or outsource) production in other regions of China. Such an organizational strategy is followed by both large and small enterprises as well as by foreign MNCs. It is therefore important to remember that the development of Beijing as a center for R&D-intensive, services-based, second-generation innovation has been so successful specifically because the city is a node in an integrated, national innovation system, not a stand-alone local system. Beijing's companies rely on the production and fabrication capabilities of China's other regions; at the same time, other regions look to Beijing to help them flourish by specializing in innovation around different stages of the IT production network. The overall result is that China's run of the Red Queen is significantly strengthened.

The impact of China's structured uncertainty is apparent in the R&D strategies of Beijing's IT companies. By following an approach that concentrates on R&D in proven technologies, with the aim of developing products for the local market, Beijing companies can hedge and minimize risk and gain access to external financing while still making the most of the region's greatest strength. Nonetheless, within the ever-changing political economy of China, successful companies are those that manage to plot a steady course, which allows them to enjoy the state's goodwill without becoming fully captured.

In the next two chapters, we analyze the development of the other two prominent nodes of China's IT industry. In Chapter Five, we examine the evolution of the PRD, which followed an opposite route from Beijing's—building its innovational capacity from the shop floor upwards. Before we do that, however, we consider the development of IT in the only other city in China whose research infrastructure can compete with Beijing's—Shanghai.

Chapter 4 Shanghai

In fact, under globalization, these foreign companies are Chinese
companies too, because they registered in Shanghai.
—*Government official, Shanghai*

Everything is bigger, better, and faster in Shanghai; even the roads are
elevated to a height equal to the tallest buildings in many Chinese
cities. Shanghai projects an image of cosmopolitan sophistication, a
gleaming metropolis of global big business, and it is the only Chinese
city with a university system comparable to Beijing's.[1] Furthermore,
because it has a long history of working with foreigners and MNCs,
a strong and capable local government, and the most rule-bound environment on the mainland, Shanghai sees itself as China's business
capital. Its IT industry has an impressive array of large-scale companies, both foreign and domestic, such as SMIC, General Electric, and
Shanghai Bell. In addition, China's newest, fastest-growing semicon-
ductor-industry subsector—pureplay foundries, represented by Hua-
hong NEC, Grace Semiconductor, China Semiconductor Manufacturing Corporation, and SMIC—is centered in Shanghai.

As part of its outward-looking policy, Shanghai heavily relies on MNCs to rapidly upgrade the capabilities of domestic companies and meet ambitious growth targets. Through joint ventures, local (state-owned) partners gain access to foreign experience and technology as well as to overseas markets. Our interviews, along with both Susan Walcott's (2002) and Yu Zhou and Xin Tong's (2003) research, show the success of this strategy by pointing out that over the past decade, the presence of leading foreign MNCs has pushed Chinese firms to ratchet up their R&D.

Unlike those in Beijing, IT-hardware companies in Shanghai keep their manufacturing in the region, supplying jobs to those who lack high-level academic educations. Shanghai prides itself on hosting MNCs such as Transcend, a Taiwanese company that is developing large R&D facilities there to go along with its large-scale manufacturing facilities in the region.[2] Shanghai's manufacturing emphasis is a cornerstone of its government's development plans.[3]

Also in marked contrast to Beijing, which allows only one science park, ZGC, Shanghai aggressively fosters the creation of multiple parks, each managed independently. Again in distinction to those in Beijing, Shanghai's parks are located far away from the city proper, in the suburban outskirts, particularly in the Pudong New Area, the Minhang District, and the Songjiang District. Similarly, the universities' main campuses and research centers are also located on the periphery, far away from downtown. On average, a drive from Shanghai to one of the region's two premier engineering universities, Jiaotong and Fudan—or a drive between them—takes more than an hour.

Many statistics are marshaled to support the image of Shanghai as a powerful, rising center of the IT industry. In 2007, Shanghai attracted $7.92 billion in FDI, accounting for 10.59% of China's total (NSBPRC 2008a; Shanghai SB 2008). Shanghai produces 16.7% of China's high-technology exports and 14.06% of its electronics. In IC design, Shanghai accounted for 38% of all new designs registered in China during 2007 (Shanghai Gov 2007). While Beijing does not even merit attention in the Chinese press as a center for IC exports, Shanghai represents approximately 40% of the country's total. Shanghai's IC production accounts for 21.65% of China's total (China Customs 2007).[4]

Shanghai's approach to development is often conceptualized as one of sophisticated local-government control. For example, city leaders have attempted to rectify some of China's widespread weaknesses in financing by offering direct state investments, subsidies, and tax breaks as well as R&D grants and cooperative programs. And since Shanghai's rapid growth has outstripped the availability of skilled personnel in targeted sectors such as IC design and software, the local government has created, both independently and in cooperation with foreign enterprises such as IBM and Infosys, training institutes designed to upgrade the skills of existing graduates and increase the absolute number of graduates able to enter the workforce in these sectors.

Nonetheless, even in the midst of all these policy initiatives and impressive growth statistics, Shanghai's weaknesses are as glaring as its strengths. Although Shanghai hosts R&D centers for many of the world's leading IT MNCs, including Intel, Hewlett-Packard, IBM, Google, and Alcatel (through Shanghai Bell), the actual R&D conducted in these centers revolves around second-generation innovation and is less sophisticated than the work done in Beijing (authors' interviews). At an extreme, some of our interviewees, who included both MNC executives and government officials, argued that many of the MNC R&D centers in Shanghai should be called development centers, not research centers. The same emphasis on second-generation innovation is also apparent in the behavior of Shanghai's domestic champions.

One of the most conspicuous exemplars of such behavior is Shanghai Bell, the city's leading telecommunications-equipment firm. Shanghai Bell has access to some of the most advanced mobile-transmission technology in the world and boasts of its global capabilities, yet engages only in work that will reach the Chinese market within three years. Similarly, SMIC, the premier IC foundry, does not have the ability to fabricate ICs from the world's current wafer generation, focusing instead on the production of less sophisticated, mass-market chips to be used in domestic electronics-assembly businesses, usually for foreign clients. Indeed, in semiconductors, the sector most crucial to city development plans, Intel, the global leader, has just announced that it is moving its production activities away from Shanghai to Chengdu.[5] Given weaknesses in the local semiconductor industry, it is not surprising that Elena Obukhova (2008) repeatedly found that the more successful and technologically sophisticated of Shanghai's IC design firms source all their production to Taiwan and shy away from the local pureplay foundries. Such behavior fits our arguments about the "run of the Red Queen development strategy," and hence, we do not see this behavior as inhibiting economic growth. However, unlike Beijing and the PRD, where local officials support Red Queen behavior against the formal wishes of the central government, Shanghai prospers from a Red Queen run that is a far cry from the technologically sophisticated and business-savvy city its planners envision.

A much more worrisome development in Shanghai is state control of the best and most successful IT companies. While state ownership by itself does not preclude development, as discussed in Chapter Three, excessive control and intervention constrains the ability of companies to respond to market needs and opportunities. Additionally, when state control enables access to cheap financing without regard to commercial success, enterprise management focuses more on pleasing its political masters than on successfully running the business. This is the case in Shanghai. Many China scholars have argued that state control is directly responsible for the lukewarm performance of the IT industry (Fuller 2005b; Segal 2003; Segal and Thun 2001; Steinfeld 1998, 2004). Consequently, in Shanghai the strong, guiding hand of the state is partly the cause for the less than stellar growth in employment and GDP.[6]

Thus, Shanghai exemplifies an altogether different approach to economic development than that taken in Beijing or the PRD—an approach that truly believes in state-led planning and command and control, relying on local elites and established enterprises to lead the way in accordance with local government dicta. Shanghai, once known as the Pearl of the Orient, has become the one Chinese city in which the dogma of comprehensive economic planning and state leadership is still celebrated, albeit with MNCs now seen as the joint heroes along with SOEs.

A systematic analysis reveals that the IT industry in Shanghai has three central characteristics that define its place in China's run of the Red Queen:

- Shanghai's large IT enterprises are mostly state owned or state controlled and tend to form conglomerates.
- Unlike Beijing, Shanghai has purposely moved its universities, research parks, and manufacturing facilities outside the city limits and far away from one another. Hence, whereas in Beijing there is one closely knit research-oriented IT cluster, in Shanghai, university campuses and industrial centers are far from the financial and service centers, which are predominantly located in the downtown.
- Shanghai's officials not only target specific industries but also particular niches within these industries. The favored companies in these niches are lavished with funds and subsidies but are also carefully managed to ensure that they adhere to the city's plans, whether or not the reality of the market makes this a prudent strategy.

On the bright side, the local state, acting in alliance with the central government, has transformed Shanghai into a leading IT industrial manufacturing and engineering center as well as a base for high-technology research in China. In 2007, Shanghai's total economy grew at 13.3% year on year, with the service industry growing even faster, at 15.2%. In education, Shanghai, with its nine top-ranked schools and dozens of other universities, has an annual output of 297,000 vocational, university, and graduate-school graduates (Shanghai SB 2008; Wu et al. 2008). Enterprises in the city filed more than 24,500 patents in 2007 (8.11% of the national total), including 3,259 invention patents, second only to Beijing (BSB 2008; Shanghai SB 2008). Showcasing its strength in connecting research to industry needs, Shanghai boasted 133 MNC regional or national headquarters and 177 foreign-invested R&D centers in March 2006 (Shanghai Foreign 2006b; Shanghai SB 2008). Collectively, these R&D strengths have enabled the city to grow dramatically.

Nevertheless, even in these statistics, Shanghai's limitations are apparent. The most obvious is the large amount of state ownership in Shanghai's economy. In a city that aims to become the center of China's modern market economy, the public economy (公有经济) still accounted for 54.9% of regional GDP in 2007, and the private economy accounted for a paltry 17.5%.[7] The figures for total exports are even more striking: state-owned and foreign enterprises accounted for 87.83%, while private enterprises accounted for only 11.31% (Shanghai SB 2008). These realities have led many researchers, some in admiration and some in desperation, to describe Shanghai's development strategy as one that favors large (mainly state-owned) urban-based industrial enterprises and strongly disdains entrepreneurial SMEs, particularly township and village enterprises (TVEs) (Huang 2008; Huang and Qian 2008; Segal 2003; Segal and Thun 2001; Thun 2006).

What is the significance of these statistics and characteristics for the structure and capabilities of Shanghai's IT industry?

The city is the center of post-reform-era China as envisioned by Shanghai's leaders and their central allies—cosmopolitan, globally influential, and possessing the requisite global brands as well as key strategic industries. The government's strategy has distributed education, research, high-tech businesses, and manufacturing around relatively remote locations on the urban periphery. At the same time, Shanghai has concentrated finance and other business services in the city center, which prevents both the emergence of a Beijing-style research-oriented cluster and the close integration of production and enterprise R&D, which are the main strengths of the PRD. Furthermore, constant intervention by the local state has led to an IT industry dominated by large state-owned or foreign enterprises. Smaller enterprises have been left to fend for themselves in a hostile business and regulatory environment. The large number of foreign-invested enterprises and MNC research centers means the city has become a primary contact point for high-end foreign production technologies and procedures. Their contributions to building up Shanghai's basic industrial capabilities have helped make the city a national leader in the production and mastery of technologies that are at the core of a nationally strong IT industry. However, these technologies, brands, and standards still remain the domain of foreign enterprises.

This overall structure raises several questions. What are the R&D and innovation implications of Shanghai's dependency on large enterprises, both foreign and state-owned? How does the local state influence the development path of the IT industry? What is the long-term impact of the Shanghai model on economic development and job creation? Finally, what does the Shanghai model mean for the whole of China's IT industry and its future development?

To answer these questions, the chapter is structured as follows: we first provide a historical introduction to Shanghai, analyzing its historic place at the center of China's economy as well as the continued influence of central-government control and the planned economy. We then consider Shanghai's advantages and limitations in both large and small enterprises. In so doing, we look at how local institutions and capabilities affect variously sized enterprises in the city. We conclude by reflecting on the implications of Shanghai's development path for the overall development of China's IT industry.

THE INSTITUTIONAL HERITAGE
OF SHANGHAI'S IT INDUSTRY

Shanghai sits near the confluence of the Huangpu and Yangtze rivers. The Huangpu bisects the city into two main areas: Pudong, in the east, and Puxi, in the west. Historically, the urban core has been in Puxi, although much of the rapid high-technology industrialization since 1990 has occurred in Pudong. Within its 6,340.5 square kilometers, or 2,448 square miles (including surface water), the city is home to 13.79 million hukou-holding residents and 4.79 million migrants, or temporary residents (Shanghai SB 2008). A heavily industrialized suburban countryside has grown up around Shanghai's Puxi urban center and now blends into Kunshan, Suzhou, and Wuxi in southern Jiangsu. Together, these areas form a discrete industrial region with Shanghai as its coordinating center.

Shanghai has the reputation of being a "big business" town dominated by powerful conglomerates. This reputation predates the centrally planned economy. Although Shanghai has hundreds of years of history, until the First

Opium War (1839–1842), Shanghai remained a small walled city and county seat. From the end of that war through 1949, Shanghai became China's most populous, wealthiest, most international, most industrialized, and most modern city. British trading conglomerates such as Jardine Matheson and other foreign concerns developed Shanghai by using foreign investment and local labor to drive trade, manufacturing, and finance. During the Republican Era (1911–1949), Shanghai dominated the Chinese economy. Three-quarters of China's trade passed through Shanghai (Hooper 1986). Foreign-run utilities provided extensive electrification, gas, and telephone services. Light industry, especially silk and cotton textiles, boomed under the supervision of British and Chinese merchant families. Chinese "bureaucratic capitalists" working in close relation with the Kuomintang (KMT) leadership controlled Shanghai-based commercial and industrial empires.

The Japanese invasion during World War II and the postwar wave of nationalizations by the KMT disrupted many foreign business, industrial, cultural, and political interests in China. Shanghai was the last great remaining center of this once-extensive presence (Naughton 2007). The pattern of large-scale enterprise-based development was presaged by the British economic presence in particular. Shanghai received 80% of all British investment in China, and seven giant concerns controlled 60% of all British investment. After the arrival of the CCP in 1949, the new authorities began to pressure foreign interests to turn over their property to the government, a process that was completed by 1954 (Hooper 1986).

During the late Qing and Republican periods, an extensive university infrastructure developed in Shanghai. Foreign missionaries and business interests established a comparatively large number of missionary schools and universities. Four of Shanghai's top universities—Jiaotong, Fudan, Tongji, and the Shanghai University of Finance and Economics—trace their roots to this period. Shanghai enjoyed a wealth of intellectual capital and infrastructure at the dawn of the People's Republic. The availability of locally educated engineering and other high-end human resources greatly facilitated the development and expansion of new industries during the 1950s and 1960s.

During the Soviet reorganization of the Chinese university system in the 1950s, Shanghai gained five more top universities. However, unlike those in Beijing, the university campuses were not clustered within a single area of the city. And throughout the second half of the twentieth century, again in contrast to Beijing's universities, Shanghai's expanding universities moved their centers of activity away from the city center to new, remote campuses on the periphery. The Soviet period's greatest influence was in the creation of specialized schools differentiated by discipline. To this day, Jiaotong University is best known for its engineering prowess, and East China Normal University is known as a school for educators. Although universities in Shanghai and Beijing are similar in the number of their quality institutions and their capacity to produce graduates, the relative dispersion of Shanghai's universities strongly differentiates them from those in Beijing.

As Shanghai's universities have grown in size and capability, and as the structure of the city's overall urban and economic layout has changed, Shanghai's schools have opened branch campuses across the city. Eighty percent of Jiaotong University's 38,000 students and most of the degree-seeking students at East China Normal University study in remote Minhang District campuses rather than in the historic Puxi-area campuses (authors' interviews). Students are thus separated from the emerging urban-based IT service economy. The Minhang campuses and remote branch units in Zhangjiang High-Tech Park (ZHTP) and other HTDZs encourage, to some degree, cooperation between companies and university labs and professors. However, entreprencurial service companies, which prefer to locate in the urban area, have grown farther and farther apart from Shanghai's universities. As a consequence, Shanghai does not enjoy the full benefits of the spatial concentration of research and industry that its impressive aggregate numbers of graduates and higher-education institutions might lead one to expect (see map 4.1).

Shanghai's great economic transition came between 1954 and 1956. The central government removed the last vestiges of the foreign economic presence and completed the nationalization of local industry and its incorporation into the scope of the national five-year plan (Naughton 2007). Through the 1980s, Shanghai was at the center of the planned economy. Under the plan, large-scale heavy-industrial projects in chemicals, steel, and machinery were extensively developed. Shanghai's planned industrialization focused on the construction of integrated factory complexes in industrial suburbs surrounding the city core (Walcott 2003). The local manpower administration assigned the graduates of local universities to the suburban factories according to the projected needs of each five-year plan. Many newly minted graduates resented these forced relocations; this resentment led to the coining of the modern Shanghai adage: "Better a bed in the city [Puxi] than an apartment in the suburbs [Pudong]."[8]

In the first years of the reform era, Shanghai remained tightly bound to the economic plan and the central government's finance-procurement organs. In

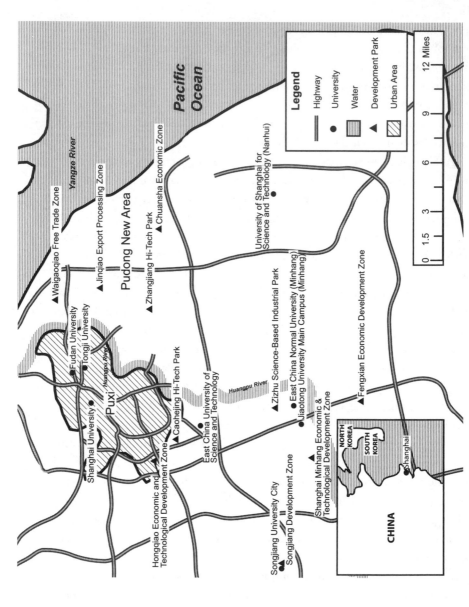

Map 4.1—Puxi and Suburban Industrial Parks and Universities

Source: Chuang et al. 1990; Sohu.com 2009; TeleAtlas and Google.com 2009.

comparison with the PRD, where the provincial government paid one, rather low, lump sum to the central government, and Beijing, which remitted 63.5% of revenues from 1980, Shanghai was still forced to remit 88.8% of all revenues to the center (W. Hong 2003; Shirk 1993; Wei and Leung 2005). Despite such close central scrutiny, Shanghai enacted some critical reforms during the 1980s. Shanghai's reform policies tended to adhere to a tradition of seeing large conglomerates as the anchor of growth and generally ignoring SMEs. Large SOEs began outsourcing certain manufacturing tasks and plan quotas to TVEs established in southern Jiangsu's now heavily industrialized Kunshan-Suzhou-Wuxi region. Unlike the more private (in practice if not in name) TVEs of the PRD, those in the Shanghai region preserved their system of nonindividual ownership. Regional TVEs benefited from the subcontracting agreements and technical assistance provided by large SOEs in Shanghai. As a consequence, Shanghai-region TVEs were larger and more technologically sophisticated than those in other regions. Both TVE development and outsourcing reinforced the viability of Shanghai's integrated SOEs while reintroducing them to market principles (Naughton 2007).

Foreign investment in Shanghai also began during the 1980s. Whereas FDI in the PRD concentrated in labor-intensive export processing, foreign investors in Shanghai aimed to establish a presence in the Chinese market. To achieve domestic-market access, many foreign MNCs agreed to form joint ventures with SOEs in exchange. For example, Bell Telephone Manufacturing's 1983 partnership with the Ministry of Posts and Telecommunications (as the Posts and Telecommunications Industry Corporation) in Shanghai created the first company to provide digital telecommunications switches in China. Today, in its current form as Shanghai Bell, the company is one of China's largest IT-equipment companies, providing one-third of all digital switches sold in China as well as dominating in digital subscriber line (DSL) and voice-over-Internet protocol (VoIP) equipment (authors' interview; Grivolas 2003; Harwit 2005, 2007; X. Liu 2006). By 1987, direct investment from large American enterprises was significant enough to justify the reestablishment of the American Chamber of Commerce in Shanghai after a thirty-eight-year hiatus (authors' interviews).

In 1987, Shanghai's municipal government under Jiang Zemin and Zhu Rongji announced "A Comprehensive Development Program for Shanghai," which was an ambitious plan to remake the city (Huang and Qian 2008). The program declared that Shanghai's goal was to become an international city and that therefore Shanghai must "internationalize" its economy by using foreign technology and global brands. In accordance with this vision, local authorities decided that Shanghai had to eliminate old economic elements that made the city appear backward, such as petty entrepreneurs and rural markets (Huang 2008). Under the plan, land-use rights were procured at below-market rates and then sold at market rates as a way to finance industrial-policy-based development programs (Huang and Qian 2008; Walcott and Pannell 2006).

Starting in 1989, Jiang and Zhu rose to power in the central government. The two served as president and premier, respectively, until 2003.[9] Accordingly, Shanghai's development became a national priority. Jiang and Zhu formed the nucleus of the so-called Shanghai Clique (上海帮), a strongly pro-coastal-development faction in the central government. In the 1990s, Shanghai enjoyed central-government patronage to such a degree that central leaders personally ordered new nationally critical FDI projects to be located in Shanghai. For example, Premier Li Peng decreed that new foreign-investment projects in semiconductors would be located in Shanghai rather than elsewhere in China (authors' interviews).

The State Council renegotiated Shanghai's relations with the central government in 1990. In April, it declared the marshy farmland and warehouse area on the east bank of the Huangpu River a special economic zone (SEZ) with the same rights as existing SEZs. Foreign investment rapidly boomed. From 1978 to 1991, Shanghai attracted a total FDI volume of $1.63 billion, but in 1992 alone its contracted FDI totaled $1.86 billion (Shanghai Foreign 2003). To attract foreign investment, Shanghai copied many policies adopted in the PRD, including land and utility subsidies, duty-free imports of components and machinery necessary for the production of exports, and tax breaks. Unlike the PRD, however, Shanghai had industrial and large state enterprise networks into which foreign investment could be integrated.

To promote foreign direct investment and encourage the development of large-scale businesses, the Shanghai municipal government allotted land for industrial parks. In Puxi, the Shanghai municipality established the Caohejing High-Tech Park in 1984 (elevated to a national-level HTDZ in 1991) and the Songjiang Industrial Zone in 1992. In 1990, State Council planners divided the Pudong New Area SEZ into zones that emphasized different areas of foreign investment (Wei and Leung 2005). On the Huangpu River, they established the Lujiazui Finance and Trade Zone. East of Lujiazui was the Waigaoqiao Free Trade Zone, which quickly became a center for foreign investment. Ninety-five percent of the firms in the zone are foreign invested (Walcott 2003). Two parks dedicated to manufacturing were also established: the Jinqiao Export

Processing Zone (1990) and the national-level ZHTP (1992). Today, there are forty-one municipal- and district-level industrial zones and five national-level zones in Shanghai, a significant difference from Beijing, where all parks are subsumed within Zhongguancun (Shanghai Economic 2006; authors' interviews).[10] Nominally, each zone has a different industrial focus, but in reality, they all strive to become innovation bases and integrated business environments, incorporating residential, commerce, political, technology, and manufacturing sectors. Some of the more remote parks, such as Zhangjiang or Jinqiao, developed amenities that allow them to resemble self-contained cities: foreign, local, and bilingual schools; apartments; shopping centers; community centers; and even churches (authors' interviews; Shanghai Gov 2006; Walcott 2003; ZHTP 2008).

During the 1990s, Shanghai debated what its target industries should be. Zhangjiang has changed its industrial focus twice since 1992. This exemplifies the best and worse outcomes of these debates. The park began as a national base for biopharmaceutical research. Because the development, testing, and approval of medicines involves high costs and extended research periods, the park quickly accumulated net losses (Walcott 2003; ZHTP 2006). Disappointment in the inability of Zhangjiang to register rapid economic growth in less than five years led the Shanghai government to launch the "Focus on Zhangjiang" campaign in 1999. The program switched the park's focus to IT, with the initial aim of building local activities in niches that had already demonstrated global success. Since 2000, with the adoption of a municipal policy package of tax incentives, financing, and stock-listing facilitation, Zhangjiang (as well as Caohejing and Songjiang) has focused mostly on the semiconductor and software industries.[11] In 2000, Zhangjiang's first Taiwanese-style pureplay foundry, SMIC, commenced operations. United Microelectronics Corporation (UMC), Taiwan Semiconductor Manufacturing Company (TSMC), and other Taiwanese producers have since opened subsidiaries as well, complementing joint-venture and indigenous foundries such as Huahong-NEC and Grace Semiconductor.

The impact of economic planning is still strong in Shanghai, as evidenced by the five-year plans issued by the city's Development and Reform Commission. The Eleventh Five-Year Plan (2006–2010) ambitiously aimed to accomplish many of the goals from Jiang and Zhu's 1987 initiative (Shanghai Foreign 2006a). Planning and policy writing aside, the implementation of development programs in Shanghai has had mixed results. On the one hand, growth is strong, investment levels are high, and Shanghai is considered a highly desirable residence. On the other hand, the manner in which Shanghai's municipal leaders and their national allies have pursued development has stifled entrepreneurship (Harwit 2005; Huang 2008; Huang and Qian 2008). Policies in effect through 2005 restricted the development of both Beijing-style university spin-offs and PRD-style small-scale enterprises. Professors, civil servants, and general managers in SOEs were largely barred from even participating in entrepreneurial ventures. To register a new business, a would-be entrepreneur had to show proof that all projected capital needs could be met before business commenced. This is a difficult task in a country whose financial system largely excludes private enterprises. Finally, while foreign enterprises and joint ventures could reduce their taxes by deducting labor costs, domestic enterprises could not (Huang and Qian 2008).

The result of Shanghai's reform and half-reform efforts has been a strong preference for foreign investment channeled through joint ventures with local SOEs. Shanghai's local government also strongly interferes in the location decisions of industries and investment. Government plans rely on large-enterprise conglomerates, disdaining smaller private enterprises. These trends are strengthened by a development paradigm partially influenced by the era of the planned economy, which distrusts private enterprises and entrepreneurs and values size above all else. Since implementing its series of reforms, Shanghai has come to fully adhere to the idea of a socialist market economy achieved through market-based economic planning and a strong interventionist state that largely maintains direct ownership of the modes of production.

THE TALENT ADVANTAGE? RESEARCH, UNIVERSITY, AND INDUSTRIAL STRUCTURE IN SHANGHAI

Shanghai's development trajectory is influenced by the relative abundance of highly educated labor and the extensive use of technology development zones and industrial parks. When we interviewed representatives from both MNCs and domestic small and large enterprises, almost every Shanghai-based executive noted the importance of local human resources, just as their Beijing counterparts did.

In addition to the availability of engineers and scientists, the ways in which land for development is allocated—specifically, the concentration of industry into large but geographically distant development zones—are central features of Shanghai's IT industrial system. Half of our interviewees from large enterprises specifically mentioned incentives offered by their industrial parks as a major factor in their final investment decisions, showing that industrial parks and their promotional policies play a large role in the distribution of investment. In keeping with Shanghai's historical reliance on the idea that bigger is better, the incentive schemes of Shanghai's S&T parks are oriented toward large enterprises—and largely ignore the needs of start-ups and SMEs. To elaborate on these findings, this section discusses Shanghai's educational system and its science-zone policies.

Shanghai has a large and growing supply of highly trained labor and an excellent university system. In 2007, 149,000 students completed four-year university degrees, and 23,900 completed post-graduate education (*Shanghai Daily* 2008a; Shanghai SB 2008). For a single metropolitan area, this quantity is second only to Beijing's. Efforts to further increase the availability of educated entry-level or experienced workers follow three approaches: reforming university degree programs, encouraging local and foreign companies to establish training centers, and attracting skilled workers from other regions.

University reforms are changing the courses and degree programs offered to students. New programs are designed to match industry needs and internationalize the universities. For example, in 2000, after software became a targeted industry under the reform known as Document 18, the government encouraged more local universities to begin offering software-engineering and software-programming degrees (Shanghai Municipal Government 2000). For existing programs, the Shanghai Information Commission worked with the universities and software-programming training schools to increase their gross enrollment (AsiaInfo 2003). As an incentive to increase enrollment, universities' budget allocations increased for each student enrolled. While this incentive was quite successful at increasing the number of students, the student-to-faculty ratio in many institutions skyrocketed (authors' interviews).

Concerns over the quality of education in Shanghai are widely shared. Even if the city is fast progressing in the quantity of graduates it produces, again in striking similarity to our findings in Beijing, the quality of the graduates, especially those conducting high-level R&D, is a different matter.[12] In our interviews, representatives from Shanghai enterprises, mirroring their Beijing counterparts, were quite adamant about the limited capabilities of a Shanghai university graduate in comparison with those educated in the West or even in non-Mainland universities in the Greater China region. The concerns about education are so similar in the two cities that this statement from the director of a global-level MNC research lab in Shanghai could well have been uttered by his Beijing counterpart: "In general, a foreign-educated employee is preferable to a domestically educated one. We find that it is a lot easier to connect foreign-educated researchers to our international research channels and practices. Domestic hires take two or three years to train to a comparable level. For that reason, *all* of our project and team leaders are Sea Turtles" (authors' interview).

This gap is widely and publicly recognized by universities. To close the gap, many of Shanghai's elite universities have programs to "internationalize" their curricula. Leading global scholars are recruited to offer seminars and courses, and English is increasingly used as an instructional language. Jiaotong University goes so far as to encourage most of its students to study abroad for at least a semester. Efforts to internationalize are also changing traditional methods of recruitment and advancement. Universities increasingly make competitively lucrative offers to overseas Chinese scholars to return and direct laboratories or centers. Jiaotong now recruits approximately one-third of its new hires, including senior hires, abroad. A further one-third are recruited domestically, but not from among its own graduates. This is in marked contrast to Beijing's Tsinghua University, which heavily relies on promotion from within its own ranks.[13]

Another approach by Shanghai's government to improve the fit between skills and needs is to encourage MNCs to establish training centers in collaboration with local-government training programs or facilities. Such efforts are especially prevalent in the case of software.[14] Lately, such efforts have been used to close the gap in other skills that are deemed necessary for business success, such as management training. For example, in 2008, the China Europe International Business School (CEIBS) signed an agreement with the Zhangjiang Institute for Innovation to establish the Zhangjiang Centre for Innovative Entrepreneurship (CEIBS 2008).[15]

The brisk expansion of training programs for so-called blue-collar software engineers brings up two interrelated issues. First, Shanghai's economy has a large demand for technicians, not only university-trained engineers and scientists. In response to that need, programs to improve universities have been augmented since 2008 by similar policies designed to increase the number and quality of vocational-school graduates. Vocational schools are encouraged to connect with manufacturing companies in order to train workers jointly and produce skilled vocational graduates in one to three years (*Shanghai Daily* 2008b). Former vocational schools that had recently become four-year colleges have been told to give priority to training skilled technicians. Setting a planned-economy-style target, Shanghai hoped to raise the percentage of skilled technicians in the skilled-manufacturing workforce from 19% in 2007 to 21% by December 2008.

The second issue regarding the fit between labor-force skills and market needs has to do specifically with the still strongly planned economy of Shanghai. Since Shanghai fully adheres to a view that large integrated enterprises conducting the majority of their production within the region should be the basis of development, it is not clear whether there is a severe misalignment between the highly educated workforce, which Shanghai invests so much in producing, and the actual needs of the expansive industrial system the city has built. These problems of fit between labor supply and demand are already causing significant problems.

Manufacturers like Transcend, a Taiwan-based IT and digital hardware firm, need line workers and foremen, not engineers and university-educated researchers. Pureplay semiconductor foundries do not require their operators to have college degrees, only vocational ones. Shanghai's manufacturers recruit heavily in China's central and western provinces (authors' interviews). Electronics and semiconductors, high-growth industries powered by foreign investment, generate thousands of jobs, but not the high-end ones sought by Shanghai's growing number of university graduates.[16] Even enterprises that need theory-oriented and R&D-capable employees, typically prefer experienced workers, not graduates. This concentration on manufacturing and high-end R&D has perpetuated an employment problem for fresh graduates, who find themselves unable to secure work suited to their skills and interests. Although the IT industry is growing, its needs differ from those of the local, expensively educated and trained workforce.

The greatest irony of this misalignment between skills and jobs is that the large-enterprise-based development policy was intended to modernize the city's industry as rapidly as possible, provide the most technology transfer, and lead to independence from foreign control. However, Shanghai has not leveraged foreign investments into distinct local capabilities. It remains as dependent as ever on foreign direction, training, and investment to sustain growth. It offers fewer incentives to young and talented graduates seeking to start their own companies, which decreases the amount of entrepreneurial churn in the economy. Economic growth relies on the extensive application of resources and investment. Shanghai has been able to sustain high rates of growth only by relying on outsiders—both foreigners and non-Shanghainese workers.

Since the demand for both high-skilled labor and experienced craftsmen and workers is so high in Shanghai, and misaligned with the locally available talent, many companies are recruiting outside the region.[17] Shanghai officially encourages the recruiting of skilled human resources from other provinces in order to meet the immediate needs of industry (AsiaInfo 2003; *Shanghai Daily* 2008b; Shanghai Municipal Government 2006). Starting in 2006, the Shanghai municipal government adopted a new raft of policies to facilitate such efforts. The government announced plans to list the specific job skills in short supply in the local economy and publish them in the "Catalogue of Shanghai's Talent Development in Major Fields." Nonlocals who supply these skills have a better chance of securing a local hukou for themselves and their families. The government similarly offers desired personnel "convenience" in seeking apartments and completing new-residency registration (Shanghai Municipal Government 2006). Starting in 2009, unemployed graduates of local universities who are not Shanghainese will, for the first time, be explicitly eligible for loans from the local government to help them start entrepreneurial ventures. Those ventures that hire Shanghainese locals "will be given preferential treatment if they apply for a Shanghai residence permit or *hukou*" (Fei 2009).

This approach to the internal migration of skilled workers is a complete reversal of the official policy in practice. Since 2004, Shanghai has sharply restricted and limited access to hukou. In our research we found that securing a hukou was still a major concern for both employees and employers in Shanghai, despite the new policies. In a classic example of structured uncertainty, at the same time the city was enacting recent policies allowing highly skilled labor to secure hukou, it simultaneously increased restrictions for hukou transfers. During our interviews, we found that the ability to offer a hukou to employees in Shanghai is a strong advantage for a company competing for scarce resources. Shanghai also seems to apply hukou restrictions so as to enhance the attractiveness of its own local SOEs at the expense of both MNCs and domestic SMEs. An MNC lab director bluntly described his company's situation: "Our competitors for human resources are mostly other MNCs and R&D-conducting SOEs. In the last few years, the SOEs pay higher salaries, offer more benefits, and can provide a hukou with no questions asked. This gives them an advantage in recruiting talent" (authors' interview).

Similarly private entrepreneurs perceive the system to be unpredictable, even politically biased. For example, most entrepreneurs assess the situation as an overall denial of hukou: "The Shanghai government used to have the bar set at a level where if you had a BA and a job from a Shanghai company, then you were good enough to get a hukou. But that policy changed in 2005. So in the past, we did have quite a few of our staff get the hukou under that policy, but in recent years, it has been difficult. They only get a working permit, not a hukou" (authors' interview).

By comparison, representatives of large-scale joint ventures or SOEs repeatedly told us that they had no difficulty securing a hukou for their employees. According to one director: "The hukou is not a problem. The requirement seems to be that the employee works in Shanghai for one year and then they are eligible. There is no obstacle in this respect. We apply for a hukou for our designers because there is no obstacle for our company and there are no limiting quotas" (authors' interview).[18]

Small companies, even those owned by the state, cannot overcome the hukou bias against them. The hukou quota a company receives is less related to its current needs than to its investment in the local economy and its output—proxy measurements for its size (authors' interviews). The current relative scarcity makes the hukou an exceptional award for many motivated IT workers in Shanghai.

To summarize, Shanghai has a university system comparable to Beijing's in enrollment as well as in the capabilities and limitations of its graduates. The local government has taken a highly activist approach in attempting to address these limitations and create graduates with the requisite skills for the type of advanced manufacturing and service economy the planners envision. Unfortunately, these efforts have fallen short of their goals in both directions. Emphasis on attracting the highest-end R&D and retaining manufacturing has created jobs for experienced researchers and managers as well as for lower-skilled and lower-cost migrants, but fewer jobs for locally educated graduates. The hukou system, even when reformed, limits the options of young outsiders seeking employment and channels them toward large SOEs, thus stifling technological entrepreneurship. Finally, all these competing and, at times, conflicting goals —in education reform, planned development, population control, and fostering entrepreneurs—have created a climate of structured uncertainty about the direction and sustainability of local policy.

SHANGHAI'S INDUSTRIAL PARKS

Shanghai's main policy vehicle for the development of high-technology industries and encouraging FDI is S&T parks. The parks are seen as the future industrial base for the city. To ensure rapid achievement of the city's ambitious development goals, the municipal government views the securing of large and ever-growing amounts of FDI in manufacturing and services as a priority. The first zones, the Caohejing High-Tech Park and the Hongqiao Industry Zone, were established in the 1980s and were located on the edge of the urban area, near access to sea and air transport. Since the 1990s, Shanghai's parks have been increasingly established in ever more remote suburban locations such as Fengxian and Chuansha (see map 4.1).

While both Shanghai and Beijing use technology parks to develop the IT industry, there are three main differences between Beijing's Zhongguancun and Shanghai's science parks. First, Zhongguancun has a single, unified administrative authority, which is a branch of the Beijing municipal government. Shanghai has forty-one municipal-, district-, or local-level development zones, and five at the national level; each park runs independently of the others and has its own administrative structure. There is no single authority to which all the various zones are ultimately responsible. For example, national-level parks receive official guidance from multiple sources, including State Council–level officials, the Shanghai municipal government, the district authorities for their respective region of the city, and the development company, which operates the parks' business and infrastructure functions. Other parks answer to different masters, including universities, district or municipal governments, and institutional investors. The competition between parks to secure investment has become so brazen that interviewees commented on the overall inefficiency of the park system as a tool for driving innovation.

All parks, regardless of their focus—electronics, semiconductor fabrication, software, or simply IT more generally—compete for occupants. All consider investments by large foreign enterprises to be a mark of distinction. Since park officials have a strong incentive to attract investment and increase revenues from renting land and facilities, they sometimes engage in what might be considered a destructive, "race to the bottom" approach to investment. Officials seek investments so heedlessly, and with so little regard for official development goals, that they will go after projects that may have negative impact on other parks and the overall development of the city. Examples of such noninvestment strategies are abundant: the Zizhu Science Park, a supposedly high-end science park operated as a joint venture between the city, Jiaotong University, and an industrial conglomerate, proudly showcases the plant, packing facility, and regional headquarters of Coca-Cola.[19] Additionally, the confusing array of incentives offered to companies has led to unfulfilled promises and great uncertainty with regard to which incentives will be granted once a company commits to investing in a particular park (author's interviews).

The second major difference between the two cities' science parks is that while Beijing's Zhongguancun aims to strengthen an urban IT cluster within the Haidian District and its multiple universities, the dispersion of Shanghai's parks exacerbates the effect of geographically isolating the city's universities from the parks and from one another. This effect is further strengthened by the fierce and growing independence of the park administrations.[20] Interpark rivalry and competition for the same enterprises prevent the organized clustering of industrial activities. This is in marked contrast to the policy in the Pearl River Delta, a finding we will discuss in Chapter Five.

In the case of semiconductors, where the central and provincial leadership's goal was specifically to create the national leading industrial cluster in Shanghai, the result of such internal rivalry is disheartening. IC design houses are scattered in multiple parks around the periphery and throughout the city (authors' interviews; Obukhova 2006). The largest foundries are primarily located in Zhangjiang and Jinqiao, but the assembly and test facilities are concentrated in Nanhui, to the southeast of Pudong, or in the more remote western parks in the Songjiang District (Y. Wang 2008). Meanwhile, many design houses have limited interaction with local foundries, and so they orient their production activities toward overseas foundries. Shanghai's foundries concentrate on the production of chips for foreign clients, using designs from abroad. To date, the primary way the IC industry has grown in Shanghai has been through continual, extensive investment from abroad.

Last but not least, Shanghai's science-park policy has further increased the importance of established large enterprises, foreign and domestic alike, to the detriment of SMEs and new entrepreneurial ventures. Since large manufacturing facilities require large swaths of (preferably inexpensive) land, they inevitably spread to increasingly distant industrial parks. Production facilities for Shanghai's IT-hardware industry are distant from the urban center (Walcott 2002; Wei and Leung 2005). Many of these companies engage in labor-intensive production that is dependent on migrant labor and so do not require proximity to the city center. However, when employees with R&D skills are needed, many companies find that Shanghainese are disinclined to move far from the city center. The outcome is an internal geographic division between R&D and production facilities. This discourages the types of closely intertwined production, marketing, and research seen in factories in the Pearl River Delta or among the research and service companies of Beijing, discussed in Chapters Three and Five.

Apart from the overt political preference of Shanghai for the kinds of large SOEs and MNCs that fill parks faster, development policies are designed with large investors in mind. This benefits state-owned or coinvested companies such as the new pureplay foundries or large foreign enterprises looking to establish a production base in China. The negative impact of such a focus on large enterprises and production facilities is that, according to all the representatives of small and start-up enterprises whom we interviewed, the development zones and their promotional policies are seen as highly irrelevant. The parks, with their emphasis on tax incentives and greenfield developments for large established companies, offer very little to meet the needs of start-up enterprises, which usually do not have large sales volumes during their start-up phase and, hence, neither benefit from tax incentives nor need to build large facilities.

Furthermore, for small enterprises competing in Shanghai's labor market, convenience for commuting employees and a prestigious in-town office location are two of their sole advantages in recruiting and retaining employees. Small enterprises worry that if they were to relocate into the suburban parks, they would have greater difficulty attracting and keeping talent.[21] In our interviews, many entrepreneurs were quite explicit in stating the need to locate their offices in the Puxi urban core:

> We also registered our company in Zhangjiang, but our offices are here [downtown]. We think most of the engineers would want to live close to Puxi and not in Pudong. In Pudong, after they finish work, they have nothing to do, so if they must, they would like to live in Puxi and work in Pudong. But if they can also work in Puxi, then they feel more comfortable, so it is easier for us to keep them.
>
> A place in the science parks would be nice because the rent would be lower. However, it is far away from the city. Many of my employees used to work in the parks, and they were not very happy with their arrangement, which is partly why they work for me now; living in the city is highly valued. (authors' interviews)

The municipal government and district or development-zone authorities are acutely aware of the difficulty of attracting high-quality engineers to work in the suburban parks. To make the parks more attractive, the latest policy aims to transform the zones into full-service communities. Apart from the fact that most such efforts have so far failed to change opinions regarding suburban living, this policy, if successful, will only augment the problem of geographic isolation and increase the industrial ghettoization of Shanghai.

The net impact of Shanghai's policies and practices on industrial parks has been mixed. From a purely economic perspective, it appears quite positive. The parks are growing and enjoy high occupancy rates. They also employ large

Table 4.1—Distances between Shanghai's Universities and Industrial Zones

Location		Distance	
From	To	Kilometers	Miles
Jiaotong University Xuhui Campus	Zhangjiang High Tech Park	19.10	11.87
Jiaotong University Xuhui Campus	Fengxian Industrial Zone	35.70	22.18
Jiaotong University Minhang (Main) Campus	Zhangjiang High Tech Park	41.00	25.48
Fudan University	Fengxian Industrial Zone	60.60	37.66
Fudan University	Zhangjiang High Tech Park	16.50	10.25
Songjiang Industrial Zone	Fengxian Industrial Zone	48.40	30.07
Songjiang Industrial Zone	Zhangjaing High Tech Park	49.10	30.51
Zhangjiang High Tech Park	Caohejing High Tech Park	37.80	23.49
Zhangjiang High Tech Park	Fengxian Industrial Zone	50.10	31.13

numbers of line workers and serve as bases for production, which increases tax and export earnings. However, the zones do not encourage the development of small-scale enterprises. Overall, the parks are less effective than those in Beijing at generating an innovation-rich (much less novel-product-rich) environment. The flexibility and independence of Shanghai's parks increase competition and allow policy innovation. But this flexibility and independence significantly diminishes the ability of the region to cluster activities together. This further increases the geographic isolation of the IT industry in Shanghai.

The distances between the technology zones, between the zones and the city, and between the zones and the university campuses greatly influence the behavior and integration of Shanghai's IT industry. Table 4.1 provides some of the driving distances between a few of the central parks and universities in Shanghai. All such drives involve the use of Shanghai's elevated road or highway system, which is usually congested. If Shanghai's goal is to integrate education, industry, and investment, the geographic dispersion of parks and universities is a most efficient way to prevent it.

LARGE ENTERPRISES IN SHANGHAI

Shanghai's economy is shaped by its large enterprises and conglomerates, which are neither wholly foreign nor entirely domestic. Their hybrid ownership resembles that of leading research institutions' spin-off enterprises in Beijing, such as CATT's Datang Telecommunications and the CAS's Legend Holdings. However, in Shanghai, the hybrid ownership of public, private, and foreign enterprises distinctively incorporates the experience, scale, and capital of leading MNCs. Unlike those in Beijing, these large enterprises keep their production activities in Shanghai, thus generating different employment needs. To elaborate on the behavior of Shanghai's large enterprises, we will focus on Shanghai Bell and SMIC, two companies that set the national Chinese standard in their industries—telecommunications equipment and semiconductor fabrication, respectively—revealing the comparative strengths and weaknesses of Shanghai's developmental model. Specifically, the two companies display the influences of Shanghai's planned economy, the geographic isolation of park-based industrialization, and the labor supply.

In 1983, the Shanghai branch of the MPT and the Belgian subsidiary of the ITT Corporation, BTM, formed Shanghai Bell (上海贝尔) (Harwit 2005, 2007).[22] Shanghai Bell utilized BTM's digital-switch technology, importing components to produce switches for the domestic market. The locally produced content of the switches increased from around 20% in 1988 to more than 68% in 1995 (Harwit 2007). Most notably, negotiations between BTM representatives, at the behest of the Chinese government, and the U.S. export-control regime led to a lifting of restrictions on the export of semiconductor-fabrication technology to China in 1988. Now able to produce its chips in-country, Shanghai Bell spun off Shanghai Belling (上海贝岭) to produce ICs for its telecom switches.[23] The Shanghai government directly supported the development of Shanghai Bell through tax exemptions intended to help the company continue its overseas component procurement and advantageous foreign-exchange policies. Promotional policies continued through the 1990s. In 1992, when Shanghai Bell was already highly profitable, the local branch of the People's Bank of China awarded the company a loan of $50 million (Harwit 2005). Through 2002, despite the rise of domestic competitors such as Huawei, ZTE, and Julong, Shanghai Bell retained more than 30% of China's telecommunications-switch market. Today, Shanghai Bell employs more than 10,000 workers nationwide. In Shanghai alone there are more than 1,660 R&D employees (authors' interviews).

Shanghai Bell is a perfect example of the sort of state-led hybrid conglomerate that dominates Shanghai's economy. Foreign investment is encouraged but controlled and channeled through existing state and industrial mechanisms. Although it was initially a joint venture, since 2002 Shanghai Bell has operated as an independent Chinese-incorporated company (authors' interviews; Business

Wire 2002). Alcatel controls a majority (by a single share) of the new company. Despite this majority-foreign ownership, the Chinese partners strongly exert state influence. Of the members of the board of directors, two are chosen from the state-owned shareholding portion of the business, one is appointed from one of the Chinese telecommunications operators, and a fourth is appointed from the Chinese government. The chairman of the board, from Alcatel, maintains close personal relations with SASAC to ensure smooth operations for the company and strong procurement relationships with national SOEs.[24]

Like Lenovo, which capitalizes on its partial state ownership to develop its supercomputing business, Shanghai Bell penetrates state-dominated or closed markets as a "domestic" enterprise. The company combines the greatest advantages of a local R&D-intensive enterprise, an SOE, and a foreign-export oriented enterprise. Unlike other foreign joint ventures or foreign companies in China's telecommunications-equipment market, Shanghai Bell has maintained its market share and revenue since the 1980s (Harwit 2005).

As far as innovation and Shanghai's goal of technological independence, however, the hybrid ownership structure of Shanghai Bell has not brought hoped-for technology-transfer benefits into the local economy. Alcatel freely transfers technology to Shanghai Bell, and the products are then localized through Shanghai Bell's R&D division; however, as it has become more and more like a state-owned national champion, the company has begun to behave like one, including relying on soft-budget constraints. For example, Shanghai Bell partnered with the local MPT commercial branch, which was also its primary customer. The company could thus easily increase sales and access state financing when needed. The result has been a lack of technology transfer and few efforts at indigenizing the foreign technology it so readily accesses. The potential technology-transfer benefits of the joint venture have been muted.

If Shanghai Bell has been the leader of Shanghai's telecommunications companies, SMIC has led Shanghai's aggressive foray into semiconductors. In 2000, Richard Chang, the founder and former CEO of the Worldwide Semiconductor Manufacturing Corporation, the third-largest pureplay IC foundry in Taiwan, decided to launch a pureplay foundry business in China, which he called the Semiconductor Manufacturing International Corporation (SMIC). Ambitious and rapid expansion has given the company a production footprint comprising wholly owned foundries in Shanghai, Beijing, Tianjin, and Shenzhen, and operation contracts for state-owned foundries in Chengdu and Wuhan. This wide array of foundries has made SMIC the dominant pureplay-foundry company in China. With a sales volume of 117 billion RMB in 2005, SMIC surpassed Singapore's Chartered Semiconductor (now part of Global-Foundries) to become the world's third-largest IC foundry company, behind the Taiwan Semiconductor Manufacturing Company (TSMC) and the United Microelectronics Corporation (UMC), both of Taiwan (LaPedus 2006). The scale of its predominance in the Chinese market is apparent when we take into account that the second-largest chip producer in China, Shanghai's Huahong-NEC, had only 24 billion RMB in sales during 2005 (McIlvaine 2007). SMIC now employs more than five thousand workers in Shanghai. Despite or perhaps because of its rapid expansion, SMIC has struggled with profitability since 2008; its overall revenues showed a strong decline that year (CTN 2009a; Lemon 2008b).

SMIC officially began as a foreign-invested private enterprise. The majority of its start-up capital came from overseas, but unlike a purely foreign-invested enterprise, it is closely tied to the Chinese market and state (Business Wire 2006; Fuller 2005b). Thus, while the company is officially private and foreign, local- and central-state influence and investment in the company have grown as rapidly as the company itself. A major investor in SMIC is the Shanghai In-dustrial Investment Holding Company, a local SOE whose majority-owned (52.18%) flagship subsidiary, Shanghai Industrial Holdings Limited, controls 10.09% of SMIC, making it the second-largest single investor (Sung and Shen 2009a). Since semiconductor fabrication is a critical industry, the national gov-ernment has taken an interest in SMIC as well. In November 2008, SMIC sold 16.6% of its shares to the CATT's Datang Telecom, making Datang and, by extension, the MII (which controls CATT), SMIC's top shareholder (CTN 2009c). This dominant shareholder position has been particularly significant for SMIC's gradual drift into state ownership: although SMIC has sought strate-gic investors in exchange for ownership stakes since March 2008, the company chose Datang instead of a foreign entity or other semiconductor fabrication firm (CTN 2008b). With the advent of TD-SCDMA licensing, Datang re-quired a large dedicated provider of TD-SCDMA chips, making SMIC an ideal investment. Thus, SMIC ended up with an SOE as its partner. Today, Datang, the leading developer of equipment for TD-SCDMA, nominates two of SMIC's board members and appoints SMIC's vice president for TD-SCDMA technol-ogy. The companies agreed to make each other's businesses a priority. As a re-sult, between the Shanghai Industry Investment Company, Shanghai Indus-trial Holdings Limited, and Datang, SMIC has effectively become state-owned, a trend that is widespread among Shanghai's large conglomerates.[25]

As it becomes nestled within the Chinese state, SMIC is becoming increasingly entangled by the conflicting interests of its various state sponsors and by those sponsors' goals and its own wish to maximize commercial success. For example, Datang's investment was seen by many as a maneuver by the MII to align related equipment industries for the launch of TD-SCDMA in 2009, while the Shanghai government, through its own investment vehicles, aims to maximize job creation in Shanghai. Needless to say, neither of these goals correlates perfectly with the maximization of profits.

We now consider the direct influence of Shanghai's technology-park development policy on both Shanghai Bell and SMIC. In the early 1990s, as parks proliferated in Pudong and the city embarked on its industrial restructuring, Shanghai authorities seeking to reshape the layout of local industry offered Shanghai Bell land in the Jinqiao Export Processing Zone. This was part of a drive to concentrate foreign-invested enterprises in the new zone to fill it as rapidly as possible (authors' interviews). The industrial clustering in Jinqiao placed Shanghai Bell in close proximity to its suppliers, which may have facilitated the localization of components, but the move also separated the company from the urban research infrastructure. Shanghai Bell maintains relations with academics in leading Chinese universities, including Fudan and Jiaotong, but only on a project-by-project basis. Unlike other companies, Shanghai Bell has never opened or sponsored a permanent research facility at a university (authors' interviews).

Shanghai's land and technology-park development policies made possible the development of SMIC and other foundries such as Grace and Huahong-NEC. Establishing a semiconductor foundry requires massive start-up capital and a large area footprint. SMIC opted to open its first facility in Shanghai, not in Shenzhen or Beijing, partly because Shanghai's Zhangjiang High-Tech Park offered both inexpensive land and direct investment, while Shenzhen and Beijing offered, at best, only one of the two. Shanghai's government offered these subsidies in order to help develop the city's semiconductor industry by completing the industry chain. However, to become profitable as quickly as possible, SMIC uses foreign semiconductor designs for 88% of its output (author's interviews). Although 60% of Chinese IC design houses say they would prefer to source their chips' fabrication domestically, most of the companies continue to source internationally (authors' interviews; Obukhova 2008).

For the city of Shanghai, Shanghai Bell is an asset because it trains new researchers and conducts globally integrated high-end R&D. It also fills a very specific need in the local economy by supplying specially tailored telecommunications solutions for local state clients, such as the subway system. However, it has proved limited in its ability to generate employment. Where technology spillovers from the movement of personnel have occurred, as in the large-scale movement of engineers to Huawei and ZTE, the engineers and their skills have not remained in Shanghai.[26] Thus, as far as generating entrepreneurs and jobs, companies like Shanghai Bell have not proved to be a great asset to Shanghai's growth.

Furthermore, although SMIC obtains the workers it needs, and the government helps house, educate, and entertain them, the company now exists within a campus-like ghetto in the distant reaches of Shanghai. Also, as primarily a manufacturing company, SMIC employs mostly operators, who need only a vocational school education, not top-end researchers. As we found in our interviews, a large number of SMIC's line operators are hired in China's hinterlands, not locally. They do not receive a local hukou and are typically brought in alone, without their families. For its management, business, and R&D divisions, SMIC receives the same local incentives as other leading companies, including tax breaks for expenses for the R&D team and income tax and property tax breaks for Sea Turtles who return to work for SMIC (authors' interviews).

Large enterprises in Shanghai exhibit several characteristics that reflect the influence of politics and state planning. Many foreign-invested companies, and even locally initiated firms, are hybrids composed of foreign, local-government, and publicly traded companies, in addition to SOEs. To create such firms, the Shanghai government—building on its heritage of strong local, state, and existing industrial infrastructure—channeled foreign investment into large, capital-intensive joint ventures. This process of hybridization has connected ostensibly profit-oriented foreign investments with the soft-budget constraints of a state-owned economy, leading to a decrease in the effectiveness of technology transfer, potential spin-offs, and the growth impact of foreign investment in Shanghai.

The second type of large enterprise in Shanghai is locally incorporated companies or foreign-invested enterprises, which over time have become bound more tightly to the state-controlled economy. The mechanisms of control and their degree of influence vary, but in all cases, entanglement with the state apparatus pressures companies to put nonmarket concerns, such as the creation of employment or the promotion of national strategic technology, ahead of market rationale, particularly in the strategic IT industries such as semiconductors.

Despite these drawbacks and limitations, large enterprises are continually attracted and fostered by the actions of the local state—most notably, suburban industrialization and investment strategy. However, investing in these far-flung zones compounds existing problems by introducing difficulties from non-spatial clustering and the industrial ghettoization of the region. Finally, the labor demands of these firms are not aligned with the skill sets of local university graduates, but rather cluster around two extremes: experienced and skilled managers and researchers, and lower-wage line workers. Thus, a focus on catering to large enterprises has made it difficult for Shanghai to generate sufficient employment for the burgeoning educated population or to spur entrepreneurship.

SMALL ENTERPRISES IN SHANGHAI

It is a lonely, winding road that R&D-based SMEs in Shanghai face in their march forward. As we have learned, the city's institutions of growth and innovation are geared toward supporting the needs and interests of large enterprises. As a result, Shanghai's government favors foreign investment and existing SOEs with joint ventures, largely ignoring, if not actively discriminating against, SMEs. Second, the centrality of S&T parks to Shanghai's development plans has clearly shaped the development of SMEs, particularly through the importance assigned to land allocation and finance. Third, education and manpower policies, especially with regard to the hukou, have made it difficult for many Shanghai SMEs to access or, more importantly, retain the critical talent they need to conduct long-term projects and develop new products. Finally, the relationships between SMEs, the state, and larger companies exemplify the negative impact of the conglomerate-building business model of Shanghai's large enterprises. This is not to suggest that small entrepreneurial start-ups in Shanghai cannot or have not succeeded. There are cases of extremely successful firms, such as the software-outsourcing company Augmentum, which grew in four years from a start-up to a company employing more than 1,200 engineers and managers worldwide. However, as our interviews revealed, even among many largely successful SMEs, the misalignment between Shanghai's local-government developmental programs and the needs of SMEs restricts their ability to grow or forces them into the arms of the state apparatus.

Local economic-development statistics showcase the comparative strengths and weaknesses of Shanghai's policies. Through June 2008, revenues from IC design were only 8.11% of Shanghai's IC-industry total (*Semiconductor Inter-*

national China 2008). By comparison, revenues from packaging and testing and from fabrication were 53.14% and 33.68% of the total. When Shanghai is compared with China's other IT industrial regions, its difficulties in creating an entrepreneurial market economy are apparent. In 2003, although Shanghai had 34% of China's software companies, the region generated only 20% of national software revenues. Beijing and the PRD combined had 37% of the software companies but generated 60% of revenues (Saxenian 2003). In the fabless, IC-design subsector, the number of companies is growing rapidly, in accordance with city plans for a complete IC industrial chain. Yet while Shanghai had approximately 39.5% of China's IC design houses in 2006, it accounted for only 12% of national IC-design revenues (Y. Wang 2008).

A representative example of the misalignment between programs, their stated intentions, and their actual outcomes is the promotional support offered to SMEs in the technology development zones. Shanghai's government, in pursuing its ideal conception of a technology park, encourages start-ups to locate in purpose-built facilities within the zones. Enterprises are eligible to receive grants of 50,000–60,000 RMB and free rent for the first year. As in Beijing, incubators also tend to highly subsidize rents as part of an effort to combat high operating costs. Shanghai has also established both a Property Rights Exchange and a Scientific and Technological Achievements Transformation Center to encourage technology transfer and thus increase the innovation capabilities and technology mastery of SMEs.[27] Despite good intentions, a grant of approximately $10,000 is not sufficient to allow a new enterprise to conduct any meaningful R&D.

Furthermore, the offer of highly subsidized facilities, while welcome, does not address the core needs of SMEs for capital support and reliable human resources. The greatest difficulty facing Shanghai's SMEs, according to our interviewees, is to attract and keep the best-quality talent necessary to conduct their product development. Among software enterprises in particular, comments such as this were frequent: "There are many difficulties facing start-up companies, but the brain drain is currently the main challenge. Excellent talents go to the big companies, both SOEs and foreign enterprises, although it seems foreign companies get the best talent. Since we are a software company, our technology is in our employees' minds, so if they leave, then the technology leaves with them" (authors' interview).

For companies that consider locating in the technology parks, there is a strong fear of their best employees being poached by large companies. Even local government officials admit that within the technology development zones, rates of employee turnover are higher than anywhere else in the city. For rational SME managers, this acts as a disincentive to move or set up facilities in the zones. But by not being located in the parks, SMEs are cut off from many of the support programs designed by the local government.

Enterprises hoping to compensate for the loss or lack of state support by seeking VC or bank loans are similarly stymied in Shanghai. As one entrepreneur explained, "We cannot secure bank loans, since we do not own physical property." In interviews, government officials stated that in Shanghai, local government agencies are forbidden to serve as loan guarantors. On the other hand, while the government cannot serve as a loan guarantor, local-government units operate and run one-third of Shanghai's VC firms—a pure example of structured uncertainty. This makes the local government, particularly when combined with the funds operated by cash-rich SOEs and other domestic champions, a particularly powerful force in local finance. Once again, however, such finance is more likely to be accessed by enterprises that follow the guiding hand of the local government and locate in technology parks than by enterprises operating outside the ideal image constructed by city planners.

Therefore, to tap into these local funds, small enterprises must acquiesce in the conglomerate-forming tendencies of Shanghai's large companies, particularly the SOEs. The case of a small logistics-software start-up is particularly representative. Founded in 1999, the company entered a market, Shanghai's rapidly expanding trade-services sector, hungry for its software. Like many start-ups, it chose to locate in the urban core, where its address would confer prestige, allow it to attract and hold employees, and give it convenient access to clients across the city. However, as the company grew, it needed capital to finance the expansion of its labor force, and so it initially approached banks in search of loans: "We did not manage to secure a loan. The current bank-loan situation works in this way. You must have independent corporate entities or individuals with mortgageable property. When we were first established, it was very difficult for us to obtain loans from banks. In those days, all we had were a handful of professionals, a little registered capital, and a company license. It was not enough" (authors' interview).

Rebuffed by the state banking sector, the company looked toward VC. It turned to "Chinese-style" VC firms owned by the local government. As a company operating in a strategically important and rapidly growing service sector, particularly one well-placed in local government plans, the firm secured investment from a VC firm operated by the Shanghai Municipal Science and Technology Commission. While the investment allowed the company to continue to operate and even to expand, its manager quickly found that the investment came with strings attached. In essence, the company became a SOE ultimately responsible to its municipal owners.

This was not the only case of the aggressive expansion of local SOE authority. A separate case reveals the desire to expand the power of local SOEs and bring entrepreneurial companies into line with state goals. In this, admittedly extreme, case, the enterprise was a small foreign-invested hardware firm whose founder came back to China after being educated overseas. The company was certified as a high-technology enterprise and maintained cooperative technology-transfer relations with a leading local university. It even recruited interns from local vocational schools to work in the workshop during periods of high demand, thus generating employment and experience for the types of skilled technicians sought by the local government. Nonetheless, even with these relationships, the owners found that they could not secure bank loans and felt that the lack of financial support would keep the firm small: "HSBC found us too small, and Chinese banks found us too small, so even with a contractual export order, we could not secure credit and thus could not fill the order. So now we sell to local companies and act like a local company under the radar. Local financial policy keeps our kind of company small. You can never grow to be big in Shanghai and stay private" (authors' interview).

When the company's successful product caught the eye of the Municipal Science and Technology Commission in the late 1990s, the commission tried to pressure the company into forming a technology-sharing joint venture with a local SOE. After being rebuffed by the owners, the commission's representatives purchased several units and replacement components from the company in 2003. It then reverse engineered, built, and sold their own versions while still using the private company's brand name. Only when customers called and demanded service for the ostensibly branded goods did the private start-up discover the IPR theft. While extreme, this case illustrates the degree to which many local government officials or units seek to expand SOEs, regarding SMEs merely as tools toward this goal.

Despite the difficulties they face, many SMEs report that the talent they are able to attract (when they succeed in bringing it in) often works diligently and loyally for them. This does not contradict the difficulties, explored above, pertaining to high levels of turnover and difficulties with the hukou. We found that for SMEs to secure such talent, many IC-design, electronic-hardware, and software enterprises recruit outside of Shanghai as much as, and maybe more than, they do locally. Thus, in this respect they exhibit the same tendency as large enterprises. The types of careers generated even by entrepreneurial start-ups seeking stable workforces are not predominantly for Shanghainese, but rather for outsiders. One of our interviewees was quite direct in explaining hiring practices: "Actually, except for me and one other employee, everyone else on my staff is from outside of Shanghai. I don't hire Shanghainese. Normally, people outside of Shanghai work harder and seem to have better morals in many senses. They are less likely to run out on you. We have people from all over China. The best students and workers are always from the poorest places" (authors' interview). For this reason, it is only logical that Shanghai's government has passed ordinances conferring special benefits on university graduates who employ Shanghainese in their start-ups. The economic structure of the city has yet to find a way to meet the demands of its growing, educated labor force.

Nonetheless, within the urban core, SMEs find a vibrant workforce with foreign exposure, a cosmopolitan outlook, and a willingness to experiment. Life in the city is exciting and sets the business and cultural trends for much of China, making it the destination for many starry-eyed entrepreneurs. SMEs that establish offices downtown frequently find high-quality employees, though they may be tempted to change jobs every six months and may not necessarily be Shanghainese. However, in the IT Industry, the geographic dispersion that separates urban-based SMEs from the industrial base, technology parks, and university learning centers prevents SMEs from making the types of innovation advances and the rapid entrepreneurial growth one would expect in such a fertile environment.

CONCLUSION

This chapter explored the rapid development of Shanghai after it was belatedly released from the control of central authorities and began, in the 1990s and 2000s, to develop its IT industry. Shanghai's experience sheds light on the themes of center-local tensions, the particularities of regional history, the impacts of structured uncertainty, and local implications of the global fragmentation of production. During this period, Shanghai was alternately tightly controlled by the central government and lavished with support and encouragement. As a result of early constraints, Shanghai did not develop the quasi-legal entrepreneurial economy of Beijing during the 1980s, and thus was forced to rely on its existing economic structure as it opened to the world. Since Shanghai had a comparatively well-developed industrial economy scattered outside the urban core, the city channeled foreign investment into its perimeter. Hence, Shanghai developed capabilities for both high-end design and research while maintaining a strong manufacturing base. During the 1990s and 2000s, it became the preferred location for large-scale prestige investments.

Building on its strong university and research base and the industrial infrastructure inherited from the planned economy, Shanghai has successfully developed a strong large-enterprise and state-led IT industry. Capital-intensive projects thrive, and Shanghai is a national leader in telecommunications hardware as well as in the fabrication, assembly, and testing of ICs. The land requirements for these enterprises have only enhanced Shanghai's existing tendency to establish facilities and universities on the periphery of the city. This has led to a divergence between clusters of knowledge-intensive service-based start-ups and more distant industrial bases. SMEs thus face difficult decisions regarding whether to locate in the dynamic and prestigious urban core or seek more affordable and strongly government-encouraged locations in the suburbs. SMEs face the brunt of the interventionist and controlling hand of the local state and SOEs; to secure financing, many are forced to turn to local-government-owned VC firms, which can lead to the incorporation of the smaller firms into state-owned holding and investment companies. As noted in the Beijing chapter, excessive state influence stifles entrepreneurship and growth. In Shanghai, for want of alternatives to the local government, SMEs are often forced to seek partnerships with it.

Structured uncertainty in Shanghai is especially visible in the behavior of the local government toward non-Shanghainese hukou residents: local authorities simultaneously encourage the in-migration of the best and the brightest, yet erect larger barriers to their permanent relocation. Similarly, although the city officially states that SMEs are the key to generating employment and building the city, in practice, policies discriminate against SMEs in favor of large-scale incumbents and foreign enterprises. The impact of both sets of policies on R&D is that large enterprises, which benefit from state support and soft-budgetary constraints, do not engage in novel-product R&D, and small enterprises are constrained in their ability to attract and hold the talent necessary to conduct long-term R&D projects. The hiring practices of large and small enterprises—highest-end talent for R&D and lower-skilled workers for manufacturing—have created difficulties for newly minted Shanghai graduates caught in the middle.

In the long-term run of the Red Queen, Shanghai will continue to serve as an important base for foreign investment, research, and development. Its large-scale fabrication facilities will supply the semiconductors needed by IT-hardware producers upriver in Jiangsu province and in the Pearl River Delta. By attracting foreign investment—while not as efficiently as it might, because of the hybridization process—Shanghai will serve as a conduit for foreign technology and managerial expertise. As in the past, Shanghai will train leaders who can then transfer to other cities and companies to help raise China's overall technological and innovative capacity. The city will remain a magnet, but its institutions affecting innovation will continue to ensure that in the midrange at least, the greatest advances will come from large-scale legacy enterprises and not from entrepreneurial ventures on the outside, looking in.

Chapter 5 Shenzhen and
the Pearl River Delta

We think of innovation as something China didn't have before, something we can now conceive of and do. Let me give you an example. Take this teacup. The first people who made this type of cup made a lot of money. Then people followed and began making the cup as well. Then more people began to make the cup. What happened? The cup was overproduced and was worth less money. When products come out and make a lot of money and everyone wants to follow, we the government encourage them to innovate around the idea instead of just following others. Even if you want to make cups, you can make a smaller cup. This is innovation.
—*Government official, Dongguan*

Prevailing wisdom contends that the Pearl River Delta has no technological innovation capabilities. The PRD has come to be known in the Western world as a region of the Dickensian factory towns where poor migrants toil in sweatshops to produce commodities for export, to the joy of foreign consumers. Chinese, especially Beijingers and Shanghainese, look down on the entire region and its capacity for industrial R&D. When we spoke with entrepreneurs in Beijing and asked about their companies' innovation activities in Shenzhen, a typical reaction was laughter followed by: "Shenzhen? Shenzhen is nothing but a manufacturing center—not a place to do R&D" (authors' interview). A drive through the PRD from Shenzhen's Nanshan District, where the financial and commercial high-rises give way to industrialized suburbs, through Dongguan and into Guangzhou, serves to strengthen this image. Thousands of small, soulless factories run by nameless OEM companies line the highway, and billboards advertise their ability to produce standardized electronic components, paper products, and light consumer goods for whoever is willing to rent their manufacturing prowess.

The region is dismissed by journalists, businessmen, and academics alike, who describe it as nothing more than an agglomeration of assembly and processing facilities that can be easily replicated and replaced if they lose their cost advantage. Adam Segal's comparison (2003) of China's regions of innovation found the PRD and Shenzhen areas to be the least innovative by far. Susan Walcott's study (2003) of Shenzhen and Dongguan concluded that while there is a necessary division of labor between the PRD and Hong Kong, the PRD's economy has been built on cheap labor and manufacturing facilities. It is far from innovative in high-technology activities. Even local and regional government officials bemoan their industrial structure's reliance on low-cost, low-skilled migrant labor (authors' interviews). Many observers foresee that the region will suffer severe economic difficulties when manufacturing moves en masse to interior provinces or abroad in search of cheaper labor.[1]

Therefore, it might come as an utter surprise that three of China's leading IT innovators are in the PRD: Huawei, ZTE, and Tencent. Of the three, Huawei and ZTE are particularly noteworthy. They are the only Chinese telecommunications-equipment companies feared by MNC executives for their in-house R&D capabilities. Huawei's success is even more interesting because central-government plans in the 1980s and 1990s did not designate the company as the telecommunications national champion it has become (authors' interviews; Harwit 2007). This elevated status was to be reserved only for select SOEs: Julong, Datang, Jinpeng, and ZTE, on which the central government lavished investment and favors. Even ZTE was considered a stepchild, since it is a locally owned SOE and not one of Beijing's favorites.[2] In a different domain, Tencent Holdings is China's leading Internet portal and value-added content provider. It thrives by taking the best ideas from foreign technology service providers and Internet content companies and adapting their systems to the Chinese market. Through clever marketing and rapid innovation, the company has become a leader; its QQ brand is now one of the most valuable and recognized in China.

Beyond its leading enterprises, the PRD also shines in market niches critical to the IT industry, and yet it is disdained by most innovation scholars. These niches include the production of computer-hardware peripherals in the Qingxi and Tangxia townships and uninterruptible power supply (UPS) devices in Dongguan. As a matter of fact, we found that the PRD is the only region where one can clearly discern growing industrial clusters whose operations resemble those of celebrated northern Italian industrial districts in form, function, and capabilities (Kenney 2000; Markusen 1996; Piore and Sabel 1984; Saxenian 1994).

We argue that the common conception of the PRD is wrong. By following "run of the Red Queen" logic, the region has become at least as successfully innovative in the IT industry as Beijing and Shanghai. It has done so by building from the bottom up—from production to industrial engineering, design, development, and research. One of our interviewees, an entrepreneur who moved from Beijing to establish his business in the PRD, summed up the core principles that are behind Shenzhen's success: "Here we view incremental innovation on existing platforms very much as indigenous innovation. So long as there is improvement or new features, it counts; we do not need to come up with a wholly new product to have self-innovation" (authors' interview).

This open perspective on innovation, shared in practice by all the officials, entrepreneurs, venture capitalists, and academics we met in the PRD, profoundly shapes the development of the local IT industry. When one considers innovation across the whole IT production network, the wide range of capabilities developed by PRD enterprises makes it clear that in some respects, the PRD is considerably more innovative than either Beijing or Shanghai. Government statistics, even with their limitations, clearly strengthen this finding: Shenzhen and Dongguan alone received 7.4% of China's domestic patents granted in 2007. By comparison, Beijing and Shanghai received 5.0% and 8.1% respectively.[3] When the remaining IT centers of Guangdong province (including Guangzhou, which has the region's only major concentration of universities and research centers) are included, the region accounted for 18.7% of China's total patents (BSB 2008; DSB 2008; GSB 2008; NSBPRC 2008a; Shanghai SB 2008; SSB 2008).[4]

Furthermore, in 2007, Guangdong accounted for 37% of China's high-technology exports, with Shenzhen and Dongguan accounting for 20.9% and 5.7% of the national total (DSB 2008; GSB 2008; SSB 2008). And growth rates for high-technology-product exports in those two cities remain high: 18.2% year on year for Shenzhen and 21.8% for Dongguan. Moreover, these statistics consider only goods that are officially certified as "high technology" and hence do not account for the production and sale of components that are not considered to possess enough indigenous proprietary-knowledge content to ensure certification.[5] The IT industry currently dominates the region's economy. In 2007, IT hardware accounted for 49% of Shenzhen's entire industrial value added. Electronic exports made up 43.2% of all of Shenzhen's exports. In spite of rising labor and input costs, the total volume of exports grew at more than 32% year on year (SSB 2008).

Such impressive rates of growth would not be possible without significant innovations across a wide range of the IT production network. How could such innovational capabilities develop in an area that historically focused on low-cost contract manufacturing and that lacks the type of research or academic infrastructure typically associated with, and seen as necessary for, innovation?

The answer lies in five key features that define the political economy of innovation and the IT industry in the PRD:

- The region has a strong international orientation based on a pragmatic approach to OEM, ODM, and original brand manufacturing (OBM) strategies.
- The region is home to some of China's strongest and most famous IT enterprises that operate in niches deemed critical to the central government. These successful companies have developed largely without the support of the central state.
- Local governments support all firms that they view as yielding growth benefits, regardless of the firms' size or ownership type or whether they conform to central-government conceptions of technology sophistication.
- R&D is conducted and concentrated within companies rather than within academic or state research institutions, and hence it is closer to final production and the actualities of the markets. This ensures that R&D in the PRD is much more market-oriented and user-generated than it is in Beijing or Shanghai. It also enables the region to make the most of its limited inheritance of science and engineering talent and to create innovations in the absence of formal R&D infrastructure.
- The PRD has formed multiple industrial clusters, each anchored around a specific city or township and focused on a specific set of products.

These five features of the PRD's IT industry evolved primarily from a heritage lacking the trappings of an advanced planned economy such as Beijing's or Shanghai's. The region has a distinct tradition of being both externally oriented and isolated from the seat of power. This isolation has led the PRD to excel in export processing and to become a leading experimenter in new approaches to economic reform and enterprise behavior.[6] Hong Kong and Taiwanese financing has enabled expertise in OEM industrialization, sophisticated knowledge, and connections to global production networks to flow into the PRD. Early access to FDI spurred a development pathway oriented toward the demands and needs of foreign consumers as well as a highly pragmatic approach to central- and local-government regulations. The combination of experience acquired from Hong Kong and Taiwan and inexpensive labor made abundant by a relaxed attitude toward internal migrants enabled the PRD's IT producers to raise their capabilities and the quality of their output more cheaply than China's other rapidly developing regions.[7]

The region's early separation from central planning created an economic space within which new, wholly indigenous companies could emerge. The first enterprises were mostly small, export oriented, and often financed by Hong Kong interests.[8] But the skills learned and absorbed during their development created a local concentration of knowledge in IT manufacturing. The relatively open climate for policy and regulation, together with isolation from central authorities, enabled entrepreneurs to launch their own companies. Enterprises that became the corporate giants of the PRD grew first by providing IT systems and products to the then-underserved domestic market, then moved on to exporting to other emerging markets, and finally started competing head-on with leading foreign MNCs (Harwit 2007).

The PRD builds on an institutional structure developed in the Maoist era: local self-sufficiency and planning for enterprises coupled with negligible education infrastructure (outside Guangzhou). R&D capabilities in the PRD are concentrated within companies. In a marked difference to Beijing and Shanghai, only 10% of Shenzhen's R&D is conducted by universities or the CAS (K. Chen and M. Kenney 2007; Xinhua 2005).[9] In time, this R&D system gave rise to unique innovational capabilities that emphasized market and user needs, facilitated ease of production, reduced costs, and incrementally improved products.

An additional, unexpected, and positive result of the local policy to concentrate support on manufacturing and incremental innovation is that the PRD developed integrated Marshallian industrial clusters (Marshall 1920). These clusters, despite rising costs, are able to prosper by attracting foreign and local investment. The tight networks between suppliers, producers, and clients within these clusters facilitate communication and innovation. Their capabilities have effectively increased the "stickiness" of the region, that is, its ability to keep jobs and businesses (Markusen 1996).

Despite the PRD's many advantages and accomplishments, its successful Red Queen run does not mean that its brand of economic development comes without consequences. As with any policy choice, there are both positive and negative outcomes. Environmental pollution is severe. Overinvestment in infrastructure and wasteful duplication of industrial parks and facilities is widespread. Furthermore, while we argue that the PRD's development model creates and uses innovation, it has certainly relied to a large degree on a massive, inexpensive labor force performing low-value-added assembly of IT hardware. Rising costs, declining export growth, and the consolidation of thousands of small manufacturers as the SME-based industry restructures will produce economic dislocation as less effective companies fail. When interviewed in late 2008, government officials were already describing this struggle: "We are extremely busy these days. As the economic crisis is becoming more and more serious, Dongguan faces great challenges. We are optimistic that we shall overcome these hard times. We hope the winter will end soon!" (authors' interview). We argue that not only will the PRD's IT Industry survive this painful transition—it will thrive. Indeed, according to Richard Doner's study (2009) of technological and industrial upgrading in Thailand, it is the advent of existential threats or resource constraints that push industrial upgrading. As the PRD loses the ability to rely on cheap labor and resource inputs, it will be forced to move up, albeit painfully, the value chain.

The region has become a critical node of the national IT industry. PRD expertise in production, design, and logistics facilitates the development of R&D-based enterprises that are headquartered in other regions of China but lack production capacity at home. Companies in Beijing indicated that Shenzhen accounted for the majority of their production and that, for many, the PRD has become an indispensable base. Thus, in addition to sustaining itself, the PRD, as a node within the national division of labor, facilitates the growth of the Chinese IT industry as a whole.

The story of the PRD and the role it plays in the national IT industry revolve around the principle of regional independence and activism by local authorities. This chapter illustrates how the region has emerged as a leading center for the production and development of IT hardware and how it continues to mature and deepen its capabilities even as costs rise and earlier advantages erode. The chapter first considers the history of the region since the advent of reform and focuses on the capabilities and patterns of investment, research, and finance that have enabled the region's enterprises to overcome some of the same types of difficulties seen elsewhere. We then elaborate on the particular strengths of the PRD's IT industrial districts by analyzing the development of SMEs in the UPS industry in Dongguan. Finally, we conclude with the implications of the PRD model for development in China and abroad.

THE RISE OF THE PEARL RIVER DELTA

The PRD occupies the center of Guangdong province, situated at the mouth of the Pearl River with the special autonomous regions of Macao and Hong Kong to the south and east and Guangzhou on the western edge. Within the area bounded by these three cities are the major IT-industry centers of Shenzhen, Dongguan, Foshan, Zhongshan, and Zhuhai (see map 5.1).[10] Geographically, the region consists of delta plains divided by meandering river channels, low mountains, and valleys.

The economy and polity of the PRD have been externally oriented throughout Chinese history. Its political leaders frequently pursued local autonomy and rebellion.[11] During the late Qing and Republican eras, the region was second only to Shanghai as a center for trade, industry, and finance. Remittances from overseas Chinese, some 70% of whom originated in the region, financed much of the PRD's development in this period (Eng 1997). Aided by being located next to the British free port of Hong Kong, the PRD was the first region in imperial China opened to foreign trade and developed a reputation for business savvy and trading prowess. Networks of trade and information built through the diaspora helped develop a comparatively modern market economy in the region.[12]

The PRD slumbered after the founding of the PRC. Fearing U.S. or Taiwanese invasion and distrustful of the internationally connected local people, central planners underinvested in the region's industrial development (Vogel 1971).[13] In 1978, though starting as a stepchild of the planned economy, the PRD pushed further and faster than any other region along the central government's ambiguously defined path of "reform and opening" (改革开放).[14] Authorities in Dongguan and other PRD regions rapidly pushed for export-processing-based light industrialization, emphasizing investment from Hong Kong (Walcott 2003).[15] Dongguan's and Shenzhen's early experiments in "one-stop shop" bureaucratic procedures and enterprise-incorporation proceedings were copied and further developed throughout China.

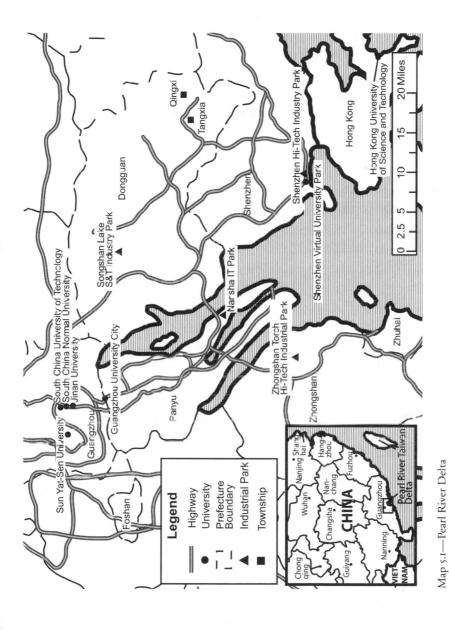

Map 5.1—Pearl River Delta

Source: Chuang et al. 1990; Sohu.com 2009; TeleAtlas and Google.com 2009

While the PRD's historic position as China's gateway to the world might make it seem logical that the region would emerge in the 1980s as a center for export-oriented manufacturing, the success of the region was far from guaranteed. As a matter of fact, one of the main reasons Guangdong was chosen as a locus of reforms between 1978 and 1981 was that the central government viewed the risk of failure for the new economic policies as high. It therefore decided to experiment with them first in what was viewed as a remote area. The PRD thus became a site of early and extensive reforms. Since Guangdong province was a site for reform, its leaders sought to gain ever-higher degrees of independence from central-government planning, although that freedom was far from certain. As early as the fiscal reforms of 1980–1981, central authorities largely freed Guangdong's economy from the national plan. The "State Council Notice on Carrying out the Financial Management System of 'Apportioning Revenues'" required Guangdong province to remit a lump sum of one billion RMB to the center and allowed the province to retain all remaining surplus revenues (Shirk 1993). Local cadres allied themselves with businessmen and Hong Kong investors in order to develop export-oriented industries using Guangdong's plentiful land and labor (Eng 1997; N. Lin 1995; Unger and Chan 1995).

The reforms permitted Hong Kong financed and locally initiated TVEs to grow. These small, early enterprises were generally engaged in the assembly of imported materials.[16] And although many of these enterprises now face significant difficulties, they represent grassroots development rather than planned actions by the central state.[17] The success of the TVEs came as a surprise to the central leadership. Deng Xiaoping himself said: "In rural reforms, what took us completely by surprise was the development of township and rural industries. All sorts of small enterprises boomed in the countryside. This is not the achievement of our central government. Every year, township and village enterprises achieve 20% growth. To this day, it has continued in this manner" (quoted in Jiang 2007).[18]

Not to discount the accomplishments and leadership of the early TVEs in the PRD, but it must be pointed out the greatest single cause of economic growth and the eventual development of the IT industry came as the result of a provincial-central bargain rather than a purely local initiative. In April 1979, Guangdong provincial officials traveled to Beijing to propose the creation of special economic zones (N. Li 2005). In their original conception, the SEZs would serve as centers for export processing and as bases for mastering foreign techniques of business management, technology, marketing, and manufacturing. The SEZs would thus earn the hard currency necessary to push the development of China's national economy (K. Chen and M. Kenney 2007; Garon and Mochizuki 1993; Garver 1993; Naughton 1995; Shirk 1993). From the SEZs' inception, the central government decided to let them develop independently. Independence was a double-edged sword: the SEZs were outside central control but also without central-government financial aid.[19] However, throughout the history of the Shenzhen SEZ, whenever the reform effort faced significant troubles, Deng Xiaoping personally intervened. In 1984 and 1992, Deng visited Shenzhen, inspecting its factories, skyscrapers, and roads to affirm its socialist essence and to encourage the local leadership to be even bolder in pushing reform. Aside from Deng Xiaoping's support, however, the central government frequently showed an unclear or even hostile intent toward the PRD and the SEZ experiments.

The central authorities agreed to allow the establishment of four SEZs (Shenzhen, Zhuhai, Shantou, and Xiamen) in Guangdong and Fujian provinces on August 26, 1980. Each was designed to target a different area of the Chinese diaspora—Hong Kong in Shenzhen, Macao in Zhuhai, Southeast Asia in Shantou, and Taiwan in Xiamen. While all have enjoyed high rates of investment and growth, Shenzhen has become by far the most successful.

In 1979, Shenzhen was little more than a series of villages and fishing communities along the Hong Kong border. The Shenzhen municipality, which covers 2,020 square kilometers (780 square miles) of land, had a population of 314,100 (Ge 1999, 46). Eighty percent of the residents worked as fishermen or farmers. Less than 20% of the GDP came from any kind of industry, and the entire area had only eight kilometers (five miles) of paved roads. Furthermore, at the end of 1979 there were only two engineers in the whole of Shenzhen. Once the SEZ project was initiated, however, Shenzhen quickly became the richest city, per capita, in China (Fu 2008). In 2007, per capita income in Shenzhen reached 79,221 RMB, four times the national average (K. Chen and M. Kenney 2007; NSBPRC 2008a; SSB 2008). Between 1980 and 1986, the economy grew at an average rate of 44% year on year, and from 1987 to 1995, GDP grew at an average rate of 29% percent year on year (Guo and Feng 2007). By 2008, Shenzhen had a GDP of 676.5 billion RMB ($96.65 billion), and the population had reached 8.615 million (SSB 2008). As the SEZ developed, manufacturing moved out from the three SEZ districts adjacent to the Hong Kong border and spread to the Baoan and Longgang districts, which lie outside the SEZ barrier fence and along the Shenzhen-Dongguan-Guangzhou corridor (Walcott 2003).[20]

The IT industry in Shenzhen emerged first, in tandem with the changes in the global industry. In the Shenzhen SEZ, Hong Kong entrepreneurs found a solution to their declining profit margins and rising costs.[21] The SEZ authorities provided subsidized land, utilities, and infrastructure to foreign manufacturing investments. As the first region opened to foreign investment, the SEZ offered a corporate income tax rate of 15%, half of the national tax rate (Shen et al. 2000).[22] By the end of the 1980s, both ZTE and Huawei had commenced operations in Shenzhen. The IT industry continued to expand within the PRD as other counties and cities began offering preferential policies and incentives similar to those available in the Shenzhen SEZ. However, as a first mover, the Shenzhen SEZ remained a major site for foreign and domestic investment.

LOCAL PLANS AND AUTHORITIES

The PRD's specific capabilities in the IT industry are built on institutional co-evolution processes between business and government (local and central) as well as on interactions between FDI and domestic capital. While partially the result of serendipitous timing and location, the PRD's emergence has been driven by the needs of the market in a region determined to spread economic growth wider, especially to rural areas, than either Beijing or Shanghai.[23] The PRD's rapid-innovation-based industrialization attempts to maximize employment, wealth, and overall economic growth benefits. Unlike the elite business-based and research-institution-based models in Beijing and Shanghai, the PRD's plans, while far from egalitarian, aim to bring the benefits of growth to more social groups, including the migrant population. The region's policies promote the development and retention of manufacturing while simultaneously slowing down, but still permitting, the failure of less capable sectors and enterprises.

To promote manufacturing, the PRD took an approach almost opposite to that of Shanghai and Beijing and adopted a highly tolerant policy toward migration. Provincial security and personnel-management officials have long permitted low-skilled workers, first from within the province and later from across China, to move into the region (Chang 2008). Local governments and industrial-zone managers included housing for assembly-line workers as part of the parks' general strategic plans.

PRD administrators further promoted manufacturing by allotting land and construction permits to all classes of enterprises: foreign and domestic, state owned, and minying. These include lower-end, high-polluting companies, although the less aesthetically appealing enterprises tend to be located on the periphery of showcase economic zones, hidden from most visitors (authors' interviews; Walcott 2003).[24] As costs rose, local administrators promoted innovation and technological upgrading in order to keep manufacturers in the region. Administrators in one PRD science park described their approach: "We always promote a view that there is no sunset industry but only sunset technology. With new technology, any industry can have new vitality" (authors' interview).

In Shenzhen, the municipal government has directly intervened to keep the production facilities of major manufacturers in the municipality (authors' interviews). In Dongguan, the municipal government offers tax rebates and duty-free imports on high-technology inputs or capital equipment used to raise local enterprise-technology levels and profitability. To support manufacturers who lack innovative or R&D capacity, local authorities have begun to cooperate with universities to develop these skills within enterprises. For example, Hong Kong University of Science and Technology's Nansha campus places master's degree and PhD candidates in enterprises so that they can conduct research and lead R&D teams as part of their graduate theses.

The collective result of such policies has been the successful recruitment and retention of enterprises working across many stages of the IT industry's production networks. In our interviews, we found the ability to source a large percentage of required services and products across stages of production to be the single greatest attraction for investment in the PRD in the last several years.[25] Representatives from enterprises, townships, and municipal governments agreed that the regionally integrated IT production network sustains their development.[26] For example, when interviewing the regional general manager of a PRD company at a branch office in Shanghai, we asked why the firm keeps its corporate headquarters, production, and R&D center in Guangzhou: "Why Guangzhou? Simple: the industrial chain is in Guangzhou. For example, within a radius of fifty kilometers, we can collect all of the components for the products we produce. But in the north, there is no condition like that. Does Shanghai have a complete industrial chain for electronics production? No, it does not! The entire Chinese electronics production chain is in Guangdong, Shenzhen, and especially Dongguan—not the North" (authors' interview).

Local authorities at all levels in the PRD are quite consistent and forceful in their attempt to spur various sectors to upgrade. Legislated wage increases, the removal of export subsidies, and new tax regulations are designed partly to force inefficient companies to adapt or fail. At the same time, to encourage upgrading, companies that invest in capital goods, R&D, and brand development are eligible for grants, tax forgiveness, and reimbursements from municipal and provincial authorities. Under this broad envelope of regional policies and practices, each city has developed its own policy framework.

Officials' willingness to experiment provides entrepreneurs and investors with opportunities to take risks that in other cities might be frowned upon or blocked by local authorities determined to pursue a highly formalized development plan. The tension between central authorities' preferences and local reality can be clearly seen in the PRD. PRD officials embrace their reputation for independence; in one of our meetings, municipal administrators even described their city's relationship with the central government as "contradictory," explaining: "Our relations with the center are somewhat contradictory. By the time the central government adopts policies we developed and tested, they have outlived their use, and we have already moved on to another stage in development" (authors' interview).[27]

Despite the many advantages provided by local state support, IT enterprises in the PRD face daunting challenges. Their explosive growth has created strong local industries, but for many enterprises, the value added per unit remains low. Although enterprises are keenly aware of the need to raise their R&D capabilities, they struggle to secure access to human and financial capital. Despite the efforts of local and provincial officials, the PRD remains rather poor in research infrastructure. If there is one weakness in the PRD industrial system, it is the lack of advanced research capabilities and high-quality universities needed to train the necessary human capital. Local authorities have engaged in many programs to overcome these two major structural constraints, with, at best, mixed success.

LOCAL GOVERNMENT INITIATIVES TO ADDRESS WEAKNESSES IN THE PRD INNOVATION SYSTEM

The greatest obstacle to technological upgrading in the PRD is the scarcity of researchers. Unlike Beijing and Shanghai, which produce hundreds of thousands of university graduates annually, the output and average quality of graduates from PRD universities is considerably lower. Apart from Guangzhou, there are few universities of note anywhere in the region. At the start of their IT booms, Shenzhen and Dongguan had no higher education infrastructure.

All PRD cities face a critical need for human resources. In response, local authorities have crafted multiple higher-education models, many of which involve attempts to build educational infrastructure overnight. In the 1990s, Shenzhen's municipal government negotiated with leading universities such as Tsinghua, Peking, and the Harbin University of Science and Technology to establish branch campuses. These universities have continued their investment in Shenzhen's educational infrastructure by establishing extended facilities, laboratories, incubators, and classroom buildings. Some, such as Tsinghua University's branch campus, have managed to produce and commercialize university technology through spin-off companies in Shenzhen (authors' interviews). Building upon these branch institutions, Shenzhen has attempted to create a critical mass of human resources and research by establishing the Shenzhen Virtual University Park (SZVU—深圳虚拟大学园). The model calls for universities across China to establish facilities—usually graduate-level minicampuses, laboratories, and representative offices—in the Shenzhen High-Tech Industrial Park. The municipal government subsidizes rent in the SZVU. By bringing in representatives from China's top universities, Shenzhen's municipal leaders hoped to instantaneously plug local industry into top-level state- and university-sponsored research and, by giving outside researchers a reason to stay in the city, to enhance local human resources. Additionally, the city hoped that the affiliation with leading schools would convince local entrepreneurs and employees to further their education by seeking part-time master's degrees or PhDs. Today, the SZVU contains offices or programs from thirty-five domestic universities, CAS academies, and Hong Kong and foreign universities. From its opening in 2000 to 2007, 69,695 students received advanced degrees or other training from the SZVU, and approximately 10,000 earned a master's degree or a PhD (Chen and Kenney 2007; SZVUP 2007).

A second, and quite different, model was developed by Guangzhou. The city has the highest concentration of universities in the PRD, including nationally ranked schools such as Sun Yat-sen University and the Huanan University of Science and Technology. To increase their output of students, the Guangzhou municipal government and the CCP Committee for Guangdong province created Guangzhou University City (广州大学城). The facility consists of a cluster of ten universities or their branch campuses from across Guangzhou, concentrated on an island in the Pearl River. Guangzhou University City's institutions enroll more than 120,000 students, mostly at the undergraduate level. While the concentration of academic talent was intended to encourage cooperation among research departments and universities, the universities themselves have frequently been uninterested in moving to the new campuses. Some, such as Huanan University, sent their peripheral programs to the new campus and kept their core labs and graduate programs on the original campus. Thus, the Guangzhou model has, in essence, become an "undergraduate factory" (authors' interviews).

A third type of educational promotion in the PRD is built more closely around explicit university-industry cooperation. In this model, university branch campuses or postdoctoral centers offer course work and high-level instruction to graduate students. The students are then paired with local enterprises to serve as directors of research teams or to conduct their thesis research in areas relevant to the sponsoring enterprise. For example, the Hong Kong University of Science and Technology manages branch-campus programs in both Nansha and Shenzhen. In addition to pairing graduate students with industry, these programs also conduct their own research and host incubators that help transfer the results from their university labs to the market.

While all these programs benefit the PRD either by connecting the region with the deep and enduring alumni networks of China's leading universities or by significantly expanding the output of undergraduates, academic education and, especially, research remain the area's weak points.[28] This low level of skill intensity and human-resource generation is augmented by the general lack of venture financing. In the PRD, much as in the rest of China, enterprises have difficulty securing sufficient capital for high-risk technology-intensive ventures. While Hong Kong has historically played a leading role in the capitalization of firms and the coordination of manufacturing and service-industry investments in the PRD, for VC, Hong Kong is no longer an important partner. Initially developed during the 1990s Internet bubble, Hong Kong's VC industry was hurt by the sudden collapse of many investments when the bubble burst in 2001. Hong Kong venture capitalists are considered more conservative and risk averse than their mainland counterparts (authors' interviews). As a result, PRD enterprises moving into new sectors or seeking a capital injection typically cannot rely upon traditional financing channels from Hong Kong.

Shenzhen conducted the main efforts to stimulate the PRD's VC industry. In 1999, the municipal government directly stepped into the gap by creating a state-owned VC company, the Shenzhen Capital Group Company, using five hundred million RMB from government resources and six local state-owned corporations.[29] In 2000, the municipality announced the creation of a VC association comprising fifty local VCs under the guidance of the Shenzhen Capital Group. Officially, the sector is to provide the necessary liquidity for the development of new industries and ventures. In practice, however, the primary benchmark is a high return on investments. The result is that the various Shenzhen VC funds behave more like private-equity firms and conduct business with companies in more established and mature industries and not only technology start-ups.

Thus, it is not a surprise that VC was not mentioned in any of our PRD interviews as a reliable source of financing for technology enterprises. However, local authorities do at times directly intervene to convince hesitant VC firms to invest in favored enterprises. The story of the funding and rapid expansion of Tencent, Huawei, and ZTE serves to illustrate the two weaknesses of the PRD—a lack of both highly skilled researchers and VC—as well as its strong points and highly responsive local authorities.

THE EMERGENCE OF THE PRD'S LEADING IT COMPANIES

In 1999, ten young Shenzhen software programmers, the owners of a small consultancy called Tencent, wrote a Chinese-language imitation of the then globally popular instant-messaging software ICQ. Under legal pressure for copyrights infringement, the Shenzhen version, OICQ, retained the look and feel of the ICQ interface but changed the name of its service to QQ (J. Li 2005). Today, QQ is the most valuable brand of Tencent Group Holdings, which has since become China's largest value-added Internet service provider, and has a base of 355.1 million active users. In 2007, Tencent's revenue reached 3.821 billion RMB.[30]

However, Tencent's beginning was less than spectacular. By 2000, less than two years after founding the company, the founders had exhausted their initial savings, and the company was on the verge of bankruptcy. The free QQ service did not generate any revenues, and its explosive growth quickly consumed the company's resources. As a young technology start-up, Tencent was shunned by the banks and refused loans. In desperation, the founders tried to sell the company for as little as one million RMB, without success. Their change of fortune came when Shenzhen's municipal government invited Tencent to participate in its annual high-technology trade fair. As a result, Tencent managed to secure support from the International Data Group, which invested $1.1 million in the company, as did Pacific Century CyberWorks of Hong Kong (authors' interviews; J. Li 2005). The capital injection enabled the firm to survive long enough to establish a revenue stream. The company's first profitable service was instant messaging for XLT phones and wireless QQ, which commenced operations in 2000. Tencent continued to grow, launching more and more services as China's Internet population exploded in the early 2000s. In 2003, the company launched its Internet portal, QQ.com, which is today the most heavily used site in China. In 2004, Tencent was publicly listed on the Hong Kong Stock Exchange.

The history of Tencent has been one of adaptation to the realities of the PRD and China. In the initial years, the company grew mostly by imitating foreign products and services, but it has thrived by developing China-specific applications. As Tencent grew and added new services and products, it increased its technology focus and started to attract top talent, including former senior employees of Microsoft Research. This technology focus has since come to be seen as Tencent's core strategic strength:

> Tencent is going to launch the Tencent Research Institute—like Microsoft Research. This kind of organization will focus on the future technology of the Internet. So Tencent will cooperate with the top talents in Internet and computing technology. Tencent is trying to build its future core competency. In the long term, the goal is to build not only the existing strength in applications but to increase innovations in storage, AI [artificial intelligence], multimedia, and computer vision. We would do anything in our power not to be just a huge dot-com, so to speak, but to be an Internet-technologies development house. (authors' interview)

However, as Tencent has grown, it has experienced difficulties in attracting sufficient human resources to accomplish these tasks. A major problem lies in the branding of the company; while QQ is universally recognized in China, the Tencent Company and its aspirations to become a technology leader are largely unknown, and hence, talented software engineers do not view the company as a desirable place to work (authors' interviews). Recognizing the difficulty of attracting top research students from Beijing and Shanghai to Shenzhen, Tencent has opened research centers in both cities. The current thinking of the company's technology managers is that these will form the core of Tencent's research while Shenzhen continues to concentrate on the development of online products. In this way, Tencent will be following the division of labor within China. Tencent currently employs 2,400 engineers, of which one-third are engaged solely in system maintenance.

Given the lack of either a strong research infrastructure or venture financing, it is not a surprise that most of the PRD's enterprises have not followed Tencent's model but instead have risen to prominence by pursuing an incremental, bottom-up improvement of low-level technologies and production operations. Since the Silicon Valley ideal of a start-up business inherently clashes with the advantages and market structure of the PRD, companies trying to follow it are likely to fail. The story of Huawei Telecommunications, which built its innovational capacity from production and assembly to a dominating position in the global telecommunications-hardware market, serves to illuminate a different model of growth, one that directly builds on the PRD's strengths.

Huawei was incorporated in 1988 in Shenzhen with an initial investment of 20,000 RMB from former People's Liberation Army officer Ren Zhengfei and several former comrades. Huawei was established as a collective enterprise whose first business was to distribute imported telecommunications switches and to assemble and repair telecommunications-transmission hardware for the domestic market. By 1990, Huawei had begun marketing its own equipment, and in 1993, the company reached an important milestone when it successfully developed its own digital telecommunications switch (Harwit 2007).[31] The system, C&C08, was both reliable and appreciably cheaper than alternative systems (X. Liu 2006). Noting that MNCs and the big SOEs concentrated their efforts on the major urban centers, Huawei adopted a market-penetration strategy of rural encirclement by selling directly to local and provincial telecommunications authorities. Huawei's offer was especially appealing to local officials, since the company was very willing to establish local joint ventures. These joint ventures immediately transformed local telecommunications authorities into profit-receiving partners as well as customers for Huawei's equipment. For example, Harwit (2007) describes how Sichuan Telecom received as much as 60%–70% of its investment in equipment back as annual dividends from Huawei. In this way, Huawei rapidly came to dominate rural and interior provincial telecommunications markets to such a degree that in 1996, it held China's second-largest market share in telecommunications switches. Building on its mastery of rural areas, Huawei quickly established a national presence before moving into export markets.

After the success of its first products, Huawei opted to eschew high-end novel-product development (W. Zhang and B. Igel 2001). Instead, it improved, simplified, and reduced the costs of existing technologies and concepts. By investing 10% of its total revenues in R&D, Huawei continually improved the quality and capabilities of its products, and today Huawei competes for 3G contracts in western Europe and North America as well as in the developing world. Huawei has been an ODM producer for leading foreign mobile-telephony companies such as Motorola and 3Com. These ODM collaborations granted Huawei access to the latest trends and technologies in mobile telephony and aided its move to specialize in incremental and design innovation. The access to foreign technology, however, probably led to repeated IPR infringements in the early days, some of which involved Huawei in a protracted lawsuit with Cisco Systems, of Silicon Valley (authors' interviews; Harwit 2007). By 2008, however, Huawei had gained the respect of its foreign competitors and clients. As several technology executives of leading MNCs fully admitted: "Huawei was definitely slower on technology in the past, but now this has completely changed. Their products in current-generation technologies are much better than ours. As a matter of fact, we can no longer compete with them on current technology. We concentrate on the next generation and let Huawei have full ODM control over a whole series of our products. In these, the design, coding, and testing are done completely by Huawei. We just sell them" (authors' interviews).

Huawei's relation with the national and local state has changed throughout its history. Since it was not a favored champion during its developmental years, it could not access bank loans to finance its expansion. In its early years, Huawei's only sources of capital were high-interest (20%–30%) loans from large SOEs (C. Li 2006). However, Ren Zhengfei enjoyed a personal relationship with Shenzhen's municipal CCP secretary. Those connections proved invaluable in allowing Huawei to secure soft loans within Shenzhen. Starting in 1997, the central government accepted Huawei as a national champion, and access to bank loans ceased to be a problem. For example, in 1998, the China Construction Bank, under encouragement from the People's Bank of China, extended 3.85 billion RMB in buyer credit to help local governments purchase Huawei's equipment (Mu and Lee 2005). In addition, the Chinese government has become actively involved in financing Huawei's export efforts; for example, the China Development Bank extended $10 billion in credit to help foreign customers purchase Huawei equipment, and Sinosure, a government insurance company, granted export credit to finance a Huawei deal in Brazil (Low 2007).

Huawei's Shenzhen headquarters employs more than 20,000 workers and engineers. Forty-eight percent of Huawei's Shenzhen's workforce is engaged in R&D, and as of 2005, 60% of those workers held master's degrees or PhDs (C. Li 2006; Low 2007). The Shenzhen facility serves as a production, business, and research base, but like Tencent, Huawei has rapidly expanded its research footprint throughout China. By the end of 2008, the company had major R&D centers in Beijing, Shanghai, and other Chinese cities as well as in Dallas, Bangalore, Stockholm, and Moscow (Low 2007). Thus, while the PRD's local support enabled Huawei to grow and prosper, the company's internal division of labor has largely tried to imitate the regional comparative advantages of Beijing and Shanghai in order to remain competitive.

The Shenzhen government's flexibility and ultimate success in building the region's telecommunications industry, compared with the stagnation achieved by central-government efforts, is even more striking when we take into account that China's second highly successful telecommunications-equipment MNC, ZTE, has even closer ties with the Shenzhen government than Huawei. ZTE was founded in 1985 by the Shenzhen government and the Ministry of Aerospace Industry as a firm to design and produce ICs for telecommunications uses (Harwit 2007). It was the brainchild of a state effort to promote domestic telecommunications-equipment manufacturing. ZTE is thus a prototypical PRD company in that it gradually moved from manufacturing to innovation (Low 2005). While the MPT and the MEI fought over their respective champions and joint ventures during the 1980s, the Ministry of Aerospace industry quietly supported the transformation of ZTE into a telecommunications-equipment company (Harwit 2007). In eerie similarity to Huawei's R&D efforts of the early 1990s, ZTE hired engineers trained at Shanghai Bell and Julong and, in 1993, launched its own digital telecommunication switch the ZXJ2000 (Liu 2006). Even without the support of the central government, ZTE had had 20% of China's telecommunications-switch market by 1998, twice that of the MPT's Julong (Harwit 2007).

In much the same way that Huawei outmaneuvered the central government by going into the rural provinces, ZTE grew to prominence by producing rugged and inexpensive mobile telephony systems and PHS-based handsets used in the infamous XLTs. As we discussed in Chapter Two, the MII opposed PHS technology as being insufficiently advanced. Currently, ZTE is the global leader in PHS technology and has continued to advance its capabilities in 2G and 3G mobile technologies. Arguably, part of the reason ZTE and Huawei grew while the designated national-champion SOEs languished was their remoteness from the MPT-MEI struggles, which included management fights and mergers motivated only by political logic. Both companies have enjoyed managerial stability and have retained the same directors since their founding in the 1980s (C. Li 2006; Low 2005).

Both Huawei and ZTE survived and thrived by avoiding novel-product in-

novation, specializing instead in the development of technologies seen as obsolete by foreign MNCs and China's national leadership. Furthermore, they
refrained from relying on the support of the central state and shunned investment in technologies that reached the market only because of regulation, such
as TD-SCDMA. By so doing, they managed to stay free of the worst perils of
central-government-structured uncertainty. Their success in managing these
complex, arm's-length relationships with the state is truly remarkable, especially because all the original state-owned telecommunications-equipment firms
designated as national champions, except Datang, have struggled.

While ZTE and Huawei are fast becoming globe-spanning MNCs, the basic
strategies they followed—specifically, the bottom-up development of innovational capacities based on production—are widespread among the PRD's small
enterprises. Even more interestingly, from the viewpoint of economic geography and the sustainability of local economic growth, many of these firms are
fully embedded in newly evolving Marshallian districts. As the following section elaborates through a case study of the UPS industry in Dongguan, the
leading hand of municipal, township, and village governments throughout the
PRD has much to do with the growth of these districts.

OF TEACUPS AND ASHTRAYS: SMALL
ENTERPRISES IN THE PEARL RIVER DELTA

The PRD is the hardware production base of China's IT industry. PRD firms
manufacture products of varying sophistication, from assembled landline telephones to ICs, the iPad, and the MacBook Air. The long-term emphasis on the
production of electronic hardware has led to the development of tightly integrated clusters of suppliers and customers. This clustering facilitates the development of new businesses and sustains established ones. Within this dense network, capabilities for incremental and production innovation are cultivated.
These capabilities enable IT companies in the PRD to win global market share
in differing niches on the basis of their own, in-house-developed products.

In the inverse of Beijing's and Shanghai's top-down, research-institution or
large-enterprise-focused approaches to innovation, manufacturers in the PRD
developed their innovational capabilities from the bottom up, beginning with
least-value-added activities and gradually moving up the value chain. To facilitate this development path, local government units intervene selectively on behalf of local industries and businesses. These policy interventions seek to improve manufacturing efficiency and complete the industrial production chain

for new products in the hope of increasing the value added locally. This pattern of self-initiated manufacturing-centric development aided by varying degrees of targeted state intervention has occurred across the PRD in support of IT niches such as laptop computers, computer peripherals, mobile phones, and telecommunications hardware. Of these clusters, the UPS-industry cluster in Dongguan illustrates the particular mode of development prevalent in the PRD.

The UPS, a critical IT-hardware technology, is frequently overlooked by innovation scholars and economists who wrongly presume it to be static and unglamorous. As we show in this case study, the opposite is true. Since Dongguan UPS companies have evolved in two decades from simple assembly operations to firms that develop their own brands, analyzing the cluster allows us to better understand the strengths and limitations of the PRD's bottom-up production-to-innovation model.

UPSs are emergency backup systems and power regulators connected to hardware systems sensitive to a sudden change or loss in voltage from the general electricity supply. They are used in data centers, telecommunications applications, power-sensitive manufacturing (like semiconductor foundries), medical applications, military technology, and space industries. UPSs can be divided into three categories of increasing sophistication. The simplest are standby UPSs, which are essentially a battery and a switch. Under normal conditions, electricity from a power source passes through the UPS directly to the connected system. However, a major interruption or outage will trip the switch connecting the battery to the system being protected. The battery backup provides typically fifteen to thirty minutes of emergency power. The second, and more sophisticated, type of UPS is the line-interactive model. Line-interactive UPSs route power through a voltage transformer to guard against partial dips (brownouts) or surges in voltage, but do so without relying on their battery systems. For major interruptions or blackouts, emergency battery backup is provided as well. The most sophisticated models are online UPSs. Power is routed through a battery charger, and the equipment runs off the battery under normal conditions rather than off the main power supply. A direct line to equipment bypassing the battery serves as backup in the unlikely event of an inverter failure on the battery side. This adds a layer of protection against surges, drops, and blackouts as well as against failure of the UPS itself. This system is used in applications like data centers or telecommunications, where it is absolutely critical that power not fluctuate or be interrupted.

UPS manufacturers in the PRD make all three types of UPSs. In addition to providing power stability and security for complex IT-hardware systems,

UPSs are information technologies in themselves. More sophisticated models use ICs to regulate such features as alternations between battery and direct power, charging, and power output in order to ensure not only a smooth energy supply but also equipment longevity. Software for user interfaces is also a major area for incremental and developmental innovation by UPS producers. The innovation process in UPS enterprises is highly representative of that throughout the PRD's hardware industry. Companies begin with the simplest assembly operations and gradually increase the amount of research they perform. As clients come to trust the producer, the degree of design freedom increases, which forces the company to increase investment in R&D and differentiate its products from others'. Companies at the top use their understanding of UPS technology to create wholly new products, such as smart lights or backup systems for complicated machinery. At the core of all these technologies are the IT-enabled aspects of UPS technology.

Dongguan lies between Shenzhen and Guangzhou along the east bank of the Pearl River. The city occupies an area of 2,465 square kilometers (952 square miles) and has a population of 6.95 million, of whom more than 5 million are migrants. The city is divided into thirty-two townships, and these are further divided into villages. Like other characteristic PRD cities, Dongguan has more than 180 industry, technology, and manufacturing zones and parks. The city developed by following an export-oriented industrialization strategy that relied closely on Hong Kong and Taiwanese investment. Today, Dongguan considers IT hardware and electronics to be its main industries. Dongguan's annual report on economic and social-development statistics states that IT-hardware production is so important that it has become the "dragon's head" of the local economy (DSB 2008). Indeed, the Qingxi and Tangxia townships consider their economic progress to be wholly the result of the computer and electronic-hardware industries, fueled by Hong Kong, Taiwanese, and, later, Japanese and Western investments. Currently, most of the investment is domestic, although local authorities continue to aggressively recruit major foreign investments (authors' interviews).

The UPS industry in the Greater China region spread from Taiwan to the mainland in the second half of the 1980s (Global Sources 2005). China's first UPS companies and manufacturing facilities emerged in the PRD cities of Dongguan, Shenzhen, Foshan, and Zhongshan. UPS firms in the early years produced the lowest-end, standby UPSs and the necessary batteries, usually low-tech lead-acid batteries. Production technology tended to be highly labor intensive, with low value added per unit.

Currently, the PRD's UPS firms are the most prominent ones in China (CA800 2008; Nanfang Ribao 2007). Altogether, Guangdong province's UPS firms produce more than 50% of the China's UPS exports (Global Sources 2005). The province is home to the most technologically sophisticated brands, such as Zhicheng Champion, East Power Company, and HSK, which are based in Dongguan (authors' interviews).

These companies began as manufacturers of batteries and transformers but have since developed into specialized UPS producers. East Company and HSK, for example, have either spun off or moved to outsource their battery production. During our fieldwork, we found that many UPS companies incorporated in the last decade continued this development pattern, moving from low-profit-margin assembly-based operations to independent brands and technology innovations.

Since their inception, the three companies have steadily upgraded their capabilities and moved into line-interactive and online systems at ever higher volt-ampere (VA) ratings.[32] Today, Zhicheng Champion designs and produces online UPSs rated at up to 300,000 VA. At this level, the company can compete with leading Taiwanese firms in the higher-value and higher-revenue online UPS market, and it is fast approaching the global technological frontier for industrial- and commercial-scale uses. Zhicheng Champion, which has grown at 40% year on year, is considered a national leader in UPS technology and cooperative research (Nanfang Ribao 2007).

Similarly, East Power Company produces high-VA models, both for the Chinese space program and for export, the latter done mainly through its foreign joint-venture partner, Schneider Electric's MGE UPS brand. HSK Power recently became fully independent from an earlier joint venture and now develops and produces higher-end UPS systems. Eighty percent of its output is sold domestically, the biggest customers being the Chinese military and the SOE sector, particularly telecommunications operators. The remainder is exported under HSK's own brand.

The Dongguan UPS cluster, therefore, has successfully upgraded its technology, and its leading companies are now widely perceived as being as capable as any foreign competitor at producing current-generation technology, with the added benefit of having lower costs. At the same time, they are rapidly approaching the technological cutting edge. To achieve such upgrading, the UPS industry has developed significant internal innovation capabilities—the common goal of local businesses and governments. Nonetheless, the local definition of innovation differs significantly from the concept of "indigenous innovation" promoted by the central government and the local governments of Beijing and Shanghai. Unlike Beijing's or Shanghai's IT companies, Dongguan's UPS companies explicitly dismissed novel-product innovation as a categorical good. In repeated interviews, entrepreneurs and officials considered the virtues of using and producing technology appropriate for market needs, making incremental improvements, and shortening the time to market to be superior to the allure of high technology and novelty. For example, when asked to define innovation, the founder of a young UPS firm gestured to the ashtray on the meeting table and answered:

> If I make something like this ashtray, then everybody else can too. You need to define your product to get an advantage. So we need to innovate. But indigenous innovation really means 'find a market need and use your own skills to fill it, not by copying or stealing.' So for us, OEM is truly an innovative activity; there may be some requirements from the client, but they don't give us the details, so I can make some suggestions that will please the customer. Then they can give us better prices. Chinese folks are really good at improving on another's base. When you give me one idea, from it we can make two or three. (authors' interview).[33]

He then elucidated the local aversion to novel technologies and the preference for technologies closer to proven markets:

> Before I started this company, I was in the CAS. Once I moved to industry, I quickly learned that the higher the technology, the less likely [that] products would enter the market, at least in a timely fashion. There are three highs: high price, high tech, and high time consumption. These are the three highs people fear. Thirty years ago, wireless technology would be unbelievable, but now it's real. If you had tried to make it thirty years ago, it would have cost a lot and failed.[34]

For these reasons, the UPS industry, in which the product itself—a backup power system for sensitive IT hardware—has long been defined, was an ideal candidate for transformation by the strengths of the PRD innovation system. While some R&D is conducted on wholly new types of UPSs or UPS-enabled technologies, such as smart lights, most R&D is invested in improving the core UPS system or its components, such as batteries, software, or user interfaces. However, the feature that allows Dongguan's UPS companies to continually excel in such innovation and rise to prominence is the gradual development of a classic Marshallian district within the city. The cluster includes specialized suppliers and companies that together encompass most of the stages of UPS development and production, from R&D to final assembly.

Networks of local suppliers in a small area enable UPS units to be produced efficiently. Because a UPS uses many of the same components as other IT-hardware products, such as personal computers and home electronics, demand from other sectors contributes to the development of niche supplier firms. As a result, the environment is highly conducive to the opening of new UPS firms in Dongguan, where both suppliers and market opportunities are abundant. For example, during our interviews, an entrepreneur explained why he chose to locate in Dongguan's Qingxi Township:

> I chose Qingxi because this industry's production base is in Qingxi. The suppliers are all located here. If I had my company in Beijing, then I would have needed to ship all the parts from here to Beijing. Since all the parts are manufactured in Qingxi, it is a great advantage for my company to be here. For example, even if, in the morning, I realize that I am missing critical parts, I just call my friends, and within a few minutes, these parts are sent and delivered to me. (authors' interview)

In opposition to the accepted wisdom in the United States and Europe about the "knowledge economy," with its obsessive focus on novel-product innovation or new technologies and its disdain for production, local leaders in Dongguan pride themselves on their locale's "complete" production chains. For example, a senior township development officer argued: "Why is the UPS industry able to operate like this? It is because the production chain is complete. Why is Qingxi able to make computer cases, LCD screens, mice, keyboards, and entire IT systems or lines? It is because Qingxi's production chain is very complete. Our full industrial chain is our greatest advantage in stimulating growth and attracting new investment" (authors' interview).

Similarly in a neighboring township, a leading official subscribed to the same logic: "Zhicheng Champion is located here because of the complete production and supplier networks we have here. It is not that we have only the final UPS companies. We have all the specialized suppliers they need. For example, there is a coordinating supplier in Tangxia that supplies all three leading UPS manufacturers. So long as we have a complete industry set, there is no reason more UPS manufacturers won't come, and no reason for these that are here to move away" (authors' interview).

The tight, dense network of related suppliers allows individual Dongguan companies to focus on a narrow set of activities that they excel in and constantly improve. Most of the UPS-manufacturer representatives we interviewed source their components locally. Even high-end components are typically sourced within Dongguan, although software and ICs frequently come from the Dongguan branch companies of foreign MNCs rather than wholly local companies. Up to 90% of the necessary components are sourced from other companies rather than produced in-house. This testifies to the degree of completeness of the local industrial chain and the extent of the integration among specialized firms.

Another reason why the UPS industry in Dongguan has managed to grow so rapidly has been the tight clustering of companies with long-term relationships. This allows trust and social capital to grow, and renegade firms and entrepreneurs to be censured. As a result, the UPS cluster has found a local solution to one of the critical issues faced by the Chinese IT industry—access to finance and growth capital.

The formal banking sector is closed to most SMEs, even in the UPS sector, where companies have land and capital equipment to be used as collateral, as well as a stable and growing revenue stream. Indeed, the banks' refusal to lend is by now so well known that most SMEs no longer bother to apply: "This is a problem for the entire nonstate sector. Minying enterprises cannot get loans. In the PRD, you could before, but not now. The national banks keep themselves really tight when making loans to minying enterprises" (authors' interview).[35]

Locked out from the central-state-run financial system, suppliers in the UPS sector must rely on other sources of capital. This is a critical issue, particularly with regard to financing start-ups and expansion. Apart from the usual sources of financing—personal savings, family and friends, and business revenues—the rich social-capital environment in Dongguan allows companies to structure elaborate credit lines and investment pools.[36] And so the cluster has come to employ some of the ideal-type positive influences of social capital (Coleman 1988; Portes 1998; Putnam 1993; Uzzi 1996). We have not found such strong interactions and trust among firms in either Beijing or Shanghai.

An example of such an informal financing institution is intercompany credit. Under such agreements, "credit" from suppliers is used to finance expansion. A typical arrangement involves obtaining components based on a commitment to pay for them once the finished products are sold. In turn, these same UPS companies extend credit to their resellers or OEM-brand clients. The system is based on promissory notes made between enterprises without the involvement of the formal financial system or legal contracts. Such a system is highly susceptible to cheating; however, the fact that the UPS industry is so spatially concentrated and tightly networked acts as a deterrent. The blacklisting of suppliers and individuals who fail to repay on time (or at all) involves excluding them not only from lines of credit but also from the industry as a whole. Since all the components for the UPS industry are produced in Dongguan, falling from favor quickly results in an enterprise or individual being forced out of business.

The nature of the constant and repeated interactions within the manufacturing-based UPS cluster of Dongguan enables enterprises to conduct transactions based on trust. This informal financial system also extends to the creation of new enterprises. Since the start-up phase for a manufacturing facility involves a large capital investment and a significant time lag before any revenue is generated, such an up-front investment would be difficult for even the wealthiest Chinese investor to sustain without credit. In Dongguan, trust-based pooled credit among enterprises enables start-ups to commence operations and secure orders in advance. For example, a founder of a UPS company recounted how such arrangements allowed him to open his company:

> The whole operation is based on trust. If you cannot be trusted, you will be kicked out of the business. In ancient China, total costs were calculated once per year. So people would trade and keep track of their balance sheets. At the end of the year, each merchant would collect their credits and pay their debts. This is traditional trust. When we first set up this company, I invested my money first. Suppliers helped me, since my own capital was insufficient. They provided me with the needed capital goods and first components, assuming I would pay once I sold the final products. We didn't borrow any money from the government. In the end, it was even better than having a loan from a bank, because had I had a loan, I would have to pay interest; now I don't. The entire business is based on trust to this day. For example, if my company needs $500,000 worth of inputs, but I only have $50,000 dollars in cash, all my suppliers support me. And I support my customers too. It's a trust cycle from beginning to end. (authors' interview)

Both the reliance on trust-based credit and the need to repay it in a timely manner have enabled the local industry to become more export oriented. Unlike many of their domestic retail or state-owned customers outside the region, which demand up to three months of credit after final delivery and usually end up deferring payment even further, foreign customers usually pay upon delivery and tend to keep to the original words of the contract. Linking exports to their domestic-supply relationships, a general manager of one of the companies remarked: "After I sell my products, I have to get money back in order to buy materials to produce again. If I sell products and the money doesn't come back soon enough, then production must stop. In domestic partnerships, sometimes it takes up to four months and I still have not received payment. I have to wait. But in the international market, once I send the products, the customer transfers their payment immediately" (authors' interview).

Consequently, while heavily reliant on the domestic market initially, Dongguan's companies have been aggressively moving toward exports. Some newer firms opt for a purely export-oriented model. Powertech, established in 2000, earned all of its 2004 revenues overseas. The move toward export has also led to the use of a divided-territory business model. UPS companies build their own brands domestically, but for their export business, they rely almost entirely on OEM-ODM agreements in which their products are sold under foreign brand names. The rapid move to exports is also evident in the changing sources of revenues of the two leading companies by sales, Zhicheng Champion and East Power Company. From 2004 to 2007, the percentage of Zhicheng's sales accounted for by exports went from 25% to 49%; for East Power, the increase was from 28% to 48%. These significant increases reflect the companies' desire for reliable clients and their increasing technological sophistication and quality.

While informal credit mechanisms are a crucial source of capital, the local state has been an important source of supplemental development capital. Realizing that the formal financial sector is largely closed to its UPS industry, the Dongguan government subsidizes expansion and capital-equipment upgrading through subsidies and tax rebates. The local government believes that savings on capital-good imports encourage UPS companies to buy more-advanced equipment and train the local workforce in its use, further enhancing the competitive advantage of the locale. The idea that successful innovation depends on raising the skill levels of manufacturing laborers is entrenched in local government policies. A local official explaining the program elaborated on this argument:

> Since 2005, we have had a program designed to improve the quality of technological sophistication of our minying enterprises. Our main method of support is that the enterprises can apply for an import permit for new high-technology equipment. The government will have an expert team review their request, and if approved, we will give them tax breaks on the imported equipment. In general, the municipality encourages enterprises to import advanced high-tech equipment. If the foreign country allows for such imports, we will certainly help our companies to receive it. Minying enterprises' product upgrades all depend on importing high-tech equipment. Once they get the equipment, they need someone to manage and train them on how to use it. They have to learn how the new equipment works, and they need to familiarize themselves with it, and during that time, they might come up with a way to improve the equipment for their use. This is the basis for our high-technology production and innovation. (authors' interview)

Leading UPS companies draw a large part of their R&D financing from local-government grants. In recent years, Dongguan's Municipal Science and Technology Commission has annually earmarked funds for projects designed to improve the R&D capabilities and technology quality of Dongguan's SMEs (authors' interviews). In 2008, the city established a new fund of one billion RMB to help SMEs and newly established enterprises (Nanfang Ribao 2008; D. Zhao 2008). These grants go directly to companies; for example, Zhicheng Champion has received approximately two million RMB in annual grants from the municipal government. Since other sources of financing are limited, the importance of local-government aid for the viability of the cluster should not be underestimated.

While all interviewees noted the importance of government support, none of them stated that their companies, including those that the MII certified as national leaders in the UPS industry, had received national-level funds. Indeed, the R&D activities of the UPS industry are mostly ignored by national authorities. While many products in other IT fields have been certified as high-technology products, several UPS firms have been unable to obtain even "high-technology enterprise" certification for the company as a whole. Many component manufacturers cannot receive any of the benefits awarded to high-technology enterprises, despite their own R&D activities. A battery manufacturer explained: "We do not have any products certified as high tech because this industry is seen as an old field. The central government doesn't award any certificates in this field. We have been officially designated a sunset field, and that is it" (authors' interview).

UPS firms in the PRD exhibit classic structured uncertainty concerning their official ownership structures. The firms explicitly describe themselves as minying. The reticence to describe themselves as "private," even among founders who started businesses with their own funds, is due to the fact that by defining themselves as minying, they do not run the risk of falling afoul of possible regulatory changes directed at a given class of enterprises. While often partly foreign invested and deeply involved in state procurement or cooperative research, managers and founders refrain from using the terms "foreign," "private," or "state owned" when defining their companies' ownership structures. Since "minying" is a largely undefined term, they are able to engage with the state, the domestic market, and global markets in whatever guise best suits the needs of the enterprise in a specific business relationship. Uncertainty over the future of property rights, combined with both the central state's disregard for the UPS industry and local authorities' particular aversion to creating SOEs, led companies to fully embrace the ambiguous and politically neutral "minying."

Apart from financial assistance, the PRD's municipal and provincial governments are also crucial in sustaining another factor critical to the success of the cluster—labor, for both production and R&D. For production, the UPS industry requires access to a large and steady supply of labor. Specifically, UPS companies require a workforce that is both low cost and relatively skillful and specially trained. Dongguan's UPS companies employ anywhere from 400 to more than 3,000 production workers each. As on the production lines of other local enterprises, the vast majority of Dongguan's UPS line operators are migrants from China's interior. They lack the independent financial resources, especially upon first arriving in the region, to purchase or rent local property. Many workers, however, stay for long periods and hence require room and board. Additionally, migrant workers must also be able to arrange the necessary work permits in order to reside and receive their salaries in Dongguan.

The local government facilitates the availability of production labor for the UPS factories in two ways: first, by supplying necessary factory housing; second, and much more importantly, by encouraging large inflows of internal migrant labor—a stark contrast to the labor policies in Beijing and Shanghai. With regard to housing, municipal-, township- and village-level administrations frequently include housing for workers when designing industrial parks. For example, Xie Kang Village built a small industrial zone that includes prefabricated factories and housing for several hundred workers per factory. Qingxi Township's Qing Hu Park includes a housing district with living space for thousands of workers. By providing enterprises with housing facilities for large numbers of migrant workers, Dongguan's government helps enterprises lower their operating expenses. From the migrants' perspective, since the minimum wage in Dongguan is 759 RMB a month and the average compensation is around 1,200 RMB, guaranteed—and often free—housing is a major attraction (*CRN* 2008).[37]

Local governments take other actions to help recruit migrant labor from all over China. For example, in Dongguan, workers arrive daily by train and bus from other areas of China. They are usually hired rapidly after submitting applications at the gates of the various factories. Authorities then arrange for readily available local work permits. For workers who remain for more than a few years, the city facilitates the transfer of hukou and, in the meantime, takes a lax attitude toward residency laws (authors' interviews). Some twenty years after the start of the reforms, government officials are happy to point to successful, though rare, cases of migrants becoming residents and successful entrepreneurs in their own right.[38]

Labor recruitment efforts are also intimately connected with local-government efforts to help build up firms' R&D capabilities. Since academic research and education infrastructure are systemic weaknesses in the PRD, local authorities aggressively help companies recruit and relocate talent from other provinces. For the purpose of recruiting educated labor, hukou regulations have been specifically restructured across the PRD. Zhongshan City grants a hukou to any applicant with a graduate degree. Similarly, Shenzhen employs an open hukou approach. In an interview, a Shenzhen official referred to this specifically as part of the city's policy: "Currently, there is an open-ended hukou for students coming into Shenzhen. In addition, we have no quota limit for those who possess academic degrees and have a job offer from a Shenzhen company. Hence, they can move and, in parallel, also transfer their hukou" (authors' interview).

In Dongguan, enterprises can apply for the hukou for their employees as long as the employee has at least a bachelor's degree. Hence, UPS firms and others with large R&D, quality control, or engineering departments do not find the hukou system to be an impediment to recruitment. However, in discussion with government officials, one stated his reservations concerning the efficiency of a lax hukou policy: "Our leaders want to have an open hukou policy to attract high-end human resources to Dongguan, but to date, I don't see it working" (authors' interview). In other interviews, it was noted that in PRD cities, including Shenzhen, the majority of workers with academic degrees who already possess a desirable hukou, such as Beijing or Shanghai, frequently choose not to transfer it. This also applies to senior researchers brought into the region for top management and research positions. It thus remains a question whether a PRD hukou is an enticing enough incentive with regard to highest-quality educated Chinese.[39]

For entry-level engineers and managers, especially from China's interior provinces, the hukou remains a major attraction in the PRD. Although large companies such as Tencent and Huawei have been forced to set up R&D centers in Beijing and Shanghai because the graduates of those cities' top universities are often emphatically unwilling to relocate to the PRD, researchers from strong universities in interior provinces, such as Hubei and Sichuan, consider the PRD hukou an important part of their job package. Fortunately, the UPS industry's needs are much better supported by such universities, since they have retained large research departments in fields that are no longer considered cutting edge by universities such as Tsinghua or Peking. Furthermore, since the prospect of moving to the PRD makes these programs more attractive, provincial universities are thrilled to work with Dongguan's UPS companies. For example, Zhicheng Champion has partnerships with Hubei's Huazhong University of Science and Technology and Wuhan University (Nanfang Ribao 2007). In its factory campus, the company runs a provincial-level R&D center that works on developing improved UPS systems and batteries. Researchers from these central China universities need access to laboratory facilities in order to conduct their thesis research, and the company benefits from hiring low-cost talent that helps build its in-house research capabilities. In a similar fashion, East Power Company maintains a postdoctoral scientific research station at its Songshan Lake campus in Dongguan. By providing facilities for PhD and postdoctoral researchers, the company improves its own R&D while keeping it within the company structure, and the arrangement provides the firm with a better selection of future employees and managers for its R&D and design teams.

Finally, local government assists the UPS industry with market research and political lobbying. The municipal- and township-level governments in Dongguan follow two models of research designed to improve the overall industry's economic growth and industrial strength. One model looks at the needs of the overall industry and specifically aims at building a "complete" production chain locally. For example, in Qingxi Township, a research group in the economic and trade office is designated to study the local industrial chain and identify components or services that are generally sourced outside the area. The group reports to the investment promotion office, which follows up by trying to locate companies that produce these components and encouraging them to invest in Qingxi. The local government does not seek to establish local SOEs to complete the industry chain. The second type of research, usually conducted at the municipal level but also by individual townships, involves sending local business and city representatives on fact-finding missions across China and abroad. During these missions, the aim is to discern best practices and subsidize lobbying by the industry on behalf of the local government.

Despite their strengths and government support, the IT clusters of the PRD still face many difficulties. The greatest cloud over the future of all of them, and in particular the UPS sector, is gross overcapacity. While the most successful firm, Zhicheng Champion, uses 75% of its production capacity on average, two other prominent Dongguan-based UPS companies, East Power Company and Kewang, use only 15% and 12% percent respectively (Global Sources 2005).

Despite this overcapacity, PRD UPS companies continue to invest in production capital and the further expansion of their production lines. It thus remains to be seen whether the newly developed industrial clusters will change the long-term trajectory of the PRD's IT industry toward greater sophistication and innovation, or whether the cutthroat competition and skewed incentives and price mechanisms will lead the industry to overexpansion and self-destruction.

CONCLUSION

In this chapter, we followed the coevolution of industry and state in the PRD, the earliest and most aggressively economically reformed region of China. Looking into our four themes—center-local tensions, the particularities of the regional history, the impacts of structured uncertainty, and the local implications of the global fragmentation of production—we analyzed how the PRD developed an innovative IT industry based on manufacturing prowess. It began with a very different history from that of Beijing and Shanghai, specifically with regard to its lack of a research and educational infrastructure, upon which the other two built their IT industries. The region moved from mastering outsourced production for foreign producers and consumers to proficiency in more sophisticated innovation, all the while eschewing the development of novel products and technologies. As a result, the PRD has developed two complementary models of successful IT companies. One model, typified by ZTE and Huawei, revolves around the creation of local MNCs. The second, epitomized by Dongguan's UPS industry, revolves around communities of SMEs evolving into thriving industrial clusters. In both cases, the unique strengths of the PRD, specifically in production and flexibility, underlie the rapid growth of the industries. Furthermore, both models have been facilitated by the global fragmentation of production, which provides PRD companies with a range of entry points to overseas markets and a number of strategies to employ when they enter different IT niches.

To enhance the growth of industry and overcome the lack of high-end research talent in the region, the local government encourages the influx of migrant workers. Further, it pays close attention to the development of highly skilled manufacturing labor as well as to the region's mastery of all stages of production. In addition, defying the definition and aims of the central government's S&T policies, local governments in the PRD have developed a much more pragmatic definition of "independent innovation" and have refrained from paying too much attention to the size of local enterprises. All in all, regional interpretations of the hukou system, of worthwhile innovation, and, to a large degree, of telecommunications-technology policy (as in the case of ZTE's focus on PHS technology) are clear examples of how the tension between the center and local government, coupled with the ever-present structured uncertainty, has allowed local entrepreneurs to thrive but has also shaped the business-strategy options at their disposal.

As they grow, the PRD and its companies are becoming a node within an overall Chinese innovation-and-production system rather than a unique, externally oriented enclave. For example, while still considered Shenzhen companies, both ZTE and Huawei have established massive R&D centers in Beijing and Shanghai. Other PRD companies, less well known and operating in less prestigious niches, opt instead to work with leading, but less famous, universities in the interior provinces. Hence, the growth of the PRD as a highly innovative production center enables and spurs the further specialization of different regions in China around divergent activities.

Conclusion The Meaning
of the Run: China and
the New Realities of
Global Production

Alice never could quite make out, in thinking it over afterwards, how it
was that they began: all she remembers is, that they were running hand
in hand, and the Queen went so fast that it was all she could do to keep
up with her: and still the Queen kept crying "Faster!" . . .

. . . Just as Alice was getting quite exhausted, they stopped, and she
found herself sitting on the ground, breathless and giddy.

The Queen propped her against a tree, and said kindly, "You may rest
a little now."

Alice looked round her in great surprise. "Why, I do believe we've been
under this tree the whole time! Everything's just as it was!"

"Of course it is," said the Queen: "what would you have it?"

"Well, in *our* country," said Alice, still panting a little, "you'd generally
get to somewhere else—if you ran very fast for a long time, as we've
been doing."

"A slow sort of country!" said the Queen. "Now, *here*, you see, it takes
all the running *you* can do, to keep in the same place. If you want to get
somewhere else, you must run at least twice as fast as that!"

—*Lewis Carroll,* Through the Looking-Glass and What Alice Found There

This book was motivated by the need to dispel two myths. The first
is the Western techno-fetishism of novelty, which equates innovation

only with the creation of new technologies and products. The second myth is about China and the rather peculiar tendency of many scholars and the popular press to judge the country's success by comparing it with an idealized conception of Silicon Valley. Throughout the book, we argue that within the current, globally fragmented production system, China has been sustaining its run of rapid economic growth, the world's longest, by innovating in many stages of production, but not in novel-product R&D. We further contend that as long as the world does not turn its back on globalization—if that happened, the worldwide economic crisis would be so severe that no nation would escape —both China's position as the global Red Queen and the economic growth deriving from that status are secure for the short and medium term, thanks to the inherent interdependencies created by such an international system.

The core of our inquiry explains how China reached this position within the global system of production—a position, we stress again, that is against the declared wishes of China's central government. The central government, like those of most advanced nations, has been fawning over the ideal of novel-product innovation for the last three decades and has done its best to steer the nations' companies toward those activities, with little apparent success. In explaining how China has become the global Red Queen, we showed how its political economy, with very high structured uncertainty and center-provincial tensions, creates a two-level innovation system. The Chinese innovation system consists of different regional models, each of which follows a different "Red Queen run" strategy, but which together constitute a competitive national innovation system.

In this concluding chapter, we look at these findings and make two inquiries. First, what do they tell us about the future of China and its role in the global economic system? And second, what might the story of China teach both emerging and advanced economies?

A RED QUEEN IN A WORLD OF DECOMPOSED PRODUCTION

Since the 1970s, the management of services and products in the international economic system has passed through a major restructuring. China's meteoric rise to economic power is directly tied to the maturation and broad international spread of the new global system of fragmented production. And as China has plugged itself into global production networks, its growth has significantly influenced their evolution.

Anyone who strolls down the aisles of any Western retailer of home-improvement goods, textiles, cosmetics, or electronics and chances to read the products' labels will quickly realize that China is very much the epicenter of the global production network in almost any industrial sector. The world's most advanced MNCs now treat China and its impressive array of capabilities and innovational capacities across stages of production as a critical node in their operations. This, in turn, is both the strength and the weakness of the Red Queen in a world of decomposed production.

So far, we have mostly looked at the Red Queen's strengths. It is now time to look at her weaknesses and to reassess why we are so optimistic that if China's leaders will continue to keep China's development on a roughly even keel, as they have for the last three decades, both China and its trading partners will enjoy continued prosperity. While maintaining the Red Queen run is decidedly different from excelling in novel-product innovation—and is, to some degree, simpler than pursuing novel-product-based models, since queues for action are set by others—mastering the run is far from easy. First and foremost, managing the parallel activities of always staying on the cusp of the latest research and at the same time being ready on time, at all times, to supply the capabilities MNCs need in order to produce their latest products is an impressive feat. Managing both sets of capabilities is especially important for preserving the Red Queen balancing act: if an investor misses a few steps, a Red Queen company might be left with massive capital investments and no orders to fill. The Red Queen is always the partner onto which MNCs try to unload as much risk as they can in capital-equipment investment and inventory holding. In a system of "just in time," if the music stops, Red Queen companies are the first to find themselves without chairs.

Second, as we detail throughout the book, moving fast enough and staying nimble enough in China is not easy. Cautious behavior is installed and reinforced by a high degree of structured uncertainty, and the financial system is not geared toward quickly deploying large sums of capital into new domains. Furthermore, as detailed in the analysis of the telecommunications industry in Chapter Two, when the state, specifically the central government, tries to infuse large amounts of capital into what it sees as critical new technologies, the result is often failure. And as Edward Steinfeld has detailed, a strategically important company's success carries the ironic risk of its being loved too much by the central state (Steinfeld 2004). Many a successful company that managed to outwit its state-owned competitors found the lure of soft-budget constraints and central-state affection too hard to resist, only to lose its way in the market and become marginalized thanks to its newfound access to large amounts of capital (Fuller 2005b; Steinfeld 2007).

Last, there is the question of institutional fit. As the production of services and goods decomposes, locales that want to excel as a central node within global networks need to develop specific innovational capabilities allowing them to master particular stages of production. However, it is an open question whether institutional systems that outcompete those of other countries in innovating around certain stages of production can also operate on the same competitive level in other stages. The evidence is that in most cases, they cannot. Once an economy becomes specialized around certain stages and becomes ever more innovative in those domains, it will find it difficult to excel in others without significant restructuring (Breznitz 2005a, 2007b). And top-down attempts to force rapid restructuring can lead to stagnation instead of growth. For instance, Israel chose to promote frontier technologies but by and large neglected to create institutional arrangements that would help their dissemination throughout the domestic economy and thereby stimulate further development. Today, Israel suffers from rapidly growing inequality and a widening gap between the few successful R&D-producing sectors and the rest of the economy, which has been left behind (Breznitz 2006, 2007a).

It is exactly here that we see the main cause of concern for China. As their behavior and rhetoric show, many in China's national leadership are keen on forcefully stimulating novel-product innovation. We argue that China would be wiser to rely on its already-impressive array of innovational capabilities, the specific institutional systems that support them, and its unique position in the global economy to ensure the country's gradual ascent to control of the whole innovation cycle. It is evident that in time, as Chinese companies battle for supremacy in global markets, many of them will move toward mastery of novel-product innovation on their own terms—as indeed some already are.

Forcing Chinese firms into novel-product innovation by government fiat, we contend, creates risks on several fronts for the continual, rapid economic growth of China. First, it is dangerous to try to impose behaviors and business models developed over decades and under significantly different institutional systems and environments, such as Silicon Valley, on Chinese companies and entrepreneurs. The central state might simultaneously prevent companies from pursuing profitable activities and condemn others to failure as they try to follow business strategies that make little sense in the Chinese market. A clear example of some of these negative results can be seen in the PRD. Companies that reach the global technological edge in market niches deemed sunset industries by the central government face significant difficulties, since they are effectively barred from the formal financial system. Additionally, forcing structural changes on a well-working, complex institutional system solely because the alternate arrangements worked for other countries presents China with the risk of getting the worst of both worlds: losing a huge competitive advantage by ending the run of the Red Queen, and getting no benefits from whatever system replaces it.

A second risk of central-government meddling, one that is becoming more and more apparent, is that many MNCs will come to consider China an untrustworthy business environment. Under conditions of interdependency, these deeply embedded MNCs cannot quickly cut their ties and leave China, but over time, they can build more of their capacities in other regions of the world, thereby acutely limiting their Chinese partners' exposure to new technologies and designs. A clear example of these dynamics is the effect of domestic technology-standards policies. As we showed in Chapter Two, on the one hand, China has used technology standards with great success as a trade-policy tool. On the other hand, China's strong-arm tactics significantly altered the behavior of several MNCs with regard to R&D and technology transfer in China. The perception that parts of the central government actively aim to force MNCs to transfer their technologies to their Chinese rivals, coupled with the already considerable ambiguities with regard to IPR enforcement in China, is part of the reason why more and more critical R&D is sourced to Indian companies rather than Chinese. This is true even in niches such as IC chip design, where, because of its massive production infrastructure, abundant skills, and enormous local market, China should have significant advantages over India as the favorite locale.

Last, there is the risk that China, by taking an overly heavy-handed approach to forcefully fostering indigenous novel-product innovation, will be increasingly seen as a security threat by other countries. It is indeed the truth that China is still very much a developing country. Around six hundred million of its citizens still live in poverty. Nonetheless, the country's brisk rise to economic power, its immense size and population, and its growing critical importance in the global economy are seen with awe and large doses of fear by its neighbors and trading partners. Under such conditions, some of China's actions to promote indigenous innovation are seen either as an unfair use of its newfound power or as an attempt to gain economic and technological superiority, to the detriment of other nations. Consequently, thanks to China's new power as the Red Queen, economic actions that many Chinese officials assume to be internal matters pursued by fair and legitimate policy tools are seen by other governments as actions taken directly against their national interests. In such an environment, there are very real risks for the prosperity of China's leading enterprises, particularly state-owned ones, if foreign partners become overly mistrustful of China.

Despite these risks, and although we are certain that many Chinese companies will face huge difficulties regardless of government action and that no small number of them will cease operation, we contend that China will continue to excel as the Red Queen of global production for at least the short and medium term. We base this prediction on several factors. First, the Chinese educational system has rapidly developed to complement the "Red Queen run" model. China's universities are producing ever-larger numbers of graduates who, while limited in their skills to conduct advanced original research, are perfectly suited, and probably significantly better suited than their foreign counterparts, to excel in other stages of innovation. Furthermore, slowly but surely, Chinese universities and research institutions are becoming the leading centers for research in many industries and domains that U.S. and European universities no longer, and perhaps never did, study. In such fields as electric power supply, heavy-metal research, and coal, China is becoming the premier place to find employees with rich domain skills. This fact has been noted not only by local companies that built their business models around these domains, but also by leading MNCs such as General Electric, which moved significant development operations in energy specifically to China in order to tap the local pool of talent in coal research. Last, there may be no other place in the world that can supply such a constant stream of science and engineering graduates oriented to factory and plant work.

A second reason why we are optimistic about China's future as the Red Queen involves the global production networks themselves. As we described in Chapter One, once an industry moves down the road of fragmentation and stage specialization, strong, positive, self-reinforcing sequences make it ever more efficient for the industry to continue with further modularization and fragmentation and to move more and more production into these global production networks. The two main mechanisms that create these cycles are "production/service-stage economies of scope and scale" and "production/service-stage specialization and capability building" (Breznitz 2007b; Sturgeon 2002, 2003). In the first—the production- or service-stage economies of scope and scale—once a specific production or service chain decomposes into discrete stages, suppliers at each stage, by pooling the demand of many customers, create economies of scope and scale that in-house divisions cannot. These economies of scope and scale enable suppliers to become more efficient and allow them to profitably operate on margins that are significantly lower than those achieved by in-house manufacturing divisions. In the second mechanism —production-stage specialization—product or service decomposition leads companies to develop superior capabilities in particular stages or components of a product or service network. Such specialization enables companies to become better and more efficient in a narrow set of activities and to acquire specialized capabilities and knowledge unavailable to more vertically integrated firms. Accordingly, inherent in the processes of global production are two mechanisms that, as we show in detail in Chapters Three to Five, make Chinese suppliers both more attractive and more innovative than their foreign peers as well as uniquely suited to their role within their global networks. Hence, the rapid and continual decomposition of production not only has made China a critical node of global production, but also has started a process through which many Chinese companies have been developing unique capabilities, including many highly innovative capacities, in various stages of production. Those, in turn, make these suppliers ever more important within the globally decomposed system of production. In time, these capabilities can be built elsewhere, though only with major outlays of capital, especially since China's capabilities change at the pace of the Red Queen run. Consequently, in the short, medium, and probably the longer term, China's position as the world's Red Queen is secure.

The third factor that adds to our optimism about China's future is the visible and growing importance of China as a market unto itself. The fact that China has become a fast-growing, major market at the same time that its companies have primed their capabilities to excel in the run of the Red Queen gives the country a unique advantage, one enjoyed by no nation since the rise of the United States in the early twentieth century. The Chinese market is unique in several dimensions, all of which are tied to "run of the Red Queen" business models. First, it has unique tastes that many local companies are best suited to fulfill. Second, China's market consists mostly of consumers, both private and commercial, that are significantly poorer than those in developed economies. Together, these characteristics lead to a market that is fast expanding and populated by consumers whose expectations regarding price, quality, and features play into the hands of fast imitators and localizers that can thrive on low margins and quickly design and manufacture cheaper products based on reliable technology developed elsewhere. This, in turn, gives local Chinese companies both significant cash flow and business experience as competitors in mature market niches, such as PCs in the case of Lenovo, or as OEM-ODMs. In addition, the growing importance of the Chinese market ensures that MNCs will continue to transfer knowledge and technology to China in their attempts to conquer a larger share of its market.

The last reason for optimism is the versatility and divergence of the regional systems of innovation in China that we describe in detail throughout the book. One of the most important advantages of China is that unlike many other emerging economies, it has used its size and its depth of talent to specialize in many IT sectors at stages of production ranging from relatively high-level design through manufacturing, components assembly, trade, and logistics. The breadth of these activities further strengthens China's hand in the global economy and enhances the benefits that accrue to China, regardless of where cutting-edge innovations are initially developed. In addition, the diverse regional models of China ensure that even if one of its regional systems suffers a downturn, China as a whole will continue to flourish. If, for example, Shanghai's model, which relies on big companies, strong state intervention, and significant FDI, becomes inflexible and stagnates, the fact that Beijing and the PRD have different strengths and their companies employ different business models gives the Chinese economy a unique capability to handle change and crisis. Hence, from the national point of view, the multitude of competing regional models gives the country the added benefits of flexibility and robustness.

ALICE'S LESSONS? EMERGING ECONOMIES
AND THE CHINESE EXPERIENCE

Is it true, as some have argued, that China is sui generis—a unique experience in human history from which no generalizable lessons can be learned?

If not, then what are the lessons that China can teach other emerging economies?

We argue that China is not sui generis and that other nations can learn both what to do as well as what not to do from China's example, particularly with regard to development and innovation policies. Like all countries, China has a unique history and some unique features, but this does not mean that theories of comparative political economy stop working when they cross its borders or that an institutional analysis of China will not provide insights relevant beyond the Middle Kingdom.

In this book, we dispel two critical myths about innovation and the rise of

China in the current age of globally fragmented production. The lessons learned from dispelling these myths speak to the problems faced by other emerging economies. The first lesson is about the impact of the fragmentation of production on the array of options available to them. Contrary to the standard myth about globalization, the current processes of intensified, globally fragmented production give emerging economies a larger number of entry points into the global economy—and, hence, more development alternatives —than they have had since World War II. In addition, the escalation of economic globalization and fragmentation limits the choices of governments, since many traditional fiscal and industrial policies no longer work, are no longer tolerated, or both.

China has taken advantage of the opportunities offered by fragmented production. After entering the IT industry's global production networks at the simplest point—assembly—China developed a massive array of capabilities around production, logistics, incremental improvements, and second-generation innovation. Because of the deep crisis facing China in 1978, it is an open question whether China's piecemeal approach to reform—groping for stones to cross the river—would have been successful, or even sufficient, without the global decomposition of production. Without the advent of spatially fragmented production, China would have had to develop missing capabilities and invest on a much larger scale than either its economic and financial resources or its political system would have permitted. Thus, emerging economies will do well to carefully analyze the entry points open to them and to devise their policies to specifically fit the stages of production (and, accordingly, innovation) at which they wish to excel. Policy deliberation and experimentation by local officials is critical, since economic development is, above all, a contextual science (Rodrik 2007). Furthermore, this process of deliberation and decision making is especially important because these choices will have long-term consequences for the development of these countries' high-technology industries (Breznitz 2007b).

This lesson about the availability of multiple entry points leads us to the second lesson China teaches the world in general and emerging economies in particular: the need for a subtler, more refined, and more comprehensive understanding of innovation. Such a Schumpeterian understanding does not equate innovation solely with novel products and technology and does not suffer from an almost religious reverence for new inventions. While invention is critical and, of course, necessary, if the main aim of a national policy is sustained economic growth, China's recent history makes it absolutely clear that in a world of fragmented production, the fetishism of novelty celebrated by policy makers and the popular press is not the only, or the best, option for emerging economies. The rapid and continual rise of China, along with the interdependencies brought about by the international decomposition of productive activities, challenges the core assumption that states must at some point master novel-product innovation if they are to sustain growth.

Emerging economies that care more about economic growth than about winning national self-esteem competitions would do well to consider all their options and all models of rapid-innovation-based industrial development. China's example shows that from a national point of view, it might be better to possess regions that excel in the Red Queen run than regions that excel in imitating Silicon Valley. California's current condition makes one wonder whether possessing a Silicon Valley, even the original one, is such a boon for states and their taxpayers as its proponents make it out to be.

However, when applying these lessons, we need to remember other important characteristics of China relevant to the particular policies other emerging economies should take. The first is, of course, size. Not many emerging economies have the same size advantages as China. Apart from perhaps India, Brazil, and Indonesia, other emerging economies should be keenly aware that size limitations, especially of labor force and market size, will prevent them from replicating the Chinese feat of simultaneously advancing in so many industries, niches, and stages of production. It is here that extra specialization and, hence, careful analysis by policy makers regarding the particular niches and stages of production that a given economy would do better to specialize in are of utmost importance.

China's ability to devise and implement policies provides another lesson for emerging economies. As we make clear throughout this book, the Chinese central state and bureaucracy have had far less influence and power than their counterparts in South Korea, Japan, or Germany did during their eras of rapid development. The trajectory and current state of China's high-technology industry are far different from those envisioned by the central government. Nevertheless, overall and at all levels, the Chinese state and bureaucracy are among the most professional and powerful in the world, specifically in comparison with those of most emerging economies. At the end of the day, especially in an economy so widely influenced by the state and party as China's, it is mostly thanks to the daily toil of officials—from provincial ones looking after their locales to mandarins in Beijing envisioning a new China—that China has managed the world's longest and fastest economic-growth miracle. An emerging economy without some semblance of a professional and publicly motivated bureaucracy will not fare well on the road to economic growth. It may very well be that a critical lesson from China, to be carefully studied not only by other emerging economies but also by international organizations such as the World Bank and the International Monetary Fund, is that state capabilities must be built first. Only then can free-market logic be enforced in developing states. If nothing else, the current financial crisis has shown that the free market cannot operate efficiently without a well-working regulatory system supervised by professional and capable civil servants.

The last implication of China's economic rise for other emerging economies stems from the fact that the world production system is now dominated by China. Consequently, other emerging economies should take China into account—its array of capabilities and its large, fast-expanding market—when devising their own paths to rapid-innovation-based industrial development. If the global fragmentation of production opens up many more entry points for emerging economies, then the rise of China may seem to close many of them. While it is true that the existence of a fast-developing, extremely big emerging economy that has not, yet, exhausted its reserve of poor rural workers poses a significant challenge to smaller and poorer emerging economies, it also opens up many opportunities. First, it is clear that many MNCs no longer feel comfortable limiting their choice of suppliers to one country or even one region. Apart from the power structure within global production networks, where MNCs move to prevent the Red Queen from amassing too much power, the current crisis, recent political turmoil, and several natural disasters, such as earthquakes and tsunamis, have sharpened the need to take a portfolio approach to managing globally fragmented production. The case of Vietnam clearly shows that a small emerging economy can quite easily plug into global production networks and successfully compete against China in its chosen market niches and stages of production. Thus, an emerging economy that carefully picks its preferred niches and stages of production can achieve success in rapid-innovation-based economic growth. A second opportunity that the rise of China opens to emerging economies is China itself. The Chinese market is rapidly growing, and Chinese consumers and companies alike are quickly developing an insatiable appetite for imports. Consequently, for the first time in many decades, emerging economies are not limited to the already saturated—and now significantly weakened—markets of the advanced economies, but also have as an export option an exponentially growing, underserved market that may very well become the world's largest market in our lifetimes.

The overarching conclusions of this book are sanguine. With regard to China, an analysis of its current political economy of innovation and its position in the global market points to the fact that its current growth, based on the "run of the Red Queen" model of development, is secure for at least the medium term. Accordingly, we argue that if its policy makers will take the long view and remember to chart an innovation-policy path that takes advantage of the impressive capabilities the country has already developed, and not a path that fights against their nation's competitive advantages, China's continued prosperity and growing global importance are assured.

The second optimistic message of this book is that if we remember that innovation is much broader than the act of inventing something new, and if we carefully read the story of China, we will quickly realize that, first, there are many ways that emerging economies can use high-technology industrial development to improve the welfare of their citizens. The second realization is that thanks to the fragmentation of production, the rise of China need not be seen as a zero-sum game by policy makers inside and outside the country.

We have entered a new age of true interdependency, where national industries and firms cannot produce many of their products and services without relying on foreign partners. This does not mean that the world is guaranteed peace and prosperity—far from it. True interdependency carries with it new dimensions of insecurity that might cause leaders to take hasty, unwise actions. The history of the first economic globalization and its violent end in World War I attests only too well to that possibility. However, true interdependency, coupled with the new opportunities open to emerging economies and the viability of the Chinese Red Queen run, provides a much more robust basis on which to build a better future for a significantly larger percentage of humanity than has ever been possible before. It falls on us and the leaders we choose to represent us to understand what this situation entails and to devise policies that bring the best of our new opportunities to fruition.

Notes

INTRODUCTION

1. China's high-technology economy has grown into a multibillion-dollar industry that is the source of a large portion of China's foreign-exchange earnings. In 2007, 28.6% of all exports were listed as high technology (NSBPRC 2008a). IT technologies dominate China's high-technology industry. In 2007, 94.9% of high-tech exports were computer, communications, electronic, or IC-production hardware technologies (NSBPRC 2008b). Thus, IT hardware alone counted for 27.1% of all of China's exports. Moreover, the R&D capacity of China continues to improve. In 2006, more than 1.5 million workers were involved in R&D activities (MOST 2007). Research spending continues to grow from both business and governmental sources. In absolute terms, China's R&D spending was expected to exceed Japan's, making it the world's second-largest spender (after the United States), with an estimated $136 billion national research budget (IHT 2006).

2. On the national system of innovation, see the studies by Carlsson et al. (2002), Edquist (1997), Lundvall (1992), Lundvall et al. (2002), Nelson (1993), and Nelson and Nelson (2002); on the regional or sectoral system of innovation, see studies by Braczyk et al. (1998), Breschi and Malerba (1997), Carlsson et al. (2002), Florida (1995), Kenney (2000), Lawson and Lorenz (1999), Morgan (1997), and Saxenian (1994).

207

3. Recent work in the evolutionary game-theoretical view of the Red Queen includes studies by Barnett (2008), Baumol (2004), Derfus et al. (2008), and Ridley (2003).

4. It is interesting to reflect that after Mattel, the world's largest toy maker, recalled over twenty million faulty or dangerous toys made by its Chinese subcontractors in 2007, Mattel felt the need to issue a formal apology to China for defaming the reputation of Chinese manufacturers. This raises interesting questions about which has more power in a world of fragmented production, the novel-product innovator or the Red Queen (*China Daily* 2007; *Economist* 2007; Story 2007).

5. The research on which this book is based, follows the tradition of institutional-industry studies, which assumes that in order to understand industries, one needs to analyze regular patterns of behavior, interactions, competition, and cooperation that constrain and support certain capabilities, as well as the forces that motivate economic actors to behave in particular ways in their search for material gain (Berger 2006; Breznitz 2005a, 2007b; Fligstein 1990; Herrigel 1996; Kenney 2000; Lester and Piore 2004; Lundvall 1992; Nelson 1993; Piore and Sabel 1984; Powell and Dimaggio 1991; Zysman 1983, 1994). To perform such an analysis within the three regions, we conducted interviews in the field with 209 stakeholders, some of whom we met with on several occasions during 2007 and 2008. We used public records of leading companies and agencies to compile lists of the established and leading local companies, multinational corporations (MNCs), and developmental agencies on the national, regional, and city levels. To supplement this initial roster, we also used a snowballing technique to tease out other companies and officials deemed critical by their peers. The interviewees included entrepreneurs, business associations, government officials, venture capitalists, and academics. The interviews were open-ended, using an instrument consisting of eight themes, all of which we touched upon during the course of each interview. We used the responses of the interviewees to draw out further information about the operation of China's IT industry. Fifty-one percent of the interviews were conducted in Mandarin Chinese or a combination of Mandarin and English; the rest were conducted in English. These interviews were then supplemented with data gathered from public resources, conferences, industry associations, archival resources, and secondary literature. Where possible, we tried to substantiate the information given by interviewees by comparing it with these data sources as well as with answers given in other interviews. Unless otherwise stated, data on company profiles were gathered through interviews and from public records such as those available from Lexis-Nexis, Securities and Exchange Commission (SEC) filings, the Hoover online database, Dun & Bradstreet, and companies' Web sites. To protect the privacy of our interviewees, we refer to all citations from interviews as "authors' interview" or "authors' interviews."

6. In the Pearl River Delta, the integrated economies of Shenzhen, Dongguan, Guangzhou, and Zhongshan dominate Guangdong's economy, particularly in high-technology activities. Within the region, Shenzhen increasingly serves as a high-tech innovation center in support of the diffuse manufacturing industries throughout Guangdong province.

7. For the purposes of this book, we define the Chinese IT industry as consisting of both the local, Chinese-owned companies and the activities carried out by foreign MNCs in China. We argue that only by understanding the industry in its entirety can we understand its influence and gauge its true innovational capabilities. This also sheds light on

the current policy debate concerning whether the research activities of foreign MNCs in China can be considered part of China's "indigenous innovation."

8. In other high-technology industries, the situation is similar to that of IT. In the case of pharmaceuticals, for example, much of the midrange, labor-intensive chemical research is now conducted by Chinese contract research firms, particularly in the Shanghai region. We opted to focus most of our research on the representative IT industry in order to enable microlevel comparative analyses of processes and mechanisms, especially since, by any measure, IT has been the most important Chinese high technology of the last two decades.

9. As detailed in Chapter Two, China's high-technology industries and economic planning are governed by multiple programs that are coordinated by different government ministries, most notably the Ministry of Science and Technology. The most significant programs for the development of the IT industry are the National High-Tech R&D Program, also known as the 863 Program; the National Key Technologies R&D Program; the Spark Program; and the China Torch Program. The fifteen-year plan for science and technology, issued in the beginning of 2006, calls on these programs to ensure that governmental research institutes and national-champion industries lead the way in high-technology development and the advancement of science and technology (S&T). Each of these national R&D programs issues research grants, selects sectors for S&T concentration, and intends to assist in the commercialization and application of research in order to develop China's economy (MOST 2008c).

10. On research paradigms, see the work by Dosl (1982).

11. The argument for the need to look at regional development efforts, and not just at planning by the central state, was first advanced by Nan Lin (1995), Yin-Ling Liu (1992), and Oi (1992, 1995, 1999), and mentioned by Shirk (1993) as well. However, it was Segal (2003) who first suggested that in the case of high technology, these regional systems developed in unique ways (see also Segal and Thun 2001). More recently, Eric Thun (2006) advanced a similar argument about the importance of local governments for the growth of the Chinese car industry. When we refer to regional economies, we are speaking specifically about those within the Chinese mainland, not the completely different economies of Hong Kong, Taiwan, and Macao.

CHAPTER 1: THE WHITE KNIGHT AVOIDED

1. Our assumption is, of course, that the global system of fragmented production, where Western companies concentrate on high-level design, marketing, and sales but move design and production of even their latest products, such as iPhones, overseas, will not be overturned. However, even if it is overturned, and the global economic system comes to a halt, it is not clear who will suffer more, the Western MNCs that no longer know how, or have the infrastructure necessary, to manufacture their own novel products, or the Chinese companies that will be cut off from their source of novel-product designs. What is clear is that everyone will feel the economic pain; however, the recent travails of Mattel, the world's largest toy manufacturer, should remind us that it is not clear who will suffer the most.

2. It is important to remember that not all companies operate according to the logic of fragmentation. For example, Seagate, a leading manufacturer of hard drives, keeps almost all of its research, design, and production in-house. Similarly, in the United States, Japan, Korea, and elsewhere, many companies seek vertical integration as opposed to fragmentation because they see internal control as central to their product success and profitability (Berger 2006).

3. The development of mass-production capabilities during the rapid-industrialization stage of national economic transformation is not new. Apart from the now world-famous Japanese and Korean production systems, in the first half of the twentieth century it was American companies that definitively mastered production innovation. The River Rouge complex of the Ford Motor Company, which in the 1930s employed more than 100,000 workers, is seen by many as the zenith of this kind of American mastery. However, we should remember that even in its prime, the River Rouge facility was the embodiment of mass (also aptly known as Fordist) production consisting of very long runs of very few products manufactured for a single customer. Foxconn specializes in flexible-length runs of a wide range of ever-changing products for a changing mix of customers. Today, one would be hard pressed to find Western companies that possess these flexible innovational, manufacturing, and organizational capabilities. For the distinction between mass production and flexible production, see the study by Piore and Sabel (1984).

4. This, of course, strengthens the basic insight of David Ricardo (1963 [1817]) about how comparative advantage and the differentiation of activities among trading nations leads all participants to grow faster as a result. However, it does not necessarily support the particular models of trade theory developed by Ricardo and others from this insight.

5. An amusing example of what most high officials view as the goal of the Chinese central government is a remark made by one of our interviewees: "Having read China's fifteen-year plan for science and technology, I now know what a planned economy is supposed to look like. Fortunately, it is not what China, or its IT industry, is" (authors' interview).

6. In official statements, this semicapitalist market economy is referred to as the "socialist market economy" or "socialism with Chinese characteristics."

7. Although first proposed by Premier Zhou Enlai and Chairman Mao Zedong in the political work report presented at the first meeting of the Third National People's Congress in December 1964, the "Four Modernizations" did not become national policy until after Mao Zedong's death in 1976 (Baum 1994). The first attempt to implement the policy under Mao's successor, Hua Guofeng, met with spectacular failure (Shirk 1993). After the Third Plenum of the Eleventh National Party Congress Central Committee in December 1978, China's leaders under Deng Xiaoping sought to accomplish the "Four Modernizations" through a broad, though then undefined, package of economic reforms (Naughton 1995; Shirk 1993).

8. In the case of the PRD, defense industrialization was also primarily the responsibility of the provincial government. Although large-scale defense plants were under the direction of central-government ministries, the exposure of Guangdong to potential Taiwanese or U.S. military threats meant that the building up of the defense infrastructure there became the responsibility of the provincial government; this was in keeping with Mao Zedong's directives concerning the "little" Third Front, in which defense-based in-

dustries were seeded throughout the country. In Guandong, the small-scale military-industrial enterprises created under the provincial aegis, particularly in military electronics, became the embryonic base for the electronics industry after the 1978 reforms. During the reform era, these enterprises either fully relocated to the SEZs or set up subsidiaries within districts opened to the market economy. From the original "little" Third Front enterprises, seven civilian electronics companies arose. Indeed, Guangdong's first joint venture in electronics was formed by a former defense electronics firm and a foreign partner (Bachman 2001).

9. For a comprehensive analysis of Chinese bureaucratic power relations, see the studies by Shirk (1993, in particular Part 2) and Lieberthal and Oksenberg (1988). Recent studies by Ling Chen (2005, 2008) focus on S&T policy, specifically the semiconductor industry.

10. There are numerous internal trade barriers between provinces in China, the most important of which are those that restrict the registration of companies to a single city or province. In the 1980s, internal tariffs made it easier for provinces to trade internationally than within one another. As stated by one academic who lived in China in the 1980s: "It was not uncommon to see the latest foreign-model TVs for sale in one province while the neighboring province only sold black-and-white Chinese models manufactured and protected within that province" (authors' interview). While the situation has improved in the last decade, it has by no means been solved. For example, in the case of Internet companies, each province has its own regulations regarding the registration of a local Internet communications protocol (ICP) or Internet service provider. Foreign Web sites must form joint ventures with local ones, and Web sites from outside the province wishing to set up servers must register within the province as well (authors' interviews). Even within the former national-state-owned mobile telephony duopoly of China Mobile and China Unicom, local protectionism and fragmentation is the rule. In both corporations, regional branch companies are insulated from one another. For example, a subscriber identity module (SIM) card number purchased in Beijing or Shenzhen cannot be serviced in another province or have credit added to it, and balance inquiries made to the automatic service are met with the automated response that the card was purchased in another province and the balance should be checked by calling from within that province. In our interviews, we found out there was no internal network or nationally unified system. When we asked why customers could not simply add value to a SIM card of the same company purchased in another province, the response was: "While they are both the same national company, our provincial companies are separate. The value added on a card will only go to the original regional company coffers, not to the other. All revenues and systems are separated; hence, we cannot add value to an out-of-province number or give it any service." Thus, for all intents and purposes, the two companies treat provinces in China in the same way that global mobile companies such as T-Mobile or Vodafone treat different countries. For more about telecommunication reforms in China, see Chapter Two of this book.

11. By the early 1990s, the opportunities for personal enrichment began to lead to direct disobedience. During an austerity period in July 1993, the central leadership imposed limits on imports, especially luxury goods like cars. However, in Shiji Town, within the

PRD, the mayor and local CCP committee chairman, Su Zhiming, not only ignored a command from Beijing to cease car imports, but even increased the import order. The cars were spoils for local officials responsible for booming township and village enterprises (TVEs). The mayor was unafraid to publicly state his actions and reasons: "A business talent like mine is worth more than one million yuan in Hong Kong. My brains are one hundred percent occupied by ideas for making money" (quoted in Lieberthal 2004, 298). Under Su Zhiming, bonuses for local leaders were as much as six times their official salaries. This made their income higher than the official income of the CCP general secretary, Jiang Zemin.

12. For example, Burns (1987, 1994) found that up until 1993, only 5,000 of the 2.8 million cadre positions were selected through the central *nomenklatura* system.

13. As we will elaborate in Chapter Two, the whole bureaucratic party infrastructure is re-created at each level of government, further cementing the allegiance of bureaucrats to their localities.

14. Original text: "必须坚持把发展作为党执政兴国的第一要务 . . . 要牢牢扭住经济建设这个中心，坚持聚精会神搞建设、一心一意谋发展，不断解放和发展社会生产力" (Hu 2007c).

15. Original text: "实施扩大就业的发展战略，促进以创业带动就业" (Hu 2007a).

16. As noted by Shirk (1993), in China, the structure of the bureaucracy is also the structure of interest representation in the policy-bargaining arena. This makes the process of policy change even more arcane and complicated, since every change considerably affects existing (and entrenched) interest groups. Indeed, as Lieberthal and Oksenburg (1998) note, at each level of governance, a given ministry or unit is responsible to its organizational superiors and to other units at the same level of government, meaning that multiple channels of command and influence—all subject to the final veto or approval authority of the CCP—must be satisfied in order to accomplish any policy activity.

17. Another possible reason for the relative ineffectiveness of the central government's industrial-innovation policies is the rise of techno-nationalism. The central government's goals of attaining or retaining both technological independence and state control of key sectors have, from time to time, gained prominence over the maximization of industrial R&D, development, or market opening and economic reform (authors' interviews). For further perspective on techno-nationalism as a coherent strategy for technology development, see Samuels (1994).

18. The idea of a pilot agency was first developed by Chalmers Johnson (1982) in his analysis of the role of the Ministry of International Trade and Industry (MITI) in the industrial development of Japan and was then elaborated on by others, most recently by Chibber (2002) and Weiss (1998).

19. Baumol (1990, 2002) and Rosenberg and Birdzell (1986) have tied the constant development of innovations, which spurs rapid economic growth under capitalism, directly to the impact of property rights and social freedoms on the behavior of entrepreneurs and companies.

20. The degree to which the economy is state owned and subject to political interference remains hotly debated. Nonetheless, even official statistics and pronouncements bear out the fact that political connections are critical to large-scale economic success. In a joint circular distributed from Shaanxi province's Party Committee and Provincial Govern-

ment, the leaders stated that in state-owned enterprises, even those corporatized under China's "Company Law," the party secretary and chairman of the board should, in principle, be the same person. For more on the subject, see the study by Holz (2007). Our research found that the term "state-owned enterprise" is itself vague and rather flexible as it is used in China. When Chinese officials speak of "state-owned enterprises," they often mean only those enterprises under the State-owned Assets Supervision and Administration Commission (SASAC). Enterprises founded by municipal governments, universities, or local holding companies, or those in which state holding companies have a dominant minority share, are typically overlooked.

21. The fifteen-year plan for science and technology, initiated in 2006, is meant to reform the tax structure in China's high-technology industries. Previously, any company in the correct industrial sector could be certified as high-tech and receive state benefits, but since 2008, China has required companies to conduct and patent their research in China in order to receive high-technology-related income tax breaks. This reform greatly concerns both foreign and Chinese firms.

22. F.-L. Wang's excellent study (2005) systematically examines the hukou system and its impact on the Chinese economy and society.

CHAPTER 2: RULES OF THE RUN

1. Arguably, the Sino-Soviet split of 1961 was in many ways the result of conflicting ideas regarding the proper method for the development of socialism. In China, Mao favored continual class struggle and revolutionary mass action, while the Soviet Union followed bureaucratic routines and a preference for management by experts (Lieberthal 2004).

2. Throughout the 1980s and early 1990s there was significant disagreement among national elites about the direction of policy reforms. In the Chinese political context, "conservatives" in this period included cadres who believed in a slower pace of reform that would preserve the essential elements of "socialist" economics and social policy. Conservative resistance to change in the state planning apparatus ran strongest in the "Petroleum Clique," a faction that wished to preserve economic planning and push development through energy-led exports rather than fundamental market-based reform. Other conservative leaders bemoaned the rise of the "bourgeois spiritual pollution" that accompanied market reform (Baum 1994).

3. The term "bird in a cage," coined by Chen Yun (a leader of the CCP for sixty-five years), best defined the intentions of conservative reformers. They agreed that markets had a role to play, but argued that market forces had to be contained within the structure of traditional socialist comprehensive planning.

4. While the fact is not widely publicized, the CCP remains entrenched in industry, establishing cells and conducting its activities even in some large foreign and nonstate enterprises. The description given by a manager of one of the largest foreign-invested enterprises in China is typical, and somewhat more forthcoming than most: "The Communist Party is still very active. We have to encourage that on the campus and allow cells in our facilities, provide venues for them to meet, facilitate events, and so on" (authors' interview).

5. DeWoskin's study (2001) of the institutional and economic impact of WTO accession

on China's telecommunications sector notes the difficulty of enacting policy changes because of the depth of vested interests throughout the national bureaucracy: "In China, the process of reform engages the vested interests of multiple ministries ranging from security entities like the Public Security Bureau and the Ministry of State Security, concerned about state security and encryption; to various press, publications and propaganda entities concerned about content; to MII, Ministries of Railroads, Energy and the other players in the provisioning sector, concerned about competition; to films, radio and television administration, that controls cable and is eyeing the 'last mile'; to the Ministry of Finance and major banks, concerned about e-business infrastructure; to the foreign investment entities like MOFTEC, concerned about foreign investment levels" (639).

6. According to the PRC constitution, all political power belongs to the people and is exercised through the People's Congresses: "All power in the People's Republic of China belongs to the people. The organs through which the people exercise state power are the National People's Congress and the local people's congresses at different levels" (PRC 1982, Article 2).

7. However, in recent years there has been increasing evidence of assertiveness by the NPC in the face of the CCP (Chao 2003). The most obvious example was the belated passage of the Property Law of the People's Republic of China, which spent years in committee and underwent seven reviews by the NPC Standing Committee before being put to a vote. Thus, while the NPC can threaten to provide only low levels of support for a bill, thereby delaying legislation and forcing its review, the body remains mostly a sounding board, since substantive matters and compromises are handled at the top (the NPC Standing Committee) or in bodies such as the CCP (Elegant 2007; *Guardian* 2007; State Council 2008).

8. This arrangement, favored by Maoists because it made politics rather than professionalism primary, proved problematic for the running of an industrializing country. In some regions, party secretaries and other locally dominant cadres were drawn from the revolutionary commanders whose military units had arrived there during the civil war. As a rule, they tended to be of peasant stock, poorly educated (even illiterate), and deeply distrustful of "experts" (Lieberthal 2004).

9. Nonetheless, guanxi networks remain critical, if only to ensure a friendly and supportive environment for businesses. According to the Chinese Academy of Social Sciences' research on China's 3,220 richest people (those with wealth in excess of 100 million RMB), 2,932, or 91%, are the children of senior officials, a fact that puts the prospect of a decline in the power of guanxi in perspective (X. Zhao 2006).

10. In Chinese: "科学发展, 共创和谐."

11. Until 1998, telecommunications were governed by MPT, which handled the operations side, and by the Ministry of Electronic Industry, which was primarily responsible for the manufacture of transmission hardware. In 1982, the MPT's hardware responsibilities were officially transferred to a state-owned enterprise called the Posts and Telecommunications Industrial Corporation (PTIC). Since the MPT remained the owner of the PTIC and the operator of telecommunications, it was still both a producer and a consumer of telecommunications equipment.

12. Using the 2006 exchange rate, the sum is about $197 billion; for more details, see the story by the AP (2007) and the study by Xia and Lu (2008).

13. For an in-depth exploration of policy making and reform in China's telecommunications industry, particularly in regard to the transition from a planned economy to state-influenced markets, see the study by Irene Wu (2009).

14. In accordance with the terms of China's WTO accession, its regulations were to permit up to 49% foreign ownership in telecommunications and 50% within two years of WTO accession. However, this has not yet taken place. Moreover, while China Telecom, China Unicom, and China Mobile have some of their stock publicly listed, the nontraded portion remains the exclusive province of China's government, and because of the companies' complicated ownership arrangements, a large portion of the traded shares are owned by various state agencies and SOEs (Kong 2000). As noted in Low's research on the evolution of the telecommunications-equipment and telecommunications-operation industries (2005, 105), the then four leading operators, China Telecom, China Mobile, China Unicom, and China Netcom, were all born of state action and control that "remains in place despite them being publicly listed."

15. In the production of telecommunications equipment, two of the largest suppliers are Huawei and ZTE. ZTE is a local SOE (Shenzhen government), while Huawei is an independent enterprise that enjoys close relations with the Chinese government and the financial system, especially with the Shenzhen government through personal ties to Shenzhen's CCP secretary (Kroeber 2007; C. Li 2006). The Datang Group, an SOE owned by the China Academy of Telecommunications Technology (CATT), is the largest producer of equipment supporting the homegrown 3G mobile standard TD-SCDMA; a TD-SCDMA network is being deployed by China Mobile. CATT is one of the two MII research branches created during the 1999 restructuring of the old MPT research institute. Although the MII is supposedly the sole industry regulator, it has two major telecommunications "research" bodies. CATT is an industrial group, while the China Academy of Telecommunications Research (CATR) is a technology, policy, and industry-planning research group (CATR 2008; Datang 2007). The final remaining major player, Shanghai Bell, is the current incarnation of a long-running joint venture between Alcatel and the MII (Zhang and Igel 2001). While the state has a strong presence in the equipment-manufacturing sector through ownership and planning, that sector is far more open and competitive than the bureaucratically controlled operations sector, a divergence that leads to significantly different innovation outcomes.

16. In western Europe and the United States, telecommunications deregulation began in earnest in the 1980s and 1990s. In the UK, telecommunications was deregulated in 1983, and the state incumbent, British Telecom, was privatized in 1984. In the United States, the private, government-licensed monopoly of AT&T was broken in 1984, leading to the formation of the so-called Baby Bells. In Germany, Deutsche Telekom was privatized in 1996, and France deregulated telecommunications and privatized France Telecom in 1998.

17. The most important of the yous have been the Beijing University of Posts and Telecommunications (Beiyou), the Xi'an Institute of Posts and Telecommunications (Xiyou), the Nanjing University of Posts and Telecommunications (Nanyou), and the Chongqing

University of Posts and Telecommunications (Chongyou). Collectively, the universities are called yous because their Chinese names all follow the same pattern: city name *you dian da xue/xue yuan.*

18. The MPT continued to set prices for telecommunications services, and, hence, China Unicom was unable to compete on price. Furthermore, users of China Unicom's initial landline services in Chongqing, Tianjin, and Chengdu could not access the local backbone, since the local MPT subsidiaries refused to give China Unicom access. China Unicom also could not access the financing necessary to build out the infrastructure for its GSM network. China Telecom, on the other hand, remained effectively owned, managed, and operated by the MPT, which also granted it privileged access to finance (MOFCOM 2008; Xia 2006).

19. According to the Chinese Academy of Social Sciences, the average *annual* per capita income for Beijing in 1995 was 4,378 RMB, putting even basic landline telephony installation beyond the reach of most Beijingers; such a luxury was unthinkable for residents of poorer regions, such as Gansu province, where the average annual per capita income was 1,226 RMB (C. Li 2006; Yao 2005).

20. Successful telecommunications expansion occurred as a result of decentralization under the centrally controlled oligarchy of companies. The national government delegated responsibility for telecommunications expansion to provincial and local governments (Kroeber 2007). This devolution created competition among local governments as they tried to increase telephone penetration, since such infrastructure helped attract investment in other industries. Decentralization also opened a window of opportunity for Huawei, which managed to circumvent the national preference for SOEs by going directly to local telecommunications authorities to sell its transmission equipment. While foreign players and larger SOEs concentrated on large urban markets, Huawei was able to conquer the countryside and the national market for transmission hardware (C. Li 2006; Low 2007; Mu and Lee 2005).

21. As the MPT began to expand its efforts in the nonstate communications market, its profits soared. This stream of revenue, which was plowed back into further expansion, enabled the MPT to break free of its reliance on the MEI. The MEI became the leader in liberalization, partly as a result of reductions in state research subsidies and partly because of the 30%–50% annual growth of the MPT's market, which led the MEI to believe that liberalization was the only way to ensure its own survival and its continued role in telecommunications. The MEI was joined by the Ministry of Railways and the Ministry of Electronic Power, whose ministry-run sector-based telecommunications networks were barred from the consumer market. To force the State Council to approve the creation of a second operator in 1994, the MEI-led coalition played on its political connections at the center and argued that in contrast to the monopoly structure, the presence of multiple operators would speed up China's informationalization and economic growth, contrary to the traditional "natural monopoly" and national-security arguments voiced by the MPT. The MEI's minister, Hu Qili, was ranked higher than the MPT minister in the state and CCP apparatus. This position, together with direct connections to the highest authorities in China—including then-president Jiang Zemin (a former MEI minister), Li Tieying (also a former MEI minister), and then-premier Li Peng

(of the Leading Group for the Revitalization of the Electronics Industry), along with other top leaders who had affiliations with the electronics bureaucracy, including Zhu Rongji (premier), Zou Jiahua (vice-premier)—helped ensure the success of the reform move (Chung 2002).

22. As early as 2001, China Telecom had become the second-largest landline operator in the world, with more than 100 million subscribers (Funding Universe 2008).

23. Until May 2008, the operators were China Telecom, China Netcom, and China Tietong in landline services; China Mobile and China Unicom in mobile telephony; and China Satcom in satellite communications. This oligarchy was heavily skewed in favor of the incumbents (China Telecom and China Mobile) that grew out of the old MPT monopoly. In 2003, China Mobile accounted for 37.7% of all telecommunications (71.7% of mobile); China Telecom, 33%; China Netcom, 18.1%; China Unicom, 10.6% (28.3% of mobile); China Tietong, 1%; and China Satcom, 0.1% (J. Chen 2003).

24. The MII's vice-minister, Xi Guohua, was appointed to that position in 2001 while he was the chairman of the Alcatel–Shanghai Bell joint venture (C. Li 2006). He currently serves as general manager and CCP secretary of China Netcom. Before his chairmanship at Shanghai Bell, he served as the Shanghai deputy director of the MPT/MII from 1994 to 2000 (China Vitae 2008). In 2003, Xi traded positions with Zhang Chunjiang, then vice-minister of the MII. Xi became vice-minister, and Zhang became president of China Netcom (Wireless Asia 2003).

25. This system is still in force despite various attempts to reform the management of SOEs. In January 2004, SASAC introduced policies intended to force the 189 largest SOEs to behave more like modern corporations. In agreements signed with SASAC, senior executives contracted to guarantee the performance of their companies or else face demotion. A related reform opened the recruitment of SOE managers to the public, including foreign nationals (HKCH 2004). However, in telecommunications, political concerns and interfirm exchanges remain commonplace.

26. While no longer officially political appointments, the top managers of SOEs are appointed, promoted, and demoted by SASAC. Since SASAC reports directly to the State Council, this makes its actions as much political and policy oriented as purely economic. While both the creation of SASAC and the transfer of ownership oversight of SOEs away from different functional ministries were designed to increase professionalism and reduce political interference, in fact these moves have only added a further layer of complication to China's state-owned economy. Now, managers of SOEs such as telecommunications companies owe allegiance to the company, SASAC, the State Council, the former ministerial owner, and their university alumni networks through the *yous*. With the dominance of the *yous*, especially Beiyou, until fairly recently, factional loyalty based on graduation year and alma mater remained strong in telecommunications policy making, regulation, and enterprise operation (Xia 2007a).

27. For more information on the significance of the separation between regulation and policy making, see the study by Irene Wu (2004).

28. Interestingly, China Unicom was also granted a landline license at its creation in 1994, yet it never exercised this right, because of extreme infrastructure development costs and difficulties with connecting to China Telecom, the incumbent (Xia 2007a, 2007b).

29. At the end of 2005, China Telecom held 92.5% of the landline market in southern China, while China Netcom held 92.3% of the market in northern China (Xia 2006).

30. On the difference between oligopoly competition based on innovation and that based on price, and the very different impact that each model has on economic growth, see the studies by Baumol (2002) and by Baumol and others (2007).

31. Further complicating the policing of the sector are the *yous* alumni networks. The leading cadres in the MII have kept their old patronage networks alive through common allegiance to their universities, the four *yous*. Such cross-allegiances have protected the companies from regulatory action when they explicitly or implicitly obstruct national goals—such as interconnection and interoperability between companies (Xia 2007a, 2007b).

32. In 2003, mobile telephony of all sorts overtook landline subscribers in China (Budde 2008; Xia 2006).

33. Xiaolingtong (小灵通): literally, "little smart." First developed by Nippon Telephone and Telegraph in the late 1980s as an easier and less costly technology than the Global System for Mobile Communications, PHS handsets function effectively like powerful cordless telephones. Base stations have a transmission power of 500 megawatts and a limited range, up to a maximum of one and a quarter miles by line of sight. PHS phones in China, offered today by China Telecom and China Netcom, can be used only in a single city. Voice service is lost outside a small, defined area, although messaging remains available. By December 31, 2006 there were 91.127 million PHS subscriptions in China (USITO 2007; Yuan et al. 2006).

34. The MII has actively discouraged the development of XLT. In October 1999, the perception of the technology as being outdated (despite its rapid market growth and obvious profitability), combined with pressure from the two mobile operators—China Mobile and China Unicom—led the MII to order provinces without XLT networks not to allow their buildup. China Telecom ignored the MII and continued to expand XLT services; it was again ordered, in May 2000, to cease XLT services and await the MII's assessment of the technology and service. In June 2000, the MII recognized XLT as a wireless supplement to landline phones, but tried to restrict it again in February 2001 by banning its use outside small to medium-sized cities in rural China. In November 2000, the MII tried attempted to erode the price advantage of XLT by requiring China Telecom and China Netcom to increase monthly and per-minute XLT fees. The companies ignored this demand, and in 2004 the MII began to loosen control over pricing in general in order to stimulate development across telecommunications. In 2003, faced with its inability to stop the growth of XLT, the MII tacitly approved the technology: "The government does not encourage its development, but it will not regulate XLT's progressive march in cities" (Yuan et al., 309). In another example that shows the dichotomy between the center and the regions, local governments much keener on enabling affordable mobile service than on questions of national innovation competitiveness invested as much as 30 billion RMB in the service in the same period—a sum as large as the entire CDMA investment by China Unicom (Yuan et al. 2006). The two official mobile operators have also tried to limit and obstruct interconnection with XLT. For example, XLT phones could not send text messages to cellular phones until 2005.

35. For many Chinese, XLT provided their first exposure to any voice telephony. It was a viable option for hundreds of millions of low-end users who lack voice telephony and could not afford mainstream mobile telephony (Yuan et al. 2006).

36. Interestingly, until 2004, the mobile duopoly had been characterized by significant competition and acrimony, which was addressed by SASAC launching the first high-level management exchange (Xia 2006).

37. In 2000, China Unicom became the sole licensed operator of CDMA networks in China after it acquired the military's Great Wall CDMA network (Jianzhou Wang 2001).

38. Licensing and construction of beta-test markets for 3G systems began belatedly in 2007, using a combination of China's homegrown TD-SCDMA and international 3G standards.

39. Those who oppose all forms of exclusive domestic standards hold that China, by overprotecting and isolating its IT industry, will end up destroying the industry in the process. They point to Japan's self-strangulation in the mid-1990s through its insistence on maintaining unique mobile telephony standards as evidence of the danger and counterproductivity of such standards (authors' interviews). On Japan, see the study by Kushida (2008).

40. In addition, standardization facilitates both the fragmentation of production and specialization because it makes it easy for differently branded product components to be compatible. A component manufacturer can broaden its customer base and potential market at a minimum of development costs, since the components, as long as they conform to the ISO or accepted industry standard, will be compatible across systems.

41. In the early 1970s, Sony released the first commercially viable home-video recording system—Betamax. The following year, JVC released a competing standard—VHS. Although both standards were technologically comparable, VHS, which offered longer recording times and was supported by multiple corporate developers (as opposed to Betamax, which was developed by Sony alone), managed to dominate the home entertainment market. The dominance was so complete that it proved impossible for other home-video technologies to overcome until both standards were swamped by DVD technology.

42. It should be noted that while these bodies are supposedly multilateral and act in the general interest, the delegations from strongly determined states or companies can usually shape the debate about, and affect the outcome of, standards decisions and royalty obligations in their interest.

43. The ISO, the ITU, and other international standards bodies are international nongovernmental organizations whose memberships are usually not limited to sovereign states. Selection of standards is typically conducted by technical committees (which are answerable to the ISO General Council) wherein experts from the countries concerned —selected by their ISO national member bodies—propose, examine, and debate standards. The technical committees consist of international panels of experts in a particular field. Standards proposals from different countries or industry groups are presented to the panel, which then votes on whether a given technology standard will be certified. Technology standards are generally weighed on their technological and economic merits as well as on their adherence to fair, reasonable, and nondiscriminatory (FRAND)

terms. To meet the fairness requirement, technology must not come with excessive IPR restrictions, such as mandatory bundling or the forcing of licensees to release their technology to the standards holder. "Reasonable" refers to the rates set for licensing fees, which should not be excessive; in addition, all standards fees should be set at a comparable level. To qualify as nondiscriminatory, a license granter must treat all applicants equally, regardless of whether they are competitors or foreign entities. Final approval of ISO standards is done by a two-thirds majority vote of all ISO member bodies. In this way, all members have a stake in the selection process. During the final vote, technological concerns may not be raised. However, suggestions and recommendations are considered during the development of future related or supplemental standards (ISO 2008).

44. In the case of 3G technology, the standards are WCDMA, which is heavily promoted in Europe; CDMA2000, which draws on support from the United States; and China's indigenous TD-SCDMA standard.

45. Both published research and many of our interviewees noted that the ISO's rejection of the Chinese WAPI standard for wireless Internet was due in whole or in part to the secretive nature of its development and the unwillingness of the Chinese partners to openly participate in the selection process. In addition, at no point during the discussion could the developers provide the ISO committee with evidence of a single product using the WAPI standard (Kroeber 2007). Nonetheless, the Chinese government deeply resented the final rejection, in 2006, of WAPI by the ISO (Suttmeier et al. 2006).

46. While most of the attention has been given to China's actions on domestic standards, we should remember that China has also become an active participant in international standards-making bodies in recent years. Therefore, China's central government is taking a dual-track approach: heavily subsidizing the development of its own standards while also trying to influence the selection of international standards that further its interests (Kroeber 2007; Suttmeier et al. 2006). This stems in part from a deeply wounded national sense that the international IT industry is biased in favor of the developed world. Participation in international bodies is seen as a pragmatic approach, better than the confrontational one adopted during the 1990s and early 2000s. It also serves to disarm fears about China's standards policies. By helping shape international standards, China's government hopes to secure a better position for its companies. This can be accomplished by encouraging the adoption of fewer proprietary standards and more open- or free-access ones, or by having China's domestic standards recognized as legitimate among equals. According to one interviewee familiar with China's negotiating position, the push for adoption of Chinese domestic standards is used as a bargaining tool in these international forums to persuade the standard bearers to lower or eliminate royalties for established proprietary standards. Should this approach fail, many Chinese government officials believe that China's market is large enough that it could sustain its own IT industry in the event of a major standards-based confrontation (*People's Daily* 2004; authors' interviews).

47. Chinese DVD-player manufacturers did not start a new industry from scratch. Video compact disc (VCD) manufacturers in China proliferated rapidly during the mid to late 1990s (Kennedy 2005). Once the VCD-player market became saturated, many manufacturers began ramping up production lines for DVD players as well. The advantages of the technology were twofold: it opened a larger export market (VCD players typically

sold well only in China and moderately well in other developing Asian countries), and it could play both DVDs and SVCDs ("super-VCDs"). The VCD sector collapsed in 1999 when more than 200 manufacturers (out of 500) in China went bankrupt. DVD manufacturing exploded, going from 3.5 million units in 2000, of which 2 million were for export, to 70 million in 2003—75% of the global output (Linden 2004).

48. Falling prices were not the only factor that increased the popularity of DVDs in China. Once the security measures had been cracked and inexpensive pirated DVD movies became available, DVD players became a viable technology in China's market.

49. From a different viewpoint, the rapid and continual entrance of ever more assemblers into the market, competing solely on price, simply eroded whatever slim profit margins had existed previously. In that case, the loss of profits was the result of the basic laws of supply and demand, not licensing fees.

50. Major shifts in mobile-telephony technology have typically been indicated through the use of generation names: 2G, 3G, and now 4G. Each generational shift represents changes in the quality and types of services available as well as in the types of transmission and data-organization technologies utilized. The switch from analog to digital technology marked the shift to 2G; 2G and 3G technologies differ primarily in their faster rates of data transfer and higher bandwidth capabilities. For example, 3G enables mobile Internet, radio, and video access in addition to standard voice telephony and text services. Transfer speeds for 3G are as high as 3 Mbps (megabits per second), while 2G could support only up to 114 kbps (kilobits per second). This limitation of the latter greatly reduces its ability to support higher-value-added and data-intensive applications. 3G technology is designed to be compatible with 2G infrastructure so that 3G handsets will continue to operate on existing infrastructure (Brain et al. 2008; Kioskea 2008).

51. The Chinese 3G standard was explicitly designed to circumvent foreign core-patent holders such as Qualcomm (Liu 2006).

52. In 1995, MOST, the MII (in the form of the MPT), and the NDRC (then the National Planning Commission) made the development of a CDMA-based 3G standard a key project of the Ninth Five-Year Plan (T. Zhou 2004). The development of TD-SCDMA technology itself began with Cwill Telecommunication, Inc., a U.S. company started by overseas resident Chinese. In November 2005, Cwill and the Chinese Academy of Telecommunication Technology (CATT) formed Xinwei SCDMA, a company devoted to developing SCDMA technology and incorporating it into a new 3G standard (Agilent 2006; X. Liu 2006). In 1998, Siemens and CATT, with Datang Telecom Technology acting as the representative for China's telecommunications industry, proposed TD-SCDMA as a 3G standard to the ITU (*People's Daily* 2007).

53. A classic example of such a failure occurred in June 2005. After five years of protected development, the TD-SCDMA system was field-tested by CATT. The system failed when the handset chips were unable to support 3G applications. The phones could send and receive calls or messages but performed poorly with other functions. This test came one month before the planned commercial launch of TD-SCDMA technology. The results of the trial led government officials to declare another delay (W. Li 2005).

54. In April 2008, China Mobile finally began selling TD-SCDMA phone numbers for test

networks in eight coastal cities. This was the first large-scale simultaneous commercial testing of the system (TD Forum 2008).

55. In September 2001, Japan's NTT DoCoMo launched the first commercial 3G network. Europe's first test network appeared in December 2001 when Manx Telecom—a subsidiary of British Telecom—launched its 3G test network on Britain's Isle of Man. In January 2002, Verizon launched the first commercial 3G network in the United States (CNN 2002; Loney 2001; D. Zhang 2008).

56. China claims to have launched the world's first 4G network in 2007. However, the validity of these claims and the viability of the technology are uncertain and unproven (Bishop 2007). The Chinese 4G system, Time Division–Long-Term Evolution (TD-LTE), builds on the TD-SCDMA system, and so the Chinese hope that even if the 3G standard fails, it will lay the groundwork for a leap into 4G. Ideally, the 3G system will provide a demonstration effect and raise the interest of global telecommunications firms in the TD-LTE system (Wei 2008).

57. For more details on the origin and operations of Datang and Xinwei, see Chapter Three of this book.

58. As was shown in the cases of telecommunications and DVD standards, the intentions of the central government (to restrict or ban XLT and to promote AVD-EVD) have been resisted by enterprises—even those owned by the central government. Here we advance this argument by pointing to the limits of central-government power over regional political actors, not just economic actors.

59. Although local governments exert great influence over the local branches of state banks, all banks in China are still subject to the policies of the People's Bank of China, the national bank. While this control is far from complete or uniform, it has prevented the emergence of a private banking sector in China.

60. In Chinese, the term minying literally means "people run." It is a category of ownership and management style that has been recognized in China since the 1980s. The term itself is ambiguous, since it can be used to define any type of ownership structure other than foreign invested (*waizi qiye*—外资企业) or state owned/operated (*guoyou/ying qiye*—国有/营企业). As a result, minying enterprises can include collective (*jiti*—集体), individual-private (*geti minying/siying*—个体民营/私营), and private (*siying*—私营) enterprises, depending on the locality and the wishes of a governmental unit or entrepreneur. Township and village enterprises (TVEs, *xiangzhen qiye*—乡镇企业) are (and were) also usually listed as minying, since they are not state owned in the traditional sense.

61. Defining what constitutes a high-technology park can be difficult. While national-level parks have specific guidelines, other parks may not. Even those with guidelines may opt to quietly ignore them. The Zhongshan Torch National-Level High-Technology Industrial Park in Zhongshan City, Guangdong province, includes the paper-and-packaging industry as one of its six promoted "high technology" pillars. The desire to attract high-technology industry and prestige investments from foreign MNCs has led to a proliferation of different types of high-technology industrial parks. Many have not been successful at attracting high-technology industry and instead serve primarily as export-processing zones. In each region we studied, the approach to macro-organization of HTDZs was different. In Beijing, the national-level Zhongguancun Science Park has

subsumed almost all parks in the metropolitan area within its structure, creating a legal-political organ overseeing the various parks (sector based and university run) within it. In Shanghai, the different parks exist largely in isolation and compete fiercely with one another. In the Pearl River Delta city of Shenzhen, there is a move to unite different parks into the Shenzhen High-Tech Industrial Belt, which runs across the manufacturing and investment zones north of the densely populated Hong Kong border area, but in general, the parks have little relation to one another. Across China, companies in the parks may be offered free or reduced-cost use of facilities, subsidized utilities, special telecommunications hookups, access to locally created development platforms, libraries, and housing and tax breaks especially designed to attract overseas Chinese.

62. Today, environmental impact is starting to be considered a factor when a municipal government grants an investment permit. However, having a polluting facility does not mean that an enterprise will not be allowed into the park; instead, it is encouraged to move the polluting activities to another location adjacent to the park itself. This allows enterprises and local officials to stay within the letter of national law and retain both the old, polluting facilities and new, cleaner ones within the local economy.

63. The Guangdong provincial government and the governments of Hong Kong and Macao hope to spearhead the development of China's interior through the Pan–Pearl River Delta Forum, which connects the PRD region with eight inland and coastal provinces in southern China. Ideally, the forum will integrate economic planning and coordination, helping move lower-value-added activities inland as a way to spur development in less developed provinces while benefiting the development of more advanced capabilities in the PRD itself.

64. SOEs and foreign-invested enterprises—both high-tech certified and not—had different tax structures and promotional policies. As with the policies for high-tech minying, SOEs and foreign enterprises could receive different benefits and support from national, provincial, local, and HDTZ governments and administrations.

65. The CCP has never renounced its belief in communism as the proper system for organizing government, society, and economics. Indeed, the General Program of the Constitution of the CCP explicitly states: "The realization of communism is the highest ideal and ultimate goal of the party" (CCP 2007). The Chinese state constitution also affirms a commitment to these principles. Article One states: "The People's Republic of China is a socialist state under the people's democratic dictatorship led by the working class and based on the alliance of workers and peasants. The socialist system is the basic system of the People's Republic of China" (PRC 1982).

66. As noted by Kellee Tsai (2002) in the case of nontechnological nonstate enterprises, different governmental bodies, including commerce offices, labor offices, finance bureaus, taxation bureaus, and the local public-security apparatus, can, and do, engage in various types of meddling in the affairs of businesses. Such interference often takes the form of seeking rents but can include attempts to control sectors of the local economy.

67. Many interviewees said that the mark of good governance in their region or HTDZ was that government officials left them "alone" and did not meddle in daily operations. The perception that the government in Shanghai is less meddlesome than those in other regions is one of its main attractions.

68. According to the 2006 draft of the law, certification will involve the national-level units of MOST, the NDRC, and the Ministry of Finance, which are primarily responsible for creating the certification criteria and setting up the catalogs of high-technology products. Actual research and certification will be the responsibility of "each province, autonomous region, or special municipality science and technology planning office. (A commission or bureau) should work with that level's economic (trade) commission (of the NDRC), finance office (bureau), and other relevant agencies, according to the stipulated requirements and prerequisites in the 'National Indigenous Innovation Work Report Directions,' concerning that region's report on overall product advances and preliminary investigations, including examinations by organization experts." Adding further complexity, the law states: "MOST, with the NDRC and Ministry of Finance, will jointly entrust related organizations, according to unified concrete confirmation requirements, to undertake the responsibility for work certifying indigenous innovation products" (MOST et al. 2006; authors' translation).

69. Two of the most famous cases of such behavior occurred when the originators of the Founder Group were pushed out after a conflict with Peking University, and when the manager of Kehai was pushed out—and ended up with nothing to show for his very successful entrepreneurial efforts—after a conflict with CAS (Lu 2000; Segal 2003). Qiwen Lu (2000) gives a detailed history of the first four highly successful Chinese IT companies—Stone, Founder, Legend, and Great Wall—describing the problems they faced in establishing and funding themselves under such conditions of ownership ambiguity.

CHAPTER 3: BEIJING

1. In the 1980s, as part of Beijing's first attempt at introducing entrepreneurial vitality and innovation into the then-critical SOE-controlled economy, large factories were required to establish enterprise incubators. Currently there are more than seventy different high-technology enterprise incubators in the city (authors' interviews).

2. An opposing perspective might find that the presence of such formalistic and state-sanctioned bodies testifies to such an environment being conspicuously missing in Beijing. However, since most other regions of innovation, including Silicon Valley, are filled with formal and informal academic, state, and civil society organs, it would appear that Zhongguancun is attempting to build similar institutions rather than hide its weakness.

3. Aigo is the brand name of the Beijing Huaqi Information Digital Technology Company. While Aigo has developed some digital products it considers world leading—such as high-end digital microscopes and a digital pen that can read written words—its main products are consumer digital electronics such as MP3 players, digital cameras, USB flash drives, and digital photo frames—all of which imitate foreign products and ideas.

4. In February 2005, Lenovo bought full control over its 2002 mobile-phone joint venture, Lenovo Mobile Communications (Nystedt 2005). Although Lenovo's mobile division was initially successful in its chosen market niche—fourth- to sixth-tier cities in China's interior—Lenovo's brand collapsed once foreign brands such as Nokia and Motorola entered China's interior markets. After suffering a more than 30% drop in sales in the fourth quarter of 2007, Lenovo sold the division in January 2008 for a mere $100

million. While pronounced a true sale, it amounted only to the transfer of ownership of the mobile division from Lenovo itself to Legend Holding, Lenovo's holding company. Legend Holding bought 60% of Lenovo Mobile through a subsidiary of Hony Capital, Legend's investment arm (X. Wang 2008).

5. ODP companies are similar to the ODM firms pioneered in Taiwan and utilized increasingly in southern China, but with one key difference. In the ODM model as practiced by Taiwanese companies such as Quanta, Acer, and Foxconn, the original equipment manufacturer (OEM) firm develops, designs, and produces the branded products for its clients. An ODP company, like TechFaith, does only the research, software development, and design. Actual production is outsourced to OEMs. TechFaith's customers include leading regional brands like Panasonic and NEC in Japan, Sprint in the United States, and T-Mobile in Europe. The company's primary success has been in offering design services for smaller brands, particularly operator brands like Sprint and T-Mobile or boutique, prestige brands like Gucci. Unlike many other Chinese mobile-phone design houses, which specialize in hardware based on a single chip set, TechFaith emphasizes the software-development component, which has a higher value added and requires greater technical sophistication.

6. Beijing's premier software park, Zhongguancun Software Park, operates as a "dual basis" park. It is both a National Software Industry Base and a National Software Outsourcing Base. In practical terms, this means that local government policies promote the development of product and outsourcing-service software companies. The MII and the Ministry of Commerce conferred the two titles on the park.

7. In interviews, entrepreneurs and foreign expatriate employees of major MNCs noted that foreign VC firms in Beijing directly encourage second-generation innovation. One interviewee described the process this way: "U.S. VCs invite top engineers from firms in China, wine and dine them, and present new ideas for software or online products they harvested in the U.S., saying, 'Here is the latest idea from Silicon Valley. If you copy the idea and start a company, we will fund you'" (authors' interview). This process further augments the quickness with which the Chinese IT industry follows the American one, reducing China's gap in new products and technologies to a matter of weeks.

8. While China's reform era officially began in 1978, it important to note that the restructuring of China's government, economy, and society after 1949 represented the most wrenching change and reform in China's history. On the scale of reformers developed by Barry Naughton, the 1949 leadership could be considered iconoclastic reformers for their willingness to fully adopt a foreign model for development in the interest of national salvation. The post-1978 reformers followed a middle way by attempting to preserve a "Chinese" (in this case, the socialist system created by the CCP) essence while adopting the practical elements of foreign economics and technology to strengthen the country (Garver 1993; Naughton 2007).

9. Despite the charge to coordinate research, CAS units became heavily isolated and insular during the 1960s and 1970s. By the 1980s, leading researchers had become somewhat disillusioned with the mission and practice of the CAS, since its research did not appear to be offering any benefit to China's development (Ling 2005).

10. In prestige, the CAE is similar to the CAS, the main difference between them being the

former's explicit focus on engineering disciplines. Academicians at both institutions are accomplished researchers in their fields, and China's top researchers are invited to join them. Membership conveys respect and influence, and facilitates access to research funds (authors' interviews). The CAS runs research institutes; however, not all researchers—even senior researchers—employed there are academicians. Accordingly, Beijing's high concentration of academicians showcases its strength in R&D both within the CAS and within academia.

11. Like its counterpart in the Soviet Union, the Central Planning Commission made plans for scientific research in China. Since science and technology were to serve the nation, and since industrial research was primarily conducted in research centers directly under the industrial ministries or in large enterprises themselves, the CAS and various universities conducted mostly basic research with strategic implications. Under the first plan, the core elements—atomic and hydrogen bombs, satellites—gave the name *Liangdan Yixing* ("two bombs, one satellite") to the entire plan and era (Cao et al. 2006). The final development of weapons systems and the applications of their technology occurred in the relevant industrial ministries or military research units.

12. Critics allege that projects linked to MOST's plans continue to lack transparency in bidding and remain largely unaccountable, as well as off-limits, to those without requisite connections (Cao et al. 2006; author's interviews). The most recent, the National Mid- and Long-Range Science and Technology Development Plan, has been criticized for its reliance on major projects and for concentrating its financial authority in MOST.

13. In 1966, the CAS Institute of Computer Science created China's first generally successful mainframe computer. It was capable of 110,000 calculations per second and was code-named Number 109-C. The computer, like other 1960s-era CAS mainframes, was used through the 1980s and participated in calculations for China's nuclear, weather study, and missile programs. The Number 109-C was far behind the global frontier even when it was first developed. It was a transistor-based computer at a time when foreign mainframes were entering the IC era. The Number 109-C was nonetheless considered a milestone and was even given military honors during its decommissioning ceremony (Ling 2005).

14. Like all urban residents, Beijing CAS employees and university professors enjoyed subsidized housing, pensions, health care, education, and access to rationed luxury and consumer goods (Andreas 2009; Naughton 2007). During the uncertainty of the 1980s, many academics and SOE employees resisted moving into the private sector, which came with high risk even though it involved high potential income.

15. The Chinese word danwei (单位) simply means "unit." In the PRC, danwei came specifically to refer to the work unit that defined urban life from the 1960s through the 1990s. Today, the danwei system has largely collapsed as even SOEs have shed most of their social-service obligations. The vestiges of danwei culture, mentality, and architecture, however, remain.

16. China's highly protected domestic market allowed for very high markups on IT hardware; a personal computer in 1985 cost 20,000 RMB at a port and more than 40,000 RMB on the consumer market (Ling 2005).

17. The first successful product sold by Lenovo was neither its own brand of computers nor a generic imported electronics item. Ni Guangnan, a senior researcher at the CAS Insti-

tute of Computing Technology (ICT), developed a Chinese-character input system for computers that increased typing speed and efficiency by 50%. The card worked by using probability to select the next character a user would input. Since the vast majority of Chinese words consist of two characters, the second character desired by a user could be probabilistically selected. This reduced the time spent searching through lists of characters to find the desired one. The Lenovo card was a spectacular success. In 1987, the first year the new card was sold, Lenovo sold one hundred cards integrated with imported PCs and earned gross profits of 400,000 RMB (Ling 2005).

18. There are some negative consequences of the passion for creating new ventures. For example, instead of conducting scientific research, graduate students find themselves working as unpaid research interns on market-oriented projects for a professor's consulting activities. There is also a concern that research in many universities has become highly applied and places less emphasis on pure or basic research. Some facts appear to support these fears; nationwide, applied and developmental work accounted for 94.8% of research spending in 2006 (NSBPRC 2007).

19. For example, Tsinghua Holdings, one of several holding companies in the university, controls thirty companies. These represent property management, construction, hardware, software, IT services, and IC design (authors' interviews). The Founder Group has five publicly traded companies and twenty wholly funded companies and joint ventures within its structure, including its core Chinese-language publishing hardware, software, chip design, pharmaceuticals, finance, and steel. Since many of the holding companies started as a desperate attempt to develop new sources of revenue for their mother institutions, they lacked a strategic vision and focus. The rapid expansion of income led to a parallel expansion of economic activities; eventually, some ostensible technology companies (like the Stone Group) were involved in international trade, retail, and even the management of real estate or food companies (Kennedy 1997). In recent years, many holding companies have cut back on their operations, and the central government has come to officially encourage universities to divest themselves from business operations (Eun et al. 2006).

20. See Chapter Four for more details on the IC-foundry case in Shanghai.

21. SMIC's business plans have changed from complete construction, ownership, and operation of IC foundries. Today, expansion occurs almost solely through agreements with local-government actors for SMIC to operate state-owned and state-constructed foundries throughout China.

22. For example, a major promotional policy for software-outsourcing enterprises states that members of the Zhongguancun Software Export Union are able to enjoy a specific rent subsidy in the park from the municipal government. According to the first director of the export union, "Software exports are an opportunity for China's software industry. Software enterprises engaged in software exports should study foreign advances in technology and ideas and create international brands as fast as possible" (Qi 2003). The government considers the development of outsourcing a necessary step toward China's mastery of software and the commencement of independent novel innovation in the field. As stated by an HTDZ representative in Beijing: "Beijing's municipal government has a strategy to transform the city toward a high-tech-industry orientation. In China, the

software industry is still weak. No matter that some of our major companies have their own intellectual property; we should learn the management practices, technology, and training when we do outsourcing. Outsourcing is a way to connect with the outside world. That is why we are encouraging outsourcing companies here in our park" (authors' interview).

23. Beijing targets individuals as well as enterprises by tailoring policies to the personal needs of entrepreneurs. For example, in the Zhongguancun Software Park, employees who earn in excess of 100,000 RMB a year are entitled to a rebate on their consumption, which includes an 80% rebate on the luxury taxes levied on a first car and apartment.

24. On several occasions, interviewees objected to the perception that many enterprises have set up R&D centers only for the political capital they earn. While not denying that this could occur, they added that with the availability of research talent in Beijing, it would be a waste of resources to set up an R&D center and then fail to use it.

25. However, the talent pool is not bottomless. Many MNC research groups noted that the top graduates tend to go overseas to continue their studies. This leaves those in the second quartile available for recruitment by large enterprises. Competition for new graduates is intense. One interviewee claimed that some Chinese companies use nationalistic appeals to win over candidates. According to the interviewee, a campus recruitment poster for Baidu declared: "Do you want to be an insect working for a foreign company or part of a Chinese dragon?" (authors' interview)

26. The university entrance examination is held once a year for third-year high school students. China's education system is primarily oriented toward teaching the material necessary to pass this exam. The final year of high school is devoted mostly to reviewing material in preparation for the exam. The school administration curtails students' holidays and mandates extra lessons. Higher scores increase the prestige of a school and attract more potential enrollees, which means greater revenues for the schools and more opportunities for administrators to advance. The exam itself is comprehensive: Chinese, English, chemistry, physics, mathematics, history, and politics (a combination of civics and the study of Marxism).

27. It should be noted that even in the 1980s, investments for small-scale pure export processing could be made without having to establish offices in Beijing. However, more complex operations, exceptionally large investments, companies in closed sectors like telecommunications, and firms seeking access to the Chinese market required the formation of a joint venture, most often with a SOE, and a presence in the capital.

28. Several interviewees mentioned that it was often beneficial to establish R&D centers in both Beijing and Shanghai. The primary reason is that graduates of universities in both cities are unwilling to relocate.

29. It is important to note this distinction: interviewees stated that IPR concerns did not determine whether to open an R&D center in Beijing, but IPR concerns did influence the type of R&D conducted and its fit within a global strategy.

30. Most of Beijing's leading large enterprises have since ended their OEM and ODM businesses in favor of their own brand-name operations. However, some, such as Tech-Faith, rely solely on ODM work for their market niche. For our purposes, we also consider the nonbranded resale and value-added resale of other brand names as a form

of OEM-ODM activity, a stage through which all of Beijing's large enterprises have passed.

31. Lenovo was known as Legend until 2003. The unchanged Chinese name of the company, Lian Xiang (联想—"linked thought") comes from the name of Lenovo's original Chinese-language card, which used a "linked thought" system for character selection.

32. Since its inception, Lenovo has diversified into many different markets. The main businesses of Legend Holdings, Lenovo's state-controlled parent company, include a supercomputing business (selling to the Chinese security and space apparatus), Digital China (a distribution and sales company), FM365.com (a now-defunct Internet portal), the Raycon Real Estate Development Company, Legend Capital, and Hony Capital.

33. Like many Chinese brands, Aigo takes pride in its Chinese identity. The company's name, Aiguozhe (爱国者), means "patriot." Also in the spirit of patriotism, the company explicitly tries to limit its reliance on foreign technologies and capital (authors' interviews).

34. By comparison, the Stone Group, as a complete outsider, never enjoyed the capital access of its state-owned or state-connected competitors during the 1980s and 1990s (Kennedy 1997).

35. Xinwei's state partner is the state-owned market arm of CATT—Datang Telecom. Like all SOEs in telecommunications, Xinwei has come under stress from state intervention. Datang demoted Xinwei's founder and then president, Chen Wei, in 2006 as part of a general management restructuring of all companies under the Datang Group's management. The motivation for his demotion to vice president was uncertain, although Datang cited a failure to effectively develop the SCDMA business (Interfax 2006). The company's first attempted IPO, in 2007, was blocked by China's stock-market regulators. Revenues remain small ($235 million in 2007) when compared with those of other telecommunications-equipment firms in China.

36. Xinwei's uncertain relationship with the central state can be seen in its developmental history. Although partly owned and championed by the MII, Xinwei was unable to get a single telecommunications operator to test its SCDMA technology and was forced to do so at its own expense in the Daqing oil-fields region of China's northeast in 2001. Mobile operators preferred to continue using established CDMA, GSM, and even PHS technologies rather than experiment with a new Chinese standard (C114 2005). In 2008, Xinwei again ran afoul of its state patrons when two test antennas in Beijing supposedly interfered with radio transmissions for the Olympic Games. Although some branches of the government had approved the technology, the Beijing Radio Administration Bureau, claiming the towers needed separate registration, confiscated the antennas (CTN 2008c).

37. Incubators reflect the critical importance of quality telecommunications infrastructure and access to the success of their enterprises. However, when asked whether the facility had access different from or superior to that available elsewhere, most interviewees stated that while they provide the connection, quality and other aspects are a matter for the telecommunications operator, not the incubator.

38. During the dot-com bubble of the late 1990s, Beijing's early VC firms bought into the global exuberance for technology companies. However, because of institutional difficulties with IPOs, M&As, and market immaturity, most of these VCs suffered great losses. As a result, many VCs remain risk averse.

CHAPTER 4: SHANGHAI

1. China's fourth- and sixth-best universities (Jiaotong and Fudan) are in Shanghai, as are nine of the top one hundred universities (Wu et al. 2008).

2. The trend to concentrate more activities in Shanghai is apparent among many Taiwanese MNCs, which are increasing their production, design, and research footprints there.

3. Manufacturing facilities, according to Shanghai's Eleventh Five-Year Plan, will increasingly be concentrated in municipal- or national-level industrial parks so that park-based manufacturing will account for 75% of the city's total industrial value added by 2010 (Shanghai Foreign 2006a).

4. China's Customs Administration calculated that Shanghai, Jiangsu, and Guangdong together accounted for 80.2% of China's IC exports in 2007. Shanghai had the largest share, followed by Jiangsu and Guangdong. Beijing was not even mentioned in the government report.

5. In a major restructuring of its China operations, Intel announced the closure of its assembly and test facilities in Shanghai's Pudong New Area and its relocation to lower-cost Chengdu, a decision that followed its 2007 commitment to build a major fabrication facility in Dalian and not in Shanghai. Intel, which will retain its R&D center and investment base in Shanghai, is offering the two thousand production workers in Shanghai opportunities to transfer to Chengdu or Dalian (CTN 2007; CTN 2009b).

6. The overall economic growth rate in Shanghai is slower than that in Dongguan, Shenzhen, or Guangdong. For growth in industry and production, Shanghai ranks behind Guangdong, Shenzhen, Dongguan, and Beijing. The one area Shanghai appears to shine in is the rapid growth of its service industry (BSB 2008; DSB 2008; GSB 2008; Shanghai SB 2008; SSB 2008).

7. As defined by China's National Statistics Bureau, the public economy consists of SOEs, state-controlled enterprises, and collectives. Foreign enterprises, Hong Kong–invested enterprises, Macao-invested enterprises, Taiwanese-invested enterprises, and private enterprises are considered part of the non-public economy (NSBPRC 2006).

8. Original Chinese: "宁要浦西一张床，不要浦东一间房。" As Pudong has developed, this saying, at least officially, no longer describes life in the suburbs. However, interviews with entrepreneurs and young Shanghai residents confirmed a continued strong preference for the urban core over the suburbs (authors' interviews).

9. Jiang Zemin joined the central government in 1989, serving as Communist Party general secretary. He became president in 1992. Zhu Rongji served as mayor of Shanghai until 1991 and then joined the central government as a member of the Politburo Standing Committee. He became premier in 1998 when Li Peng stepped down.

10. Geographers Dennis Wei and Chi Kin Leung estimate that since the 1980s, nearly 200 different development zones have opened in Shanghai (Wei and Leung 2005).

11. In 2000, the State Council released "Policies to Encourage the Development of the Software and Integrated Circuit Industries," better known as Document 18. It proposed reductions in the value-added tax for domestic IC firms, financing from MOST, and the simplification of investment-approval procedures. In 2002, to encourage the VC industry, the State Council augmented these incentives by promising that IC-design firms

would be permitted to list publicly earlier and more easily than other enterprises. Foreign firms believed the support promised by Document 18 amounted to subsidies that were incompatible with China's WTO obligations. In April 2005, China officially rescinded the promotional policies under Document 18, although these were simply replaced with a different set of policies (Kroeber 2007).

12. An additional difficulty for enterprises investing in Shanghai is comparative cost. Average starting salaries for university graduates in Shanghai are the highest in China. Shanghai's salaries are 3.4% higher than Beijing's and nearly 10% higher than Guangzhou's. Despite the difficulties faced by many firms and an increase in unemployment in 2008, Shanghai graduates continued to seek starting salaries ranging from 3,000 to 8,000 RMB a month, significantly above the market rate and higher even than the city average (Li and Fei 2009).

13. An especially frank explanation of Tsinghua's practices was given to us by one of its full professors: "You must have been a student here in order to work here and expect to be promoted. Tsinghua is very insular in this way. Although the rules officially forbid it, Tsinghua PhDs are hired as researchers as soon as they finish and are gradually, usually about two years later, converted into full faculty members. In administration, only a Tsinghua alumnus can expect to become a Tsinghua administrator. Elevation and appointment of administrators are decided by the personnel department of the university and their network within the school" (authors' interview).

14. As early as 2001, the Beijing-based joint-venture training company Aptech Jade Bird trained more than twelve thousand software engineers in Shanghai (Saxenian 2003). The pace of such efforts has increased; for example, in 2007, IBM opened the first MNC-based center devoted to developing software programmers for outsourcing. The facility was projected to train two thousand software-outsourcing experts its first year (AsiaInfo 2007). In 2008, Infosys, the Pudong Software Park, and the Shanghai Municipal Information Commission launched a major training program for software-outsourcing workers. The Information Commission provided four million RMB in seed funds for this program (Q. Chen and S. Zhu 2008).

15. CEIBS offered the first international MBA program in China. The European Union and the Shanghai municipal government jointly finance the school, which trains current and prospective managers in international best practices so that they can assist the growth of Chinese enterprises.

16. Difficulties have arisen when the local government tries to train employees in the skills needed by local companies. For example, the recent push to create a software-outsourcing sector neglected the potential difficulties arising from the high costs for Shanghai workers. As a result, the industry drive may fail altogether because of uncompetitive costs, or jobs may go to non-Shanghainese willing to work for lower salaries.

17. In the IC industry in particular, we found that many enterprises, both foreign and local, recruited heavily in China's interior rather than in Shanghai (authors' interviews).

18. While small enterprises perceive government bias against them regarding the hukou, and MNCs frequently enjoy better access to it, the system is not wholly standardized or predictable. The director of a major MNC R&D center explained the company's experience: "It was easier a few years ago to arrange a hukou for an employee. Back then, if the can-

didate had a graduate degree and secured a job with a local company, he could obtain a Shanghai hukou. Now when we hold discussions with government officials, we make it a point to mention that it has become harder to obtain a hukou for our employees. But they have not yet resolved the difficulties" (authors' interview).

19. Coca-Cola received particularly special treatment in the park because the park's largest shareholder—the Zhejiang Group—began as a packaging company working for Coca-Cola (authors' interviews; Shanghai Foreign 2008).

20. Shanghai's development zones are constantly increasing their independence and discretionary authority. Since 2000, under the provisions of Document 18, Shanghai's municipal and local authorities have received even greater autonomy and rights to approve foreign-investment projects in IC or software. The local autonomy to approve projects and land development has only increased the fragmentation among Shanghai's development zones.

21. In a classic example of the impact of ambiguity and structured uncertainty, many small enterprises are unofficially allowed to "game" the system by registering in a park while remaining in the city. These arrangements serve both sides by allowing park officials to claim that they aid small start-ups and by supplying the start-ups with some benefits and, more importantly, a bureaucratic mother-in-law (authors' interviews; W. Hong 2003).

22. France's Alcatel purchased BTM in 1987 and thus assumed responsibility for BTM's investments in China. Shanghai Bell has undergone a series of name changes. In 2004, the company became Alcatel Shanghai Bell before returning to simply Shanghai Bell after an ownership and management reorganization in 2008.

23. Shanghai Belling became a prospective national champion in the nascent IC industry in China during the 1990s. While small compared with the pureplay foundries introduced since 1998, it remains an active player and supplier of telecommunications-switch semiconductors.

24. Further evidence of the localization of the company and the blurring of the distinction between the foreign and the Chinese portion is the lack of foreign expatriates employed. The company's top research organ—the Asia Pacific Research and Innovation Group—no longer employs any foreigners.

25. State control over other Shanghai foundries is similarly increasing. The second- and third-largest semiconductor foundries, Huahong-NEC and Grace, are merging, and a new chairman has been appointed by the Shanghai government (Sung and Shen 2009b).

26. For more about ZTE's and Huawei's very successful utilization of former Shanghai Bell engineers, see Chapter Five.

27. The Property Rights Exchange is a government unit, but the Transformation Center is a local, state-led nonprofit organization that acts an intermediary between "patent holders, universities, and some science-and-technology administrations of the government" (authors' interview).

CHAPTER 5: SHENZHEN AND THE PEARL RIVER DELTA

1. The global economic crisis of 2008 accelerated the economic difficulties faced by many PRD industrial firms. Many MNCs have begun to diversify their investment plans and

now look to Vietnam as an alternative to further investment in the PRD and China (Brad-sher 2008; Wong 2008). Venerable PRD enterprises such as Foxconn announced plans to close their production facilities in the region and move inland (CTN 2008a). Small local enterprises, too, have begun to face financial difficulties and even bankruptcy (Nie 2008).

2. ZTE had a central-government patron, the Ministry of Aerospace Industry, but was not related to either the MEI or the MPT. Thus, it was also shielded from the power strug-gles between the MEI and the MPT (see Chapter Two for more details). Established as a new entity in 1985, it avoided the confused structure of companies such as Julong, which were assembled in a hodgepodge fashion from existing SOEs (Harwit 2007).

3. However, the same statistics bear out the region's reputation for limited novel innovation. Dongguan's invention patents granted in 2007 were only 0.65% of the total number of patents granted to Dongguan enterprises. The vast majority of patents were for designs or applications (DSB 2008).

4. Guangzhou, an older major Chinese city, has a much richer academic infrastructure than the newer or more recently developed cities of Shenzhen, Dongguan, Zhongshan, and Zhuhai. Guangzhou is home to six of the top one hundred universities in China, most notably Sun Yat-sen University, the Huanan University of Science and Technology, and Jinan University (Wu et al. 2008).

5. Both products and enterprises can be certified as "high and new technology" (高新技术产品/企业). In practice, the certification procedures vary slightly from re-gion to region, but are typically conducted by a combination of local officials from the tax and technology bureaus. As discussed in Chapter One, the central government is attempting to regain control by centralizing procedures for high-technology certi-fication.

6. While the PRD's leading companies have experience with exports, many began by cater-ing to underserved domestic markets, as a consequence becoming adept at offering qual-ity technology solutions at low cost and with a short time to market.

7. Traditionally, PRD cities have the most relaxed hukou and work-permit regulations in China.

8. It should be noted, however, that an export orientation did not mean that production was purely for export. During the 1980s, the imbalance caused by China's dual pricing system made sales of consumer goods on the domestic market far more profitable than exports. This led to corruption and illegal sales domestically as well as the circuitous routing of goods through Hong Kong and back into China for final sale. Through the 1990s, as long as PRD enterprises were required to export most or all of their output, daily convoys of trucks crossed into Hong Kong and then turned around and drove back into Shenzhen (Walcott 2003).

9. By comparison, 20% of R&D in Beijing is conducted at universities or state research units, and government forms a much more significant source of R&D funding wherever it is performed (K. Chen and M. Kenney 2007).

10. The PRD encompasses twenty-eight cities and counties with a total area of 41,698 square kilometers, or 16,100 square miles (Shen et al. 2000). While the total area of the PRD, as an economic and cultural region, is larger than that of the cities on which we focus, the most significant players in the IT industry are concentrated on the northern and

southern sides of the delta in a triangle whose vertices are Hong Kong–Shenzhen, Guangzhou, and Macao-Zhuhai.

11. Guangdong was home to one of imperial China's first breakaway kingdoms—the Kingdom of Nanyue, created by Zhao Tuo, a Qin dynasty general, during the second century BC. Guangdong was also the base of the Kuomintang before the Northern Expedition. With their unique language, international ties, and history of independence, Guangdong residents embody the spirit of the colorful adage: "The mountains are tall and the emperor is far away" (山高皇帝远).

12. Zhongshan City, on the southwest side of the PRD, is now publically celebrating its commercial heritage in a restored Republican-era town center. The Xiangshan Commercial Culture Museum commemorates the advanced development of the commercial economy and the different business and trading interests in the region under the Qing and Republican governments.

13. It can be argued that this underinvestment facilitated the development of new market-oriented and light-industrial enterprises. As Chris Bramall writes concerning the industrialization of Guangdong and Fujian provinces during the reform era (2003, 305): "Their industrial sectors were under-developed by the close of the Maoist era, and thus both provinces enjoyed abundant reservoirs of surplus labor. The absence of industrialization in these areas therefore paved the way for rapid future growth." Because it lacked an abundance of large planned-economy industrial centers, the PRD did not face the risks inherent in introducing market-based challengers to established high-employment enterprises. While not a determinant, the lack of entrenched interests in the existing industrial system facilitated a willingness to experiment.

14. While Zhejiang province's Wenzhou City developed the most radical production and ownership reforms and the earliest private companies in China, Wenzhou's economy was primarily oriented toward the vast domestic market. During the early reform years, Wenzhou's firms did not look outward for investment or markets, unlike the PRD's earliest manufacturers.

15. In July 1978, four months before the official start of the reforms, Dongguan established the first Hong Kong–partnered joint-venture export-oriented factory since the PRC's founding.

16. Barry Naughton (2007) considers the PRD model of TVE development to be one of three models for rural industrialization in 1980s China. The model is distinct from those in Wenzhou and Jiangsu because it used foreign capital and concentrated on exports.

17. Yasheng Huang (2008) argues that this early rural entrepreneurship has led to better, much more vibrant, and private-market-led growth than the later urban, state-led entrepreneurship of which he views Shanghai as the embodiment.

18. Original Chinese: "农村改革中，我们完全没有意料到的最大的收获，就是乡镇企业发展起来了，突然冒出搞多种行业，搞商品经济，搞各种小型企业，异军突起。这不是我们中央的功绩。乡镇企业每年都是百分之二十几的增长率，持续了几年，一直到现在还是这样。"

19. After hearing the initial SEZ proposal, Deng Xiaoping supposedly commented, "The center has no money, but it can give some policies. You go and do it yourself—make

your own success" (中央没有钱, 可以给些政策, 你们自己去搞, 杀出一条血路来) (quoted in N. Li 2005).

20. Despite the spectacular performance of Shenzhen and the PRD, their rise failed to live up to central-government hopes. The generated levels of foreign exchange remained small, especially in light of China's enormous needs (Ge 1999). Developing the SEZs' infrastructure also proved exceedingly expensive (Garver 1993).

21. We should note, however, that Shenzhen's and the PRD's success in IT hardware did not emerge from a tabula rasa. See Chapter 1, note 8 for more details on the role of little "Third Front" electronics industries in the PRD's early marketization.

22. In the first phase of reform, from 1978 to 1984, the majority of investment in the PRD region was actually in services, including hotels, tourism, and entertainment facilities, rather than in manufacturing. From 1985 to 1990, however, manufacturing accounted for 77% of all FDI in the region (Shen et al. 2000).

23. Each successful rapid-innovation-based development path leads to different outcomes in wealth distribution and overall economic growth (Breznitz 2007b). Compared with Beijing and Shanghai, the PRD has spread the fruits of its economic success more widely among the population, mainly because of the economy's reliance on rural communities, not just urban elites.

24. During our fieldwork, we found that factories engaging in plastic injection molding for electronic hardware cases or battery manufacture were relegated to areas outside the showcase industrial zones. These highly polluting industries are encouraged and welcomed as anchors for high-technology enterprises. However, they are not allowed within the new high-technology parks, since these seek to cultivate a more pristine image.

25. Beginning with the Open Cities policy in 1984 and the Coastal Development Area plan in 1985, the SEZs and creative local policy makers in Guangdong lost much of their distinctiveness in tax policy and export promotion. Today, across all three regions in our study, local administrators and entrepreneurs mentioned national tax policy and similar subsidies with a dismissive wave as they noted that these policies are now mostly uniform.

26. According to their municipal Web sites, both Shenzhen and Dongguan produce more than 90% of the necessary components for computer manufacturing.

27. In deference to central authority, local officials in the PRD did not describe their actions as making economic "policy" (政策), since only the national government makes policy. Local authorities have programs (规划) and provide support (支持). They are constrained by national policies and act within that framework. Support can include communication (沟通), research (研究), and training (培训) services (authors' interviews).

28. Analyzing the Shenzhen High-Tech Industrial Park, Susan Walcott (2003) found that the effect of alumni networks is apparent in the types of enterprises and branch companies established in the park.

29. The Shenzhen government raised two hundred million RMB from Baoan Airport, the local highway company, the Nengyuan Group, Yantian Port, the public bus company, and ZTE. The local government then ordered the Shenzhen Capital Group Company to invest in technology-intensive SMEs. However, aside from this general mandate, the local state has not attempted to control the company's investment patterns by restrict-

ing them to a given sector or even geographic region. Over time, the company's behavior has become more akin to that of a private-equity firm than a true VC firm, since it invests in more established enterprises rather than in first-stage start-ups. The company, the largest VC firm in China, invests across the country in order to follow its true mandate: "To make as much money for our shareholders as possible."

30. By comparison, Baidu's revenues were only 1.744 billion RMB in 2007 (Baidu 2008). QQ has become such a highly valued and recognized brand in China that the Chery Group decided to call their new compact car the QQ.

31. Harwit (2007) notes that Huawei and ZTE benefited from the indigenous development of the HJD-04 digital telecommunications switch in 1991. Also, many of the engineers and researchers trained through this project had worked for the Alcatel–Shanghai Bell joint venture. Many lured away from Shanghai Bell by offers of higher salaries formed the core of Huawei's and ZTE's research groups.

32. A volt-ampere is the standard unit for the capacity of a UPS system. For direct-current systems, it is the same as a watt. For alternating-current systems, the VA rating is higher than the number of watts the UPS is capable of putting out, since almost all systems contain inductors or capacitors that introduce reactance. The VA rating is usually about 60% of the number of watts. Hence, a UPS unit rated at 100,000 VA would be capable of an output of approximately 60,000 watts of power. For a UPS (which uses alternating current), the VA rating must be higher than the wattage the user expects it to output.

33. Throughout our interviews in the PRD, we were struck that the exact same explanation of innovation was given to us from both industry and government actors. Each and every time, the interviewee used one of the two prominent accessories of an interview setting in the PRD—teacups and ashtrays.

34. During our interviews in the PRD, we heard similar answers throughout the IT industry. For example, a manager of a company specializing in precision automation controls for machinery recounted the moment when management finally hit on the business model that led to their current success and planned IPO: "You know, we are all ex-university researchers, so at first we tried to design a technologically advanced and powerful product. But when we released it to the market, we found we had made a big mistake: the technology was too high-end for Chinese producers. It was too complex, and most of its features were not used by the customers. Since it was so advanced, the price was too high. After we learned from this mistake, we no longer aimed for novelty, just for slight improvements on earlier products, reliability, ease of use, and price."

35. China's central government radically loosened restrictions on loans from state banks as part of its economic stimulus package in late 2008 (*Economist* 2009a). A majority of the loans appear to have gone to SOEs and not to minying or light-industrial enterprises. Financial restraints remain a factor for minying enterprises in the PRD.

36. On the importance of social capital and trust for the creation of community-managed resources, investment, and credit pools, see the studies by Geertz (1962), Hechter (1987), and Ostrom (1990).

37. For those companies that do not use the prefabricated facilities provided by local authorities in their industrial parks, building housing attached to the factory is standard practice in Dongguan and throughout the PRD.

38. Leslie Chang, a journalist with the *Wall Street Journal* who followed migrant labor in Dongguan for three years, reported similar findings (2008). Her analysis claims that migrants have now become critical to enterprises at all levels and that they fill all but the highest management positions in most factories.

39. UPS firms noted that when they recruit the best talent, they have to offer a high salary, purchase housing in Dongguan for the prospect, and purchase housing for his or her family. If the family will not relocate, the company has to provide housing in their home city. We have found that the same system is used with some variation by many R&D-conducting OEM and ODM manufacturers throughout the PRD.

References

3mt. 2006. "*Ai Guo Zhe MP3: Ai Guo Zhe Sheng Chan Guang Shang Hua Qi Gong Si Huan Xin Ren Shi Shi Xin Zheng*" [Aigo MP3 Player: Aigo Manufacturing Company Huaqi Companies Changes Its Personality to Carry Out New Management] Shu Ma Shi Chang Diao Cha [Digital Market Survey], February 6, 2006. http://www.thethirdmedia.com/Article/200607/show40895c27p1.html (accessed on March 27, 2009).

Aghion, Philippe, and Peter Howitt. 1992. "A Model of Growth through Creative Destruction." *Econometrica* 60 (2): 323–351.

Agilent. 2006. "TD-SCDMA Market Evolution and Spec Update." Presentation given at *An Jie Lun Ke Ji TD-SCDMA Yan Tao Hui* [Agilent Technologies TD-SCDMA Discussion Meeting], October 13, 2006. Available at http://cp.literature.agilent.com/litweb/pdf/5989-5734ZHA.pdf.

Akamatsu, Kaname. 1962. "A Historical Pattern of Economic Growth in Developing Countries." *Developing Economies* 2:3–25.

Amsden, Alice. 1989. *Asia's Next Giant: South Korea and Late Industrialization.* Oxford: Oxford University Press.

———. 2001. *The Rise of "The Rest": Challenges to the West from Late-Industrializing Economies.* Oxford: Oxford University Press.

Amsden, Alice, and Wan-Wen Chu. 2003. *Beyond Late Development: Taiwan's Upgrading Policies.* Cambridge, Mass.: MIT Press.

Andreas, Joel. 2009. *Rise of the Red Engineers: The Cultural Revolution and the Origins of China's New Class.* Stanford, Calif.: Stanford University Press.

AP. 2007. "China to Be Third Largest Economy." *China Daily,* July 11, 2007. http://www.chinadaily.com.cn/china/2007–07/11/content_5433153.htm (accessed April 2,2009).

Arndt, Sven W., and Henryk Kierzkowski, eds. 2001. *Fragmentation: New Production Patterns in the World Economy.* Oxford: Oxford University Press.

Arora, Ashish, and Alfonso Gambardella, eds. 2005. *From Underdogs to Tigers: The Rise and Growth of the Software Industry in Some Emerging Economies.* New York: Oxford University Press.

Arora, Ashish, V. S. Arunachalarn, Jai Asundi, and Ronald Fernandes. 2001. "The Indian Software Services Industry." *Research Policy* 30(8):1267–1287.

Arora, Ashish, and Suma Athreye. 2002. "The Software Industry and India's Economic Development." *Information Economics and Policy* 14:253–273.

Arrow, J. Kenneth.1962. "Economic Welfare and the Allocation of Resources for Invention." In *The Rate and Direction of Inventive Activity: Economic and Social Factors,* ed. R. R. Nelson, 609–625. Princeton, N.J.: Princeton University Press.

AsiaInfo. 2003. "Shanghai in Need of Software Human Resources." AsiaInfo Services, September 8. http://www.highbeam.com/doc/1P1–79359000.html (accessed on April 2, 2009).

———. 2004. "Chinese HDV Alliance Established." SinoCast, May 10. http://www.highbeam.com/doc/1P1–94404822.html (accessed July 15, 2008).

———. 2007. "IBM Software Training Center Unveils in Shanghai." Sinocast, March 8. http://www.highbeam.com/doc/1P1–135788571.html (accessed January 13, 2009).

Avnimelech, Gil, and Morris Teubal. 2004. "Venture Capital Start-Up Co-Evolution and the Emergence and Development of Israel's New High Technology Cluster." *Economics of Innovation and New Technology* 13 (1): 33–60.

———. 2006. "Creating Venture Capital Industries that Co-Evolve with High Tech Clusters: Insights from an Extended Industry Life Cycle Perspective of the Israeli Experience." *Research Policy* 35 (10): 1477–1498.

Bachman, David. 2001. "Defense Industrialization in Guangdong." *China Quarterly* 166:273–304.

Baidu. 2008. "Baidu Announces Fourth Quarter and Fiscal Year 2007 Results." Press release, February 13. http://ir.baidu.com/phoenix.zhtml?c=188488&p=irol-newsArticle&ID=1108033&highlight= (accessed July 12, 2010).

Baldwin, Carliss Y., and Kim B. Clark. 1997. "Managing in an Age of Modularity." *Harvard Business Review* 75 (5): 84–93.

———. 2000. *Design Rules.* Vol. 1, *The Power of Modularity.* Cambridge, Mass.: MIT Press.

Bao, Daozu. 2008. "CPPCC Ends with Vow of Further Political Reform." *China Daily,* March 15, 2008.

Barnett, P. William. 2008. *The Red Queen among Organizations: How Competitiveness Evolves.* Princeton, N.J.: Princeton University Press.

Baum, Richard. 1994. *Burying Mao: Chinese Politics in the Age of Deng Xiaoping.* Princeton, N.J.: Princeton University Press.

Baumol, J. William. 1990. "Entrepreneurship: Productive, Unproductive, and Destructive." *Journal of Political Economy* 98 (5): 893–921.

———. 2002. *The Free-Market Innovation Machine: Analyzing the Growth Miracle of Capitalism.* Princeton, N.J.: Princeton University Press.

———. 2004. "Red-Queen Games: Arms Races, Rule of Law and Market Economies." *Journal of Evolutionary Economics* 14 (2): 237–247.

Baumol, J. William, Robert E. Litan, and Carl J. Schramm. 2007. *Good Capitalism, Bad Capitalism, and the Economics of Growth and Prosperity.* New Haven, Conn.: Yale University Press.

Berger, Suzanne. 2006. *How We Compete: What Companies around the World Are Doing to Make It in Today's Global Economy.* New York: Doubleday.

Berger, Suzanne, and K. Richard Lester, eds. 2005. *Global Taiwan: Building Competitive Strengths in the New Economy.* New York: Sharpe.

Besen, Stanley M., and Joseph Farrell. 1994. "Choosing How to Compete: Strategies and Tactics in Standardization." *Journal of Economic Perspectives* 8 (2): 117–131.

Bian, Yanjie. 1994. "Guanxi and the Allocation of Urban Jobs in China." *China Quarterly* 140:971–999.

Bishop, John. 2007. "3G: The Next Generation." *China International Business* (Beijing), July.

BJKW [Beijing Municipal Science and Technology Commission]. 2008. Beijing Startup Incubator Association. http://www.bjkw.gov.cn/n244495/n244682/2664927.html (accessed October 24, 2008).

Braczyk, Hans-Joachim, Philip Cooke, and Martin Heidenreich, eds. 1998. *Regional Innovation Systems: The Role of Governance in a Globalized World.* London: UCL Press.

Bradsher, Keith. 2008. "Investors Seek Asian Options to Costly China." *New York Times,* June 18, 2008. http://www.nytimes.com/2008/06/18/business/worldbusiness/18invest.html (accessed December 22, 2008).

Brain, Marshall, Jeff Tyson, and Julia Layton. 2008. "How Cell Phones Work." http://www.howstuffworks.com/cell-phone.htm (accessed March 26, 2009).

Bramall, Chris. 2003. "Path Dependency and Growth in Rural China since 1978." *Asian Business and Management* 2 (3): 301–321.

Breschi, S., and F. Malerba. 1997. "Sectoral Innovation Systems: Technological Regimes, Schumpeterian Dynamics, and Spatial Boundaries." In *System of Innovation: Technologies, Institutions and Organizations,* ed. C. Edquist, 130–156. London: Pinter.

Breznitz, Dan. 2005a. "Development, Flexibility, and R&D Performance in the Taiwanese IT Industry—Capability Creation and the Effects of State-Industry Co-Evolution." *Industrial and Corporate Change* 14 (1): 153–187.

———. 2005b. "Innovation and the Limits of State Power: IC Design and Software in Taiwan." In *Global Taiwan,* ed. S. Berger and R. Lester, 194–227. New York: Sharpe.

———. 2005c. "Software Tooling: The Development of the Israeli Software Industry." In *From Underdogs to Tigers: The Software Industry in Emerging Countries,* ed. A. Arora and A. Gambardella, 72–98. New York: Oxford University Press.

———. 2006. "Innovation-Based Industrial Policy in Emerging Economies? The Case of Israel's IT Industry." *Business and Politics* 8 (3): Article 3: 1–38.

————. 2007a. "Industrial R&D as a National Policy: Horizontal Technology Policies and Industry-State Co-Evolution in the Growth of the Israeli Software Industry." *Research Policy* 36 (9): 1465–1482.

————. 2007b. *Innovation and the State: Political Choice and Strategies for Growth in Israel, Taiwan, and Ireland.* New Haven, Conn.: Yale University Press.

Brown, C., and G. Linden. 2005. "Offshoring in the Semiconductor Industry: A Historical Perspective." Paper presented at Brookings Trade Forum on Offshoring of White-Collar Work, Washington, D.C., May 12–13.

BSB. 2008. *2007 Nian Bei Jing Shi Guo Min Jing Ji He She Hui Fa Zhan Tong Ji Gong Bao* [2007 Beijing City People's Economic and Social Development Statistics Report]. Beijing: Beijing City Bureau of Statistics.

Budde, Paul. 2008. "China—Mobile Market—Overview & Statistics." http://www.budde.com.au/buddereports/3772/China-Mobile-Market-Overview-Statistics.html (accessed June 16, 2008).

Burns, John P. 1987. "China's Nomenklatura System." *Problems of Communism* 36 (5): 36–51.

————. 1994. "Strengthening Central CCP Control of Leadership Selection: The 1990 Nomenklatura." *China Quarterly* 138:458–491.

Business Wire. 2002. "Alcatel Shanghai Bell Is Officially Launched Today; Integration of Alcatel's Key Operations in China with Shanghai Bell in Only Seven Months." Business Wire, May 28, 2002 http://www.highbeam.com/doc/1G1-86392080.html (accessed February 16, 2009).

————. 2003. "Datang Mobile, Philips and Samsung Form Joint Venture to Deliver Cellular TD-SCDMA Chipset & Reference Design." Business Wire, January 20, 2003. http://www.allbusiness.com/electronics/computer-electronics/5673690-1.html (accessed September 12, 2008).

————. 2006. "China's Largest Manufacturers in the Semiconductor Industry Account for $22.5 Billion." Business Wire, January 19, 2006. http://www.allbusiness.com/electronics/electronics-overview/5362363-1.html (accessed February 17, 2009).

C114. 2005. "Homegrown SCDMA System More Popular." C114.net, December 6, 2005. http://www.cn-c114.net/582/a307939.html (accessed April 2, 2009).

CA800. 2008. "*2007 Nian Dian Yuan Hang Ye Fen Xi Bao Gao—Wo Guo UPS Dian Yuan Hang Ye Xian Zhuang Zong Shu*" [2007 Power Supply Industry Analysis Report—China's UPS Power Supply Industry Summary Situation]. CA800.com, March 23, 2008. http://www.ca800.com/news/html/2008-3-26/n80767.html. (accessed March 23, 2008).

Cai, Hongbin, and Daniel Treisman. 2006. "Did Government Decentralization Cause China's Economic Miracle?" *World Politics* 58:505–535.

Cao, Cong. 2004. "Zhongguancun and China's High-Tech Parks in Transition." *Asian Survey* 44 (5): 647–688.

Cao, Cong, Richard P. Suttmeier, and Dennis Fred Simon. 2006. "China's 15-Year Science and Technology plan." *Physics Today* 59 (12): 38–43.

Carlsson, Bo, Steffan Jacobsson, Magnus Holmén, and Annika Rickne. 2002. "Innovation Systems: Analytical and Methodological Issues." *Research Policy* 31:233–245.

Carroll, Lewis. 2001. [1872]. *Through the Looking-Glass and What Alice Found There.* Boston, Mass: Adamant Media.

CAS [Chinese Academy of Sciences]. 2008. "Founding and Building Up (1949–1955)." Chinese Academy of Sciences. August 26, 2009. http://english.cas.cn/ACAS/history/200908/t20090826_34227.shtml(accessed June 11,2010).

CATR [China Academy of Telecommunication Research]. 2008. "Profile." China Academy of Telecommunication Research of MII. http://www.catr.cn/english/profile.php (accessed June 17, 2008).

CCP [Chinese Communist Party]. 2007. Constitution of the Communist Party of China. Beijing.

CEIBS [China Europe International Business School]. 2008. "MOU Signed for Establishing the CEIBS Zhangjiang Centre for Innovative Entrepreneurship." China Europe International Business School. May 12, 2008. http://www.ceibs.edu/media/archive/27890.shtml (accessed January 29, 2009).

Chang, L. Shirley. 1992. "Causes of Brain-Drain and Solutions: The Taiwan Experience." *Studies in Comparative International Development* 27 (1): 27–43.

Chang, Leslie T. 2008. *Factory Girls: From Village to City in a Changing China.* New York: Spiegel and Grau.

Chao, Chien-Min. 2003. "The National People's Congress Oversight Power and the Role of the CCP." *Copenhagen Journal of Asian Studies* 17:6–30.

Chen, Jinqiao. 2003. "China: The History of Telecom Reform and the Future of the Telecom Regulation." Paper presented at the Third Asia Pacific Forum on Telecommunications Policy and Regulation, Bangkok, Thailand.

Chen, Kun, and Martin Kenney. 2007. "Universities/Research Institutes and Regional Innovation Systems: The Cases of Beijing and Shenzhen." *World Development* 35 (6): 1056–1074.

Chen, Ling. 2005. "*Zhi Du, Jing Ying Yu Gong Shi: Zhong Guo Ji Cheng Dian Lu Chan Ye Zheng Ce Guo Cheng Yan Jiu*" [Institution, Elites, and Consensus: The Policy Process of China's Semiconductor Industrial Policies]. PhD diss., School of Public Policy and Management, Tsinghua University, Beijing.

———. 2008. "Bureaucratic System and Negotiation Network: A Theoretical Framework for China's Industrial Policy." Working paper, School of Public Policy and Management, Tsinghua University, Beijing.

Chen, Qian, and Shenshen Zhu. 2008. "City to Train 10,000 Software Developers." *Shanghai Daily,* July 1, 2008. http://www.shanghaidaily.com/sp/article/2008/200807/20080701/article_365246.htm (accessed April 2, 2009).

Chen, S. H. 2006. "The National Innovation System and Global R&D Strategies: The Case of Taiwan." Paper presented at the conference R&D Interplay in Northeast Asia: A Global Corporate Strategy and Host Countries' National Innovation System, Seoul, South Korea.

Chen, S. H., and Y. C. Chen. 2006. "MNCs' Offshore R&D Mandates and Host Countries' Locational Advantages: A Comparison between Taiwan and China." Taipei, Taiwan.

Cheng, Tun-jen. 1990. "Political Regimes and Developmental Strategies: South Korea and Taiwan." In *Manufacturing Miracles,* ed. G. Gereffi and D. Wyman, 139–178. Princeton, N.J.: Princeton University Press.

Chibber, Vivek. 2002. "Bureaucratic Rationality and the Developmental State." *American Journal of Sociology* 107 (4): 951–989.

Chien, Shiuh-Shen. 2007. "Institutional Innovations, Asymmetric Decentralization and Local Economic Development: A Case Study of Kunshan, in Post-Mao China." *Environment and Planning C: Government and Policy* 25: 269–290.

China Customs. 2007. *2007 Nian Wo Guo Ji Cheng Dian Lu Jing Jin Kou Zhi Chao Guo Qian Yi Mei Yuan, Ji Dai Jia Qiang He Ti Gao Zi Zhu Chaung Xin Neng Li* [2007 China IC Imports Exceed 100 Billion USD, Urgently Strengthen and Raise Indigenous Innovation Ability]. Beijing: China General Administration of Customs Press.

China Daily. 2006. "Review of China's Foreign Capital Utilization Situation and Prospect of 2005–2006." March 22. http://www.chinadaily.com.cn/Investment/2006–03/22/content_549795_2.htm (accessed April 2, 2009).

———. 2007. "Guangdong Govt May Help Toy Makers Sue Mattel." November 6. http://english.peopledaily.com.cn/90001/6297106.html (accessed April 2, 2009).

China Development Gateway. 2004. "Planning: Torch Program." China Development Gateway. http://en.chinagate.com.cn/english/446.htm. (accessed August 8, 2008).

China Mobile. 2008. "Directors & Senior Management." China Mobile Ltd. http://www.chinamobileltd.com/about.php?menu=2 (accessed June 16, 2008).

China Telecom. 2010. "Corporate Governance: Supervisory Committee." http://www.chinatelecom-h.com/eng/company/supervisory.htm (accessed August 8, 2010).

China Torch. 2008. "Huo Ju Zhong Xin Jian Jie" [Torch Center Introduction]. China Torch. http://www.chinatorch.gov.cn/intr/index.html (accessed April 10, 2008).

China Unicom. 2006. "Item 6. Directors, Senior Management and Employees." http://sec.edgar-online.com/2006/06/29/0001104659–06–044306/Section9.asp (accessed June 17, 2008).

———. 2008a. "Further Suspension and Change of Directors." Press release, May 25. http://www.chinaunicom.com.hk/files/doc/news-2008/a052500-en.pdf.

———. 2008b. "Corporate Governance." http://www.chinaunicom.com.hk/en/corpgover/Board.html (accessed June 16, 2008).

China Vitae. 2008. "Xi Guohua—Career Data." China Vitae. http://www.chinaunicom.com.hk/en/corgover/gov_bod.html (accessed January 22, 2009).

Chuang, Liu, Yao Xurong, and William Lavely. 1990. "China Administrative Regions GIS Data: 1:1M, County Level." Consortium for International Earth Science Information Network [CIESN]. ftp://ftpserver.ciesin.org/pub/data/China/adm_bnd/CTSAR90.bnd 90/ (accessed February 5, 2009).

Chung, Yousun. 2002. "Anatomy of the Decision-Making Process in China: (De)Concentration of the Internet Industry." Thesis, Graduate School of International Studies, Seoul National University, Seoul. http://gsis.snu.ac.kr/studata/0202thesis_ysjeong.pdf (accessed August 8, 2010).

CIC [China IntelliConsulting Corporation]. 2008. "China Search Engine Survey Report 2008 Released: Baidu Market Share Slightly Slips While Managing Great Lead over Google." September 16. http://www.iaskchina.cn/en/Report/view/id/13 (accessed August 8, 2010).

Clendenin, Mike. 2006. "China Taps U.S. Partner to Keep EVD Standards." EE Times India. http://www.eetindia.co.in/ART_8800407147_1800010_NT_32a4d728.HTM (accessed June 27, 2008).

Cn18dao.com. 2010. "*Di Tu Ji Jin/Han Dian Qu*" [Map Collection/Haidian District]. http://cn .18dao.net/%E5%9C%B0%E5%9B%BE%E9%9B%86%E9%94%A6/%E6%B5%B7% E6%B7%80%E5%8C%BA (accessed August 8, 2010).

CNN. 2002. "Verizon Launches First U.S. '3G' Network." CNN.com. January 28. http:// edition.cnn.com/2002/TECH/ptech/01/28/verizon.3g/index.html (accessed July 21, 2008).

Coleman, S. James. 1988. "Social Capital in the Creation of Human Capital." *American Journal of Sociology* 94 (issue supplement: "Organizations and Institutions: Sociological and Economic Approaches to the Analysis of Social Structure"): S95-S120.

CRN [*China Review News*]. 2008. "Dong Guan Gong Ren Gong Zi Bao Sheng, Pin Tiao Cao, Gang Qi San Zhao Liu Ren" [Dongguan's Industrial Worker Wage Increases, Frequent Job Changes—Three Hong Kong Enterprise Perspectives]. January 9. http://gb .chinareviewnews.com/doc/1005/3/8/7/100538773.html?coluid=2&kindid=0&docid= 100538773&mdate=0109100019 (accessed January 19, 2009).

CTN [China Tech News]. 2003. "VP5 And VP6 to Be Included in China's EVD Standard." November 18. http://www.chinatechnews.com/2003/11/18/105-vp5-and-vp6-to-be-included-in-chinas-evd-standard/ (accessed June 27, 2008).

———. 2004a. "HVD Alliance Established by 19 Enterprises." April 30. http://www.china technews.com/2004/04/30/1201-hvd-alliance-established-by-19-enterprises/ (accessed July 15, 2008).

———. 2004b. "HDV and HVD Hold Secret Discussions over EVD's Fate." December 8. http://www.chinatechnews.com/2004/12/08/2113-hdv-and-hvd-hold-secret-discussions-over-evds-fate/ (accessed July 15, 2008).

———. 2007. "Intel's Dalian Wafer Fabrication Facility Plans 2010 Opening." September 11. http://www.chinatechnews.com/2007/09/11/5868-intels-dalian-wafer-fabrication-facility-plans-2010-opening/ (accessed March 18, 2009).

———. 2008a. "Foxconn Moves Factory to Northern China to Reduce Costs." June 26. http://www.chinatechnews.com/2008/06/26/6924-foxconn-moves-factory-to-northern-china-to-reduce-costs/ (accessed October 27, 2008).

———. 2008b. "SMIC Introduces Strategic Investors." March 26. http://www.chinatech news.com/2008/03/26/6541-smic-introduces-strategic-investors/ (accessed February 17, 2009).

———. 2008c. "Two Illegal Datang Subsidiary Base Stations Closed." July 24. http://www .chinatechnews.com/2008/07/24/7055-two-illegal-datang-subsidiary-base-stations-closed / (accessed December 29, 2008).

———. 2009a. "Chips Are Down for China's SMIC." February 6. http://www.chinatech news.com/2009/02/06/8691-chips-are-down-for-chinas-smic/ (accessed February 16, 2009).

———. 2009b. "Intel to Relocate Shanghai Manufacturing Plant." February 9. http://www .chinatechnews.com/2009/02/09/8711-intel-to-relocate-shanghai-manufacturing-plant/ (accessed March 18, 2009).

———. 2009c. "SMIC Signs Cooperative Agreement with Datang." January 12. http://www .chinatechnews.com/2009/01/12/8469-smic-signs-cooperative-agreement-with-datang/ (accessed February 17, 2009).

Cusumano, Michael A., Yiorgos Mylonadis, and Richard S. Rosenbloom. 1992. "Strategic Maneuvering and Mass-Market Dynamics: The Triumph of VHS over Beta." *Business History Review* 66 (1): 51–95.

Cyranoski, David. 2004. "Biologists Lobby China's Government for Funding Reform." *Nature* 430 (6999):495.

D'Costa, Anthony P., and E. Sridharan, eds. 2004. *India in the Global Software Industry: Innovation, Firm Strategies, and Development*. Basingstoke, UK: Palgrave Macmillan.

Datang. 2007. "*Da Tang Dian Xin Ke Ji Chan Ye Ji Tuan—Dian Xin Ke Ji Shu Yan Jiu Yuan*" [Datang Telecommunications Technology and Industry Group—Telecommunications Science and Technology Research Institute]. http://www.catt.ac.cn/english/portfolio.asp (accessed June 17, 2008).

Dean, Jason. 2007. "The Forbidden City of Terry Gou, the Biggest Exporter You Never Heard Of." *Wall Street Journal*, August 11.

Dedrick, Jason, Kenneth L. Kraemer, and Greg Linden. 2008. "Who Profits from Innovation in Global Value Chains? A Study of the iPod and Notebook PCs." Paper presented at the Alfred P. Sloan Foundation Industry Studies conference, Boston, Mass., May 1–2.

Derfus, J. Pamela , G. Patrick Maggitti, Curtis M. Grimm, and Ken G. Smith. 2008. "The Red Queen Effect: Competitive Actions and Firm Performance." *Academy of Management Journal* 51(1): 61–80.

DeWoskin, Kenneth J. 2001. "The WTO and the Telecommunications Sector in China." *China Quarterly* 167:630–654.

Doner, Richard F. 2009. *The Politics of Uneven Development*. Cambridge: Cambridge University Press.

Dosi, Giovanni. 1982. "Technological Paradigms and Technological Trajectories: A Suggested Interpretation of the Determinants and Direction of Technical Change." *Research Policy* 11:147–163.

Dossani, Rafiq, and Martin Kenney. 2003. "'Lift and Shift': Moving the Back Office to India." *Information Technologies and International Development* 1 (2): 21–37.

———. 2007. "The Next Wave of Globalization: Relocating Service Provision to India." *World Development* 35 (5): 772–791.

DSB [Dongguan Statistics Bureau]. 2008. *2007 Nian Dong Guan Shi Guo Min Jing Ji He She Hui Fa Zhan Tong Ji Gong Bao* [2007 Dongguan City People's Economic and Social Development Statistics Report]. Dongguan, China.

Economist. 2007. Plenty of Blame to Go Around: Mattel Tries to Rescue Its Relationship with Its Chinese Suppliers." September 27.

———. 2009a. "China Is Spending to Recover." June 1. http://www.economist.com/agenda/displaystory.cfm?story_id=13765331&fsrc=twitter (accessed July 30, 2009).

———. 2009b. "The More the Merrier: China and India Are Creating Millions of Entrepreneurs." May 12.

Edquist, Charles, ed. 1997. *Systems of Innovation: Technologies, Institutions, and Organizations*. London: Pinter.

EEO [Economic Observer Online]. 2008. "China's Telecom Firms in the Post-Restructuring Era." Economic Observer Online.com.cn. http://www.eeo.com.cn/ens//Industry/2008/06/12/102852.html (accessed June 16, 2008).

Elegant, Simon. 2007. "China Gets a Property Rights Law." *Time,* March 16.

Eng, Irene. 1997. "The Rise of Manufacturing Towns: Externally Driven Industrialization and Urban Development in the Pearl River Delta of China." *International Journal of Urban and Regional Research* 21 (4): 554–568.

Ernst, Dieter. 2005. "Complexity and Internationalisation of Innovation: Why Is Chip Design Moving to Asia?" *International Journal of Innovation Management* 9 (1): 47–73.

Ernst, Dieter, and Barry Naughton. 2007. "China's Emerging Industrial Economy—Insights from the IT Industry." In *China's Emergent Political Economy: Capitalism in the Dragon's Lair,* ed. C. A. McNally, 47–73. London: Routledge.

Eun, Jong-Hak, Keun Lee, and Guisheng Wu. 2006. "Explaining the 'University-Run Enterprises' in China: A Theoretical Framework for University-Industry Relationship in Developing Countries and Its Application to China." *Research Policy* 35: 1329–1346.

Fan, Peilei. 2006. "Catching Up through Developing Innovation Capability: Evidence from China's Telecom-Equipment Industry." *Technovation* 26:359–368.

Fei, Lai. 2009. "Help for Graduate Entrepreneurs." Shanghai Daily, January 9. http://www.shanghaidaily.com/sp/article/2009/200901/20090109/article_387465.htm (accessed April 2, 2009).

Feng, Yimin. 1995. "Direct Foreign Investment from Hong Kong into Guangdong Province: Motivations for Investing." *Berkeley McNair Journal* 3.

Fields, Karl. 1995. *Enterprise and the State in Korea and Taiwan.* Ithaca, N.Y.: Cornell University Press.

Fligstein, N. 1990. *The Transformation of Corporate Control.* Cambridge, Mass.: Harvard University Press.

Florida, Richard L. 1995. "Toward the Learning Region." *Futures* 27 (5): 527–536.

Frauenheim, Ed. 2004. "Report: China's Next-Generation DVD Faces Hurdles." CNET News. January 29. http://news.cnet.com/Report-Chinas-next-generation-DVD-faces-hurdles/2100-1041_3-5150373.html (accessed June 13, 2010).

Fu, Jing. 2008. "Shenzhen Zen: Fishing Village Turned Boomtown." *China Daily,* August 4. http://www.chinadaily.com.cn/home/2008-08/04/content_6901116.htm (accessed January 16, 2009).

Fuller, Douglas B. 2005a. "The Changing Limits and the Limits of Change: The State, Private Firms, International Industry and China in the Evolution of Taiwan's Electronics Industry." *Journal of Contemporary China* 14 (4): 483–506.

———. 2005b. "Building Ladders Out of Chains: China's Technological Upgrading in a World of Global Production." PhD diss., MIT.

———. 2007. "Globalization for Nation-Building: Taiwan's Industrial and Technology Policies for the High-Technology Sectors." *Journal of Interdisciplinary Economics* 18 (2): 203–224.

Fuller, Douglas B, Akintunde Akinwande, and Charles G. Sodini. 2003. "Leading, Following, or Cooked Goose: Successes and Failures in Taiwan's Electronics Industry." *Industry and Innovation* 10 (2): 179–196.

Funding Universe. 2008. "China Telecom." http://www.fundinguniverse.com/company-histories/China-Telecom-Company-History.html (accessed June 17, 2008).

Galvin, P., and A. Morkel. 2001. "The Effects of Product Modularity on Industry Structure: The Case of the World Bicycle Industry." *Industry and Innovation* 8 (1): 31–47.

Garon, Sheldon, and Mike Mochizuki. 1993. "Negotiating Social Contracts." In *Postwar Japan as History*, ed. Andrew Gordon, 145–166. Berkeley and Los Angeles: University of California Press.

Garver, John W. 1993. *Foreign Relations of the People's Republic of China*. Upper Saddle River, N.J.: Prentice Hall.

Ge, Wei. 1999. *Special Economic Zones and the Economic Transition in China*. Hackensack, N.J.: World Scientific.

Geertz, Clifford. 1962. "The Rotating Credit Association: A 'Middle Rung' in Development." *Economic Development and Social Change* 10 (3): 241–263.

Gereffi, Gary, John Humphrey, and Timothy Sturgeon. 2005. "The Governance of Global Value Chains." *Review of International Political Economy* 12 (1): 78–104.

Gerschenkron, Alexander. 1962. *Economic Backwardness in Historical Perspective: A Book of Essays*. Cambridge, Mass.: Harvard University Press.

Global Sources. 2005. *UPS—China Sourcing Report*. Singapore.

Gold, Thomas B. 1985. "After Comradeship: Personal Relations in China since the Cultural Revolution." *China Quarterly* 104:657–675.

Gold, Thomas B., Doug Guthrie, and David L. Wank, eds. 2002. *Social Connections in China: Institutions, Culture, and the Changing Nature of "Guanxi."* Cambridge: Cambridge University Press.

Gourevitch, Peter. 2000. "Globalization of Production: Insights from the Hard Drive Disk Industry." *World Development* 28 (2): 301–317.

Grivolas, Julien. 2003. "The Chinese Telecoms Equipment Market." *Communications and Strategies* 52:71–90.

GSB [Guangdong Statistics Bureau]. 2008. 2007. *Nian Guang Dong Guo Min Jing Ji He She Hui Fa Zhan Tong Ji Gong Bao* [2007 Guangdong People's Economic and Social Development Statistics Report]. Guangzhou, China.

Guardian. 2007. "New Law Strengthens China's Private Property Rights." March 16. http://www.guardian.co.uk/world/2007/mar/16/china (accessed July 7, 2008).

Guo, Wanda, and Yueqiu Feng. 2007. *Special Economic Zones and Competitiveness: A Case Study of Shenzhen, the People's Republic of China*. PRM Policy Note, series no. 2. Islamabad: Pakistan Resident Mission, Asian Development Bank.

Guthrie, Doug. 1998. "The Declining Significance of Guanxi in China's Economic Transition." *China Quarterly* 154:254–282.

———. 2002. *Dragon in a Three-Piece Suit: The Emergence of Capitalism in China*. Princeton, N.J.: Princeton University Press.

Harwit, Eric. 2005. "Telecommunications and the Internet in Shanghai: Political and Economic Factors Shaping the Network in a Chinese City." *Urban Studies* 42 (10): 1837–1858.

———. 2007. "Building China's Telecommunications Network: Industrial Policy and the Role of Chinese State-Owned, Foreign and Private Domestic Enterprises." *China Quarterly* 190:311–332.

Hechter, Michael. 1987. *Principles of Group Solidarity*. Berkeley and Los Angeles: University of California Press.

Helpman, Elhanan, ed. 1998. *General Purpose Technologies and Economic Growth*. Cambridge, Mass: MIT Press.

Helpman, Elhanan, and Manuel Trajtenberg. 1998. "A Time to Sow and a Time to Reap: Growth Based on General Purpose Technologies." In *General Purpose Technologies and Economic Growth,* ed. E. Helpman, 55–84. Cambridge: Mass: MIT Press.

Herrigel, Gary. 1996. *Industrial Constructions: The Sources of German Industrial Power.* Cambridge: Cambridge University Press.

HKCH [Hong Kong–China–Hawaii Chamber of Commerce]. 2004. "Special Report— China—Northeast." Hong Kong–China–Hawaii Chamber of Commerce. October 14. http://www.hkchcc.org/chinanortheast.htm (accessed June 17, 2008).

HKTDC [Hong Kong Trade Development Council]. 2007a. *Market Profiles of Chinese Cities and Provinces: Beijing.* Hong Kong: Hong Kong Trade Development Council.

———. 2007b. *Market Profiles of Chinese Cities and Provinces: Shanghai Municipality.* Hong Kong: Hong Kong Trade Development Council.

Holz, Carsten A. 2007. "Have China Scholars All Been Bought?" *Far Eastern Economic Review* 170 (3): 36–40.

Hong, Sung Gul. 1997. *The Political Economy of Industrial Policy in East Asia: The Semiconductor Industry in Taiwan and South Korea.* Cambridge: Edward Elgar.

Hong, Wen. 2003. "An Assessment of the Business Environment for High-Tech Industrial Development in Shanghai." *Environment and Planning C: Government and Policy* 21:107–137.

Hooper, Beverley. 1986. *China Stands Up.* Singapore: Singapore National Printers.

HSB [Haidian Statistics Bureau]. 2008. *Hai Dian Qu 2007 Nian Guo min Jing Ji He She Hui Fa Zhan Tong Ji Gong Bao* [Haidian District 2007 Citizens' Economic and Social Development Statistics Report]. Beijing: Haidian Statistical Information Net.

Hsing, Y. 1996. "Blood, Thicker than Water: Interpersonal Relations and Taiwanese Investment in Southern China." *Environment and Planning A* 28 (12): 2241–2261.

Hu, Jintao. 2007a. *Hu Jin Tao Zai Dang De Shi Qi Da Shang De Bao Gao (Quan Wen): Ba, Jia Kuai Tui Jin Yi Gai Shan Min Sheng Wei Zhong Dian De She Hui Jian She* [Full Text of Hu Jintao's Report at the Seventeenth Party Congress: Part Eight, Accelerating Social Development with the Focus on Improving People's Livelihood]. Beijing.

———. 2007b. "Hold High the Great Banner of Socialism with Chinese Characteristics and Strive for New Victories in Building a Moderately Prosperous Society in All Respects." Speech by Hu Jintao to the Seventeenth National Congress, October 15. http://www.china elections.net/newsinfo.asp?newsid=12146 (accessed April 2, 2009).

———. 2007c. *Hu Jin Tao Zai Dang De Shi Qi Da Shang De Bao Gao (Quan Wen): San, Shen Ru Guan Che Luo Shi Ke Xue Fa Zhan Guan* [Full Text of Hu Jintao's Report at the 17th Party Congress: Part Three, Thoroughly Applying the Scientific Outlook on Development]. Beijing.

Huang, Yasheng. 2003. *Selling China: Foreign Direct Investment during the Reform Era.* Cambridge: Cambridge University Press.

———. 2008. *Capitalism with Chinese Characteristics: Entrepreneurship and the State.* Cambridge: Cambridge University Press.

Huang, Yasheng, and Yi Qian. 2008. "Is Entrepreneurship Missing in Shanghai?" Paper presented at the National Bureau of Economic Research conference "International Differences in Entrepreneurship," February 1–2, Savannah, Georgia. http://web.mit.edu/polisci /research/cpol/Huang%202_14_08.pdf (accessed August 8, 2010).

IHT [*International Herald Tribune*]. 2006. "OECD Says China Overtaking Japan in Research Spending." December 4.

Interfax. 2006. "'Father of SCDMA' dismissed as Xinwei Telecom President." C114.com. September 30. http://www.cn-c114.net/582/a310355.html (accessed December 29, 2008).

ISO [International Organization for Standardization]. 2008. "How ISO Develops Standards." International Organization for Standardization. http://www.iso.org/iso/about /how_iso_develops_standards.htm (accessed July 21, 2008).

ITU [International Telecommunication Union]. 2007. "Top 20 Telecommunication Operators—Ranked by Revenue, 1998." International Telecommunication Union. http://www .itu.int/ITU-D/ict/statistics/at_glance/topptor_1998.html (accessed June 16, 2008).

Jiang, Xianhong. 2007. "*Dui Xiang Zhen Qi Ye Di Wei Zuo Yong Zai Ren Shi*" [Concerning the Position and Purpose of Township and Village Enterprises]. China Modern Enterprises. September 21. http://xqj.gzlps.gov.cn/art/2008/8/15/art_5922_43551.html (accessed December 22, 2008).

Jin, Hehui, Yingyi Qian, and Barry R. Weingast. 1999. "Regional Decentralization and Fiscal Incentives: Federalism, Chinese Style." *Journal of Public Economics* 89 (9–10): 1719–1742.

Johnson, Chalmers A. 1982. *MITI and the Japanese Miracle: The Growth of Industrial Policy, 1925–1975.* Stanford, Calif.: Stanford University Press.

Kennedy, Scott. 1997. "The Stone Group: State Client or Market Pathbreaker?" *China Quarterly* 152:746–777.

———. 2005. *The Business of Lobbying in China.* Cambridge, Mass.: Harvard University Press.

———. 2006. "The Political Economy of Standards Coalitions: Explaining China's Involvement in High-Tech Standards Wars." *Asia Policy* 2:41–62.

———. 2007a. "Capitalists in the Capital: Institutionalizing Informal Business Lobbying in China." Paper presented at the International Conference on the State Capacity of China in the 21st Century, Hong Kong.

———. 2007b. "Transnational Political Alliances: An Exploration with Evidence from China." *Business and Society* 46 (2): 174–200.

———. 2009. "Comparing Formal and Informal Lobbying Practices in China." *China Information* 23 (2): 195–222.

Kenney, Martin. (2000) *Understanding Silicon Valley: The Anatomy of an Entrepreneurial Region.* Stanford, Calif.: Stanford University Press.

Kenney, Martin, and Richard L. Florida. 2004. *Locating Global Advantage: Industry Dynamics in the International Economy.* Stanford, Calif.: Stanford University Press.

Kim, Linsu. 1997. *Imitation to Innovation: The Dynamics of Korea's Technological Learning.* Cambridge, Mass.: Harvard Business School Press.

Kioskea. 2008. "Mobile Telephony." http://en.kioskea.net/contents/telephonie-mobile/reseaux -mobiles.php3 (accessed March 26, 2009).

Kong, Qianjiang. 2000. "China's WTO Accession: Commitments and Implications." *Journal of International Economic Law* 3 (4): 655–690.

Kroeber, Arthur. 2007. "China's Push to Innovate in Information Technology." In *Innova-*

tion with Chinese Characteristics: High-Tech Research in China, ed. L. Jakobson, 37–70. New York: Palgrave Macmillan.

Krugman, Paul. 1979. "A Model of Innovation, Technology Transfer, and the World Distribution of Income." *Journal of Political Economy* 87 (2): 253–266.

Kushida, Kenji E. 2008. "Wireless Bound and Unbound: The Politics Shaping Cellular Markets in Japan and South Korea." *Journal of Information Technology and Politics* 5 (2): 231–254.

Kushida, Kenji Erik, and John Zysman. 2009. "The Services Transformation and Network Policy: The New Logic of Value Creation." *Review of Policy Research* 26 (1–2): 173–194.

Langlois, Richard N. 2002. "Modularity in Technology and Organization." *Journal of Economic Behavior and Organization* 49 (1): 19–37.

Langlois, Richard N., and Paul L. Robertson. 1992. "Networks and Innovation in a Modular System: Lessons from the Microcomputer and Stereo Component Industries." *Research Policy* 21:297–313.

LaPedus, Mark. 2006. "SMIC Tops Chartered in '05 Foundry Rankings." EE Times Asia, March 28. http://www.eetasia.com/ART_8800412152_480200_NT_24aabfoe.HTM (accessed February 16, 2009).

Lawson, Clive, and Edward Lorenz. 1999. "Collective Learning, Tacit Knowledge and Regional Innovative Capacity." *Regional Studies* 33 (4): 305–317.

Lemon, Summer. 2008a. "China Announces Telecom Restructuring, Clearing Way for 3G." *PC World,* May 25. http://www.pcworld.com/businesscenter/article/146297/china_announces_telecom_restructuring_clearing_way_for_3g.html (accessed August 8, 2010).

———. 2008b. "Troubled SMIC Gets Lifeline from China's Datang." MIS Asia. November 12. http://www.mis-asia.com/news/articles/troubled-smic-gets-lifeline-from-chinas-datang (accessed February 16, 2009).

Lenovo. 2008. "Company History." http://www.pc.ibm.com/ca/about_lenovo/company history.html (accessed October 1, 2008).

Lester, Richard K., and Michael J. Piore. 2004. *Innovation: The Missing Dimension.* Cambridge, Mass.: Harvard University Press.

Levi-Faur, David. 1998. "The Developmental State: Israel, South Korea, and Taiwan Compared." *Studies in Comparative International Development* 33 (1): 65–93.

Li, Cheng. 2006. "China's Telecom Industry on the Move: Domestic Competition, Global Ambition, and Leadership Transition." *China Leadership Monitor* 19. http://media.hoover.org/documents/clm19_cl.pdf (accessed June 13, 2010).

Li, Jonsson Yinya. 2005. *Investing in China: The Emerging Venture Capital Industry.* London: GMB Publishing.

Li, Nanling. 2005. "'*Shen Zhen Su Du' Zhang Xian Xiao Ping 'Fa Zhan Cai Shi Ying Dao Li' Li Lun*" ['Shenzhen Speed' Manifests Xiaoping's 'Development Is the Only Hard Justification' Theory]. Renmin Wang. August 25. http://news.163.com/05/0825/16/1S118KL400011247.html (accessed April 2, 2009).

Li, Weitao. 2005. "TD-SCDMA Insiders Say Trial Went Badly." *China Daily,* June 22. http://www.chinadaily.com.cn/english/doc/2005-06/22/content_453509.htm (accessed April 2, 2009).

Li, Xinran, and Lai Fei. 2009. "Graduates Still Want High Pay despite Economic Down-

turn." *Shanghai Daily,* January 15. http://www.shanghaidaily.com/sp/article/2009/200901
/20090115/article_388138.htm (accessed April 2, 2009).

Lieberthal, Kenneth. 2004. *Governing China: From Revolution through Reforms.* 2nd ed. New
York: Norton.

Lieberthal, Kenneth, and Michel Oksenberg. 1988. *Policy Making in China: Leaders, Structures, and Processes.* Princeton: Princeton University Press.

Lin, Nan. 1995. "Local Market Socialism: Local Corporatism in Action in Rural China."
Theory and Society 24 (2): 301–354.

Lin, Qiang. 2003. "The Development of ZTE & PHS." ZTE Corporation. http://www
.phsmou.org/events/GMMaterials/ZTEIntroduction.pdf (accessed March 26, 2009).

Lin, Ying. 2004. "The Political Basis of China's Telecom Reform: A Bureaucratic Interest-
Group Model." Paper presented at the annual meeting of the Western Political Science
Association, May 11–13, Portland, Oregon.

Linden, Greg. 2004. "China Standard Time: A Study in Strategic Industrial Policy." *Business and Politics* 6 (3). http://www.bepress.com/bap/vol6/iss3/art4.

Linden, Greg, Clair Brown, and Melissa Appleyard. 2004. "The Net World Order's Influence on Global Leadership in the Semiconductor Industry." In *Locating Global Advantage: Industry Dynamics in the International Economy,* ed. M. Kenney and R. Florida, 232–
260. Stanford, Calif.: Stanford University Press.

Ling, Zhijun. 2005. *The Lenovo Affair: The Growth of China's Computer Giant and Its
Takeover of IBM-PC.* Singapore: Wiley.

Liu, Xielin. 2006. "Path-Following or Leapfrogging in Catching-up: The Case of Chinese
Telecommunication Equipment Industry." Paper presented at the CIRCLE Seminar Series, Lund, Sweden.

Liu, Yin-Ling. 1992. "Reform from Below: The Private Economy and Local Politics in the
Rural Industrialization of Wenzhou." *China Quarterly* 130:293–316.

Loney, Matt. 2001. "Europe's First 3G Network Goes Live." http://www.zdnet.com.au
/europe-s-first-3g-network-goes-live-120262215.htm?omnRef=NULL (accessed June 13,
2010).

Low, Brian. 2005. "The Evolution of China's Telecommunications Equipment Market: A
Contextual, Analytical Framework." *Journal of Business and Industrial Marketing* 20 (2):
99–108.

———. 2007. "Huawei Technologies Corporation: From Local Dominance to Global Challenge?" *Journal of Business and Industrial Marketing* 22 (2): 138–144.

Lu, Qiwen. 2000. *China's Leap into the Information Age: Innovation and Organization in the
Computer Industry.* Oxford: Oxford University Press.

Lundvall, Bengt-Åke, ed. 1992. *National Systems of Innovation: Towards a Theory of Innovation and Interactive Learning.* London: Pinter.

Lundvall, Bengt-Åke, Björn Johnson, Esben Sloth Andersen, and Bent Dalum. 2002. "National Systems of Production, Innovation and Competence Building." *Research Policy*
31:213–231.

Markusen, Ann. 1996. "Sticky Places in Slippery Space: A Typology of Industrial Districts."
Economic Geography 72 (3): 293–313.

Marshall, Alfred. 1920 [1890]. *Principles of Economics.* 8th ed. London: Macmillan.

Mathews, John A., and Dong-Sung Cho. 2000. *Tiger Technology: The Creation of a Semiconductor Industry in East Asia.* Cambridge: Cambridge University Press.

McDonald, Joe. 2006. "Chinese Companies Unveil Video Player with Homegrown DVD Technology." *International Herald Tribune,* December 6.

————. 2008. "Chinese Entrepreneur Dreams of a Global Brand." Associated Press, August 4. Available at http://www.usatoday.com/tech/products/2008-08-04-1970329563_x.htm (accessed June 13, 2010).

McIlvaine. 2007. "Semiconductor Update, July 2007." McIlvaine Company. http://www.mcilvainecompany.com/industryforecast/semiconductor/updates/2007%20updates/july%2007%20update.htm#_Toc174345600 (accessed June 13, 2010).

McKendrick, David G., Richard F. Doner, and Stephan Haggard. 2000. *From Silicon Valley to Singapore: Location and Competitive Advantage in the Hard Disk Drive Industry.* Stanford, Calif.: Stanford University Press.

Meany, Connie Squires. 1994. "State Policy and the Development of Taiwan's Semiconductors Industry." In *The Role of the State in Taiwan's Development,* ed. J. D. Aberbach, D. Dollar, and K. L. Sokoloff, 170–192. Armonk, N.Y.: Sharpe.

Microsoft. 2003. "Microsoft and China Announce Government Security Program Agreement." Microsoft News Center, February 28. http://www.microsoft.com/presspass/press/2003/feb03/02-28gspchinapr.mspx (accessed April 2, 2009).

Ming, Shuliang. 2008. "Telecoms Undergo Restructuring—Again." *Caijing Magazine,* June 25. Available at http://tradeinservices.mofcom.gov.cn/en/i/2008-06-25/49014.shtml (accessed April 2, 2009).

MOFCOM [Ministry of Commerce of the People's Republic of China]. 2008. "The Telecommunications Industry in China." China Trade in Services. http://tradeinservices.mofcom.gov.cn/en/e/2007-11-29/13648.shtml (accessed June 16, 2008).

Montinola, Gabriella, Yingyi Qian, and Barry R. Weingast. 1995. "Federalism, Chinese Style: The Political Basis for Economic Success in China." *World Politics* 48 (1): 50–81.

Morgan, Kevin. 1997. "The Learning Region: Institutions, Innovation and Regional Renewal." *Regional Studies* 31 (5): 491–503.

MOST [Ministry of Science and Technology of the People's Republic of China]. 2006a. "Government S&T Appropriation." http://www.most.gov.cn/eng/statistics/2005/200603/t20060317_29723.htm (accessed June 13, 2010).

————. 2006b. "Output Indicators." http://www.most.gov.cn/eng/statistics/2005/200603/t20060317_29722.htm (accessed June 13, 2010).

————. 2006c. "R&D Activities." http://www.most.gov.cn/eng/statistics/2005/200603/t20060317_29724.htm (accessed June 13, 2010).

————. 2007. "High Technology." http://most.gov.cn/eng/statistics/2006/200703/t20070309_42004.htm (accessed June 13, 2010).

————. 2008a. *2007 China Science and Technology Statistics: Data Book.* http://most.gov.cn/eng/statistics/2007/200801/P020080109573867344872.pdf (accessed March 27, 2009).

————. 2008b. *2007 Nian Wo Guo Gao Xin Ji Shu Chan Ye Kai Fa Qu Jing Ji Fa Zhan Qing Kuang* [2007 China's High and New Technology Development Zones' Economic Development Situation]. Beijing.

———. 2008c. "S&T Programmes: National High-Tech R&D Program (863 Program)." http://most.gov.cn/eng/programmes1/index.htm (accessed January 20, 2008).

MOST, NDRC, et al. 2006. *"Guo Jia Zi Zhu Chuang Xin Chan Pin Ren Ding Guan Li Ban Fa" (Shi Hang)* [National Indigenous Innovation Product Certification Administration Method (draft)]. Beijing.

Mowery, David C., and Nathan Rosenberg. 1991. *Technology and the Pursuit of Economic Growth*. Cambridge: Cambridge University Press.

Mu, Qing, and Keun Lee. 2005. "Knowledge Diffusion, Market Segmentation and Technological Catch-up: The Case of the Telecommunication Industry in China." *Research Policy* 34:759–783.

Nanfang Ribao. 2007. *"Xiao Qi Lian Yin Ji Huo Chan Ye Chuang Xin Ji Yin"* [School-Business Marriage Enlivens Industry Innovation Gene]. Nanfang Ribao. June 28. http://news.163.com/07/0628/10/3I2LBON6000120GU.html (accessed January 2,2 2009).

———. 2008. "Dong Guan 10 Yi Yuan Bang Fu Zhong Xiao Qi Ye Rong Zi Qi Ye Xu Wu Bu Liang Xin Yong Ji Lu" [Dongguan's One Billion RMB To Support SMEs—Enterprises Must Not Have an Unhealthy Credit Record]. Nanfang Ribao. October 7. http://www.gd.gov.cn/govpub/rdzt/nxcfz/knxds/200811/t20081124_73933.htm (accessed January 19, 2008).

Naughton, Barry. 1995. *Growing Out of the Plan: Chinese Economic Reform, 1978–1993*. Cambridge: Cambridge University Press.

———. 2007. *The Chinese Economy: Transitions and Growth*. Cambridge, Mass: MIT Press.

Naughton, Barry, and Adam Segal. 2003. "China in Search of a Workable Model: Technology Development in the New Millennium." In *Crisis and Innovation in Asian Technology*, ed. W. W. Keller and R. J. Samuels, 160–186. Cambridge: Cambridge University Press.

Nelson, R. Richard, ed. 1993. *National Innovation Systems: A Comparative Analysis*. New York: Oxford University Press.

Nelson, R. Richard, and Katherine Nelson. 2002. "Technology, Institutions, and Innovation Systems." *Research Policy* 31:265–272.

Nie, Peng. 2008. "Guangdong: Newly-Registered Firms Outnumber Bankrupt Ones." *China Daily*, November 11. http://www.chinadaily.com.cn/bizchina/2008-11/11/content_7194909.htm (accessed December 22, 2008).

Noble, Gregory W. 1998. *Collective Action in East Asia: How Ruling Parties Shape Industrial Policy*. Ithaca, N.Y.: Cornell University Press.

North, Douglass. 1990. *Institutions, Institutional Change, and Economic Performance*. Cambridge: Cambridge University Press.

NSBPRC [National Statistical Bureau of the People's Republic of China]. 2006. *Gong You He Fei Gong You Kong Zhi Jing Ji De Fen Lei Ban Fa* [Public and Non-Public-Controlled Economy Classification Method]. Beijing: National Bureau of Statistics of China.

———. 2007. *2006 Nian Quan Guo Ke Ji Jing Fei Tou Ru Tong Ji Gong Bao* [2006 National Science and Technology Funds Investment Statistics Report]. Beijing: National Bureau of Statistics of China.

———. 2008a. *2007 Nian Guo Min Jing Ji He She Hui Fa Zhan Tong Ji Gong Bao* [2007 Citizen's Economic and Social Development Statistics Report]. Beijing: National Bureau of Statistics of China.

————. 2008b. *2007 Nian Wo Guo Gao Ji Shu Chan Pin Jin Chu Kou Fen Xi* [2007 China's High Technology Product Import and Export Statistics]. Beijing: National Bureau of Statistics of China.

Nystedt, Dan. 2005. "Lenovo to Take Over Mobile Phone Joint Venture." InfoWorld, December 20. http://www.infoworld.com/article/05/12/20/HNlenovophone_1.html (accessed September 28, 2008).

O'Brien, Kevin J. 1988. "China's National People's Congress: Reform and Its Limits." *Legislative Studies Quarterly* 13 (3): 343–374.

————. 1990. *Reform without Liberalization: China's National People's Congress and the Politics of Institutional Change.* New York: Cambridge University Press.

————. 1994. "Agents and Remonstrators: Role Accumulation by Chinese People's Congress Deputies." *China Quarterly* 138:359–380.

Obukhova, Elena. 2006. "IC Design Industry in Shanghai." Unpublished manuscript, MIT Sloan School of Management, Cambridge, Mass.

————. 2008. "IC Design Industry in Shanghai: 2004–2008." Unpublished manuscript, MIT Sloan School of Management, Cambridge, Mass.

OECD [Organization for Economic Cooperation and Development]. 2006. "China, Information Technologies and the Internet." Chap. 4 in *Information Technology Outlook 2006.* Paris: OECD.

————. 2007. *OECD Reviews of Innovation Policy: China; Synthesis Report.* Paris: OECD. Available at http://www.oecd.org/dataoecd/54/20/39177453.pdf.

Oi, Jean C. 1992. "Fiscal Reform and the Economic Foundation of Local State Corporatism in China." *World Politics* 45 (1): 99–126.

————. 1995. "The Role of the Local State in China's Transitional Economy." *China Quarterly* 144:1132–1149.

————. 1999. *Rural China Takes Off: Institutional Foundations of Economic Reform.* Berkeley and Los Angeles: University of California Press.

Ostrom, Elinor. 1990. *Governing the Commons: The Evolution of Institutions for Collective Action.* Cambridge: Cambridge University Press.

Park, Phillip Hoon. 2000. "A Reflection on the East Asian Developmental Model: Comparison of the South Korea and Taiwanese Experiences." In *The East Asian Development Model: Economic Growth, Institutional Failure, and the Aftermath of the Crisis,* ed. E. Richter, 141–168. London: Macmillan.

Pei, Xiasheng. 2005. "Science and Technology Business Incubators, One of the Pillars of China Torch Program." Paper presented at the National Business Incubation Association's nineteenth International Conference on Business Incubation, Baltimore, Maryland, May 15–18.

People's Daily. 2003. "China to Issue Home-Developed EVD Standard." October 28.

————. 2004. "EVD Players Not Selling as Expected in China." January 10.

————. 2007. "Special Supplement: TD-SCDMA Powers China's Telecom Industry." November 8. http://english.people.com.cn/90001/90776/90884/6298946.html (accessed July 23, 2008).

Piore, Michael J., and Charles F. Sabel. 1984. *The Second Industrial Divide: Possibilities for Prosperity.* New York: Basic Books.

Porter, Alan L., Nils C. Newman, J. David Roessner, David M. Johnson, and Xiao-yin Jin. 2009. "International High Tech Competitiveness: Does China Rank #1?" *Technology Analysis and Strategic Management* 21 (2): 173–193.

Portes, Alejandro. 1998. "Social Capital: Its Origins and Applications in Modern Sociology." *Annual Review of Sociology* 24:1–24.

Powell, Gareth. 2006. "Out DVD, in EVD." *China Economic Review,* December 1. http://www .chinaeconomicreview.com/it/2006/12/01/out-dvd-in-evd/ (accessed June 14, 2010).

Powell, Walter W., and Paul Dimaggio, eds. 1991. *The New Institutionalism in Organizational Analysis.* Chicago: University of Chicago Press.

PRC [People's Republic of China]. 1982. Constitution of the People's Republic of China. Beijing.

———. 1993. Amendment to the Constitution of the People's Republic of China. Beijing.

Putnam, D. Robert. 1993. *Making Democracy Work.* Princeton, N.J.: Princeton University Press.

Qi, Guotao. 2003. "*Zhongguancun Ruan Jian Qi Ye Chu Kou Lian Meng Cheng Wei*" [Zhongguancun Software Enterprise Export Union Established].Zhong Guo Ji Suan Ji Bao, December 18. http://industry.ccidnet.com/art/1548/20031218/765161.html (accessed September 30, 2008).

Qian, Yingyi. 2003. "How Reform Worked in China." In *In Search of Prosperity: Analytic Narratives on Economic Growth,* ed. D. Rodrik, 297–333. Princeton, N.J.: Princeton University Press.

Qian, Yingyi, and Barry R. Weingast. 1996. "China's Transition to Markets: Market-Preserving Federalism, Chinese Style." *Journal of Economic Policy Reform* 1 (2): 149–185.

Ricardo, David. 1963 [1817]. *The Principles of Political Economy and Taxation.* Homewood, Ill.: Irwin.

Ridley, Matt. 2003. *The Red Queen: Sex and the Evolution of Human Nature.* New York: Harper Perennial.

Rodrik, Dani. 2007. *One Economics, Many Recipes: Globalization, Institutions, and Economic Growth.* Princeton, N.J.: Princeton University Press.

Romer, M. Paul. 1990. "Endogenous Technological Change." *Journal of Political Economy* 98 (5, part 2: "The Problem of Development: A Conference on the Institute for the Study of Free Enterprise Systems"): S71–S102.

Rosenberg, Nathan. 1983. *Inside the Black Box: Technology and Economics.* Cambridge: Cambridge University Press.

Rosenberg, Nathan, and L. E. Birdzell, Jr. 1986. *How the West Grew Rich: The Economic Transformation of the Industrial World.* New York: Basic Books.

Rottenberg, Boaz. 2007. "TD-SCDMA: Much Ado About Nothing?" Maverick China Research. http://www.maverickchina.com/TD-SCDMA-and-3G-in-China/TD-SCDMA-Much-Ado-About-Nothing.html (accessed July 23, 2008).

SASAC [State-Owned Assets Supervision and Administration Commission of the State Council]. 2003. "Main Functions and Responsibilities of SASAC." http://www.sasac.gov .cn/n2963340/n2963393/2965120.html (accessed June 16, 2008).

Samuels, Richard. 1994. *Rich Nation Strong Army: National Security and the Technological Transformation of Japan.* Ithaca: Cornell University Press.

Saxenian, AnnaLee. 1994. *Regional Advantage: Culture and Competition in Silicon Valley and Route 128*. Cambridge, Mass.: Harvard University Press.

―――. 2003. "Government and Guanxi: The Chinese Software Industry in Transition." DRC [Development Research Centre] Working Paper 19. Global Software in Emerging Markets, Centre for New and Emerging Markets, London Business School. http://www.research4development.info/PDF/Outputs/CNEM/drc19.pdf (accessed June 14, 2010).

Saxenian, Annalee, and Jinn-Yuh Hsu. 2001. "The Silicon Valley-Hsinchu Connection: Technical Communities and Industrial Upgrading." *Industrial and Corporate Change* 10 (4): 893–920.

Schumpeter, Joseph Alois. 1961 [1934]. *The Theory of Economic Development: An Inquiry into Profits, Capital, Credit, Interest, and the Business Cycle*. Cambridge, Mass.: Harvard University Press.

Segal, Adam. 2003. *Digital Dragon: High-Technology Enterprises in China*. Ithaca, N.Y.: Cornell University Press.

Segal, Adam, and Eric Thun. 2001. "Thinking Globally, Acting Locally: Local Governments, Industrial Sectors, and Development in China." *Politics and Society* 29 (4): 557–588.

Semiconductor International China. 2008. *"Jin Nian Shang Ban Nian Shang Hai Ji Cheng Dian Lu Chan Ye Fa Zhan Gai Kuang"* [First Half-Year Shanghai IC Industry Development Summary]. *Semiconductor International China*, October 1. Available at http://www.dzsc.com/news/html/2008-10-13/86480.html (accessed August 8, 2010).

Serger, Sylvia Schwaag, and Magnus Breidne. 2007. "China's Fifteen-Year Plan for Science and Technology: An Assessment." *Asia Policy* 4 (July 2007): 135–164.

Shanghai Daily. 2008a. "Too Many Graduates Lead to Lower Pay." June 6. http://www.shanghai.gov.cn/shanghai/node17256/node18151/userobject22ai29442.html (accessed June 6, 2008).

―――. 2008b. "City Combats Shortage of Technicians." July 6. http://www.shanghai.gov.cn/shanghai/node17256/node18151/userobject22ai29700.html (accessed April 2, 2009).

Shanghai Economic. 2006. *Investment Guidebook on Industry and Commerce in Shanghai*. Shanghai: Shanghai Economic Committee.

Shanghai Foreign [Shanghai Foreign Investment Commission]. 2003. "Shanghai Foreign Direct Investment Contract by Year up to Dec. 2002." http://www.smert.gov.cn/.

―――. 2006a. "White Paper: Environment for Foreign Investment in Shanghai." Shanghai: Shanghai Foreign Investment Commission.

―――. 2006b. "Research & Development Center of Multinational Company." Investment Shanghai. August 7. http://www.investment.gov.cn/2006-08-07/1152500440530.html (accessed April 2, 2009).

―――. 2008. "New Project of Coca Cola Officially Settled in Minhang Shanghai." Investment Shanghai. November 6. http://www.investment.gov.cn/2008-11-06/1225591333637.html (accessed April 2, 2009).

Shanghai Gov. 2006. *"Shang Hai Jin Qiao Chu Kou Jia Gong Qu"* [Shanghai Jinqiao Export Processing Zone]. http://www.shanghai.gov.cn/shanghai/node2314/node2318/node9364/node9423/node9440/index.html (accessed January 13, 2009).

―――. 2007. *2007 Nian Shang Hai Shi Guo Min Jing Ji He She Hui Xin Xi Hua Gong Bao* [2007 Shanghai Citizen's Economic and Social Informationization Report]. Shanghai.

Shanghai Municipal Government. 2000. "Regulations on Encouraging Shanghai Software

Industry and Integrated Circuit Industry Development." http://www.isoip.sh.cn/English
/Module/Policy/ShowDetail_eng.aspx?sj_dir=ENG_Policy_City&ct_id=8347 (accessed
June 14, 2010).

———. 2006. "Suggestions regarding Promoting the Development of Shanghai Service
Outsourcing Development." http://www.isoip.sh.cn/English/Module/Policy/ShowDetail
_eng.aspx?sj_dir=ENG_Policy_City&ct_id=8336 (accessed June 14, 2010).

ShanghaiSB [Shanghai Statistics Bureau]. 2008. *2007 Nian Shang Hai Shi Guo Min Jin Ji He
She Hui Fa Zhan Tong Ji Gong Bao* [2007 Shanghai City People's Economic and Social
Development Statistical Report]. Shanghai.

Shen, Jianfa, Kwan-Yiu Wong, Kim-Yee Chu, and Zhiqiang Feng. 2000. "The Spatial Dynamics of Foreign Investment in the Pearl River Delta, South China." *Geographical Journal* 166 (4): 312–322.

SHIP [Shenzhen High Tech Industrial Park]. 2003. "Park Profile." http://www.ship.gov.cn
/en/index.asp?bianhao=20 (accessed August 8, 2010).

Shirk, Susan. 1993. *The Political Logic of Economic Reform in China.* Berkeley and Los Angeles: University of California Press.

SIP [Suzhou Industrial Park]. 2007. "How the 'New Silicon Valley' Becomes Prosperous."
SIP Science and Technology Development Center. March 17. http://fjt.sipac.gov.cn/gate
/big5/stipc.sipac.gov.cn/sipstipcEN/News/200704/t20070410_21447.html (accessed June
14, 2010).

Smith, Tony. 2003. "China Unveils 'DVD Killer' Video Disk Format." The Register. November 20. http://www.theregister.co.uk/2003/11/20/china_unveils_dvd_killer_video/
(accessed June 27, 2008).

Sohu.com. 2009. Map of Beijing Industrial Development Zone. http://oldimages.house
.focus.cn/upload/photos/895/AOUrAche.jpg (accessed February 5, 2009).

Solinger, Dorothy J. 1996. "Despite Decentralization: Disadvantages, Dependence and Ongoing Central Power in the Inland—The Case of Wuhan." *China Quarterly* 145:1–34.

Solow, Robert M. 1956. "A Contribution to the Theory of Economic Growth." *Quarterly
Journal of Economics* 70 (1): 65–94.

SSB [Shenzhen Statistics Bureau]. 2008. *Shenzhen Shi 2007 Nian Guo Min Jing Ji He She Hui
Fa Zhan Tong Ji Gong Gao* [Shenzhen City 2007 People's Economic and Social Development Statistics Report]. Shenzhen, China.

State Council [State Council of the People's Republic of China]. 2008. "White Paper: China's
Efforts and Achievements in Promoting the Rule of Law." Beijing: Information Office of
the State Council. Available at http://news.xinhuanet.com/english/2008-02/28/content_
7687418.htm (accessed June 14, 2010).

Steinfeld, S. Edward. 1998. *Forging Reform in China: The Fate of State-Owned Industry.* Cambridge: Cambridge University Press.

———. 2004. "China's Shallow Integration: Networked Production and the New Challenges for Late Industrialization." *World Development* 32 (11): 1971–1987.

———. 2007. "Innovation, Integration, and Technology Upgrading in Contemporary Chinese Industry." In *The Economic Geography of Innovation,* ed. K. Polenske, 289–309. New
York: Cambridge University Press.

Stevenson-Yang, Anne, and Ken DeWoskin. 2005. "China Destroys the IP Paradigm." *Far
Eastern Economic Review* 168 (3): 9–18.

Story, Louise. 2007. "An Apology in China from Mattel." *New York Times*, September 22.

Streeck, Wolfgang. 1996. "Lean Production in the German Automobile Industry: A Test Case for Convergence Theory." In *National Diversity and Global Capitalism*, ed. S. Berger and R. Dore, 138–170. Ithaca, N.Y.: Cornell University Press.

Sturgeon, Timothy J. 2000. "Turnkey Production Networks: The Organizational Delinking of Production from Innovation." In *New Product Development and Production Networks*, ed. U. Jurgens, 67–84. New York: Springer.

———. 2001. "How Do We Define Value Chains and Production Networks?" *Institute of Development Studies Bulletin* 32 (3): 9–18.

———. 2002. "Modular Production Networks: A New American Model of Industrial Organization." *Industrial and Corporate Change* 11 (3): 451–496.

———. 2003. "What Really Goes on in Silicon Valley? Spatial Clustering and Dispersal in Modular Production Networks." *Journal of Economic Geography* 3:199–225.

Sturgeon, Timothy J., and Richard Florida. 2004. "Globalization, Deverticalization, and Employment in the Motor Vehicle Industry." In *Locating Global Advantage: Industry Dynamics in the International Economy*, edited by M. Kenney and R. L. Florida, 52–81. Stanford, Calif.: Stanford University Press.

Sturgeon, Timothy J., and Richard Lester. 2004. "The New Global Supply-Base: New Challenges for Local Suppliers in East Asia." In *Global Production Networking and Technological Change in East Asia*, ed. S. Yusuf, A. Altaf, and K. Nabeshima, 35–88. Oxford: Oxford University Press.

Sunami, Atsushi. 2002. "Industry-University Cooperation and University-Affiliated Enterprises in China, a Country Aspiring for Growth on Science and Education: Building New System for Technological Innovation." *RIETI Research and Review* (May). http://www.rieti.go.jp/en/papers/research-review/001.html (accessed June 14, 2010).

Sung, Claire, and Jessie Shen. 2009a. "SIHL Increases Stake in SMIC." DigiTimes, February 3. http://www.digitimes.com:8080/news/a20090203PD212.html (accessed February 16, 2009).

———. 2009b. "China Steps Up Consolidation of Foundries, Sources Say." DigiTimes, February 17. http://www.digitimes.com:8080/news/a20090217PD217.html (accessed February 17, 2009).

Suttmeier, Richard P., Xiangkui Yao, and Alex Zixiang Tan. 2006. *Standards of Power? Technology, Institutions, and Politics in the Development of China's National Standards Strategy*. Seattle: National Bureau of Asian Research.

SZVUP [Shenzhen Virtual University Park]. 2007. "*Shen Zhen Xu Ni Da Xue Yuan 2007 Nian Jian Jie*" [2007 Introduction to the Shenzhen Virtual University Park]. http://www.szvup.com/Html/xydt/2007/671209610040.html (accessed December 22, 2008).

TD Forum. 2008. "TD-SCDMA, Good Experience in Trial Use and an Uncertain Future." TD Forum, TD-SCDMA News. May 26. http://www.tdscdma-forum.org/EN/NEWS/see.asp?id=5365 (accessed April 2, 2009).

TeleAtlas and Google.com 2009. Map data. Retrieved February 5, 2009 (http://maps.google.com/).

Teubal, Morris. 1983. "Neutrality in Science Policy: The Case of Sophisticated Industrial Technology in Israel." *Minerva* 21:172–197.

Thun, Eric. 2004. "Keeping Up with the Jones': Decentralization, Policy Imitation, and Industrial Development in China." *World Development* 32 (8): 1289–1308.

———. 2006. *Changing Lanes in China: Foreign Direct Investment, Local Governments, and Auto Sector Development.* Cambridge: Cambridge University Press.

Trajtenberg, Manuel. 2001. "Innovation in Israel, 1968–1997: A Comparative Analysis Using Patent Data." *Research Policy* 30 (3): 363–389.

Tsai, Kellee S. 2002. *Back Alley Banking: Private Entrepreneurs in China.* Ithaca, N.Y.: Cornell University Press.

Unger, Jonathan, and Anita Chan. 1995. "China, Corporatism and the East Asian Model." *Australian Journal of Chinese Affairs* 33:29–53.

USITO [U.S. Information Technology Office]. 2007. "USITO Weekly China Market Summary, 12/25/2007." http://www.usito.org/08/news_dls.php?id=480&category=USITO %20Weekly%20China%20%20Summary (accessed August 8, 2010).

Uzzi, Brian. 1996. "The Sources and Consequences of Embeddedness for the Economic Performance of Organizations: The Network Effect." *American Sociological Review* 61 (4): 674–698.

Vernon, Raymond. 1966. "International Investment and International Trade in the Product Cycle." *Quarterly Journal of Economics* 80 (2): 190–207.

Vogel, Ezra. 1971. *Canton under Communism: Programs and Politics in a Provincial Capital, 1949–1968.* New York: Harper.

Wade, Robert. 1990. *Governing the Market: Economic Theory and the Role of the Government in East Asian Industrialization.* Princeton, N.J.: Princeton University Press.

Walcott, Susan. 2002. "Chinese Industrial and Science Parks: Bridging the Gap." *Professional Geographer* 54 (3): 349–364.

———. 2003. *Chinese Science and Technology Industrial Parks.* Burlington, Vt.: Ashgate.

Walcott, Susan M., and Clifton W. Pannell. 2006. "Metropolitan Spatial Dynamics: Shanghai." *Habitat International* 30:199–211.

Walder, Andrew G. 1989. "Factory and Manager in an Era of Reform." *China Quarterly* 118:242–264.

———. 1995. "Local Governments as Industrial Firms: An Organizational Analysis of China's Transitional Economy." *American Journal of Sociology* 101 (2): 263–301.

Wang, Fei-Ling. 2005. *Organizing through Division and Exclusion: China's Hukou System.* Stanford, Calif.: Stanford University Press.

Wang, Jianzhou. 2001. "China Unicom Limited." Paper presented at Credit Suisse First Boston Global Telecommunications CEO Conference, New York, March 5–7.

Wang, Jici, and Jixian Wang. 1998. "An Analysis of New-Tech Agglomeration in Beijing: A New Industrial District in the Making?" *Environment and Planning A* 30:681–701.

Wang, Shuguang, Yulin Wu, and Yujiang Li. 1998. "Development of Technopoles in China." *Asia Pacific Viewpoint* 39:281–301.

Wang, Xing. 2008. "Lenovo to Offload Handset Unit." *China Daily,* February 1. http://www.chinadaily.com.cn/bizchina/2008-02/01/content_6436473.htm (accessed April 2, 2009).

Wang, Yan. 2008. "IC Design Houses Cement Shanghai's Stardom." *EE Times India,* January 22. http://www.eetindia.co.in/ART_8800498761_1800000_NT_d17c2c64.HTM) (accessed January 15, 2009).

Wank, D. L. 1996. "The Institutional Process of Market Clientelism: Guanxi and Private Business in a South China City." *China Quarterly* 29:820–838.

Weber, Max. 1952 [1920]. "The Essentials of Bureaucratic Organization: An Ideal-Type Construction." In *Reader in Bureaucracy,* ed. R. K. Merton, A. Gray, B. Hockey, and H. C. Selvin, 19–27. New York: Free Press.

Wei, Michael. 2008. "China's 3G Standard Could Wither on the Vine." Reuters, December 4. Available at http://www.cn-c114.net/583/a367462.html (accessed August 8, 2010).

Wei, Yehua Dennis, and Chi Kin Leung. 2005. "Development Zones, Foreign Investment and Global City Formation in Shanghai." *Growth and Change* 36 (1): 16–40.

Weingast, Barry R. 1995. "The Economic Role of Political Institutions: Market-Preserving Federalism and Economic Development." *Journal of Law, Economics and Organization* 11 (1): 1–31.

Weiss, Linda. 1998. *The Myth of the Powerless State.* Ithaca, N.Y: Cornell University Press.

Whittaker, D. Hugh, Tianbiao Zhu, Timothy J. Sturgeon, Mon Han Tsai, and Toshie Okita. 2008. "Compressed Development." MIT IPC [Industrial Performance Center] Working Paper 08-005, Massachusetts Institute of Technology, Cambridge, Massachusetts. http://web.mit.edu/ipc/publications/pdf/08-005.pdf (accessed August 8, 2010).

Wilson, James Q. 1968. *Varieties of Police Behavior: The Management of Law and Order in Eight Communities.* Cambridge, Mass.: Harvard University Press.

Wireless Asia. 2003. "Beijing: China Netcom President Xi Guohua Will Swap Jobs with MII Vice Minister Zhang Chunjiang." Wireless Asia. May 15. http://www.highbeam.com /doc/1G1-103193261.html (accessed March 2, 2009).

Womack, James P., Daniel T. Jones, and Daniel Roos. 1990. *The Machine That Changed the World : The Story of Lean Production.* New York: Harper Perennial.

Wong, Edward. 2008. "As Factories Close, Chinese Workers Suffer." *International Herald Tribune,* November 14.

Woo-Cumings, Meredith. 1991. *Race to the Swift: State and Finance in Korean Industrialization.* New York: Columbia University Press.

———, ed. 1999. *The Developmental State.* Ithaca, N.Y.: Cornell University Press.

Wu, Irene. 2004. "Traits of an Independent Communications Regulator: A Search for Indicators." International Bureau Working Paper 1. Federal Communications Commission, Washington, D.C. http://hraunfoss.fcc.gov/edocs_public/attachmatch/DOC-248467A1 .pdf (accessed June 14, 2010).

———. 2005. "Traits of an Independent Communications Regulator: A Search for Indicators; with Teaching Module on Ethics and Corruption." Federal Communications Commission, Washington, D.C. Available at http://web.si.umich.edu/tprc/papers/2005 /406/FCC%20IB%20indpt%20reg%20aug%2005.pdf (accessed June 14, 2010).

———. 2009. *From Iron Fist to Invisible Hand: The Uneven Path of Telecommunications Reform in China.* Stanford, Calif.: Stanford University Press.

Wu, Shulian, Jia Lu, and Guo Shilin. 2008. "*Wu Shu Lian 08 Zhong Guo Da Xue Pai Hang Jie Mu Qing Hua Lian Xu Duo Kui*" [Wu Shulian's 08 Chinese University Rankings— Tsinghua Leads for 12 Years in a Row]. Sina Kao Shi. January 7. http://edu.sina.com.cn /gaokao/2008–01–07/1653116647.shtml (accessed on April 2, 2009).

Wu, Yuihui, and Yao Sha. 2008. "*Zhong Guan Cun Zhang Da Le*" [Zhongguancun Comes of Age]. *Renmin Ribao*, November 5.

Xia, Jun. 2006. "Head-to-Head or Hand-in-Hand: Does Structural Reform Have Led to Meaningful Competition in China?" Paper presented at the 34th Annual Research Conference on Communication, Information, and Internet Policy, Arlington, Virginia, September 29–October 1.

———. 2007a. "Market Forces or *Qian Gui Ze*? Interpreting Market Behavior in the Chinese Telecommunication Industry." Paper presented at 35th Annual Research Conference on Communication, Information, and Internet Policy, Arlington, Virginia, September 28–30. http://web.si.umich.edu/tprc/papers/2007/801/Market%20Force%20or%20Qian%20Gui%20Ze-TPRC07-Jun%20Xia.pdf (accessed June 14, 2010).

———. 2007b. "Regulatory Incentive and Regulatory Governance: An Institutional Perspective on USO Regime in China." Paper presented at 35th Annual Research Conference on Communication, Information, and Internet Policy, Arlington, Virginia, September 28–30.

Xia, Jun, and Tingjie Lu. 2008. "Bridging the Digital Divide for Rural Communities: The Case of China." *Telecommunications Policy* 32 (9–10): 686–696.

Xinhua [Xinhua News Agency]. 2005. "Shenzhen Encourages Home-Bred Innovation." Xinhua News Agency, December 14. Available at http://english.gov.cn/2005-12/14/content _220712.htm (accessed April 2, 2009).

———. 2006. "Feature: Chinese Businessman Blazes Trail to His Digital Dream." Xinhua News Agency, February 17. Available at http://www.highbeam.com/doc/1P2-16017297.html.

Xinwei. 2008. "About Chongqing Xinwei." http://www.xinwei.com.cn:8080/en/zjxw/index .asp?InfoTypeID=178&InfoTypeDescription=About+Chongqing+Xinwei (accessed December 11, 2008).

Xu, Chenggang, and Juzhong Zhuang. 1998. "Why China Grew: The Role of Decentralization." In *Emerging from Communism: Lessons from Russia, China, and Eastern Europe*, ed. P. Boone, S. Gomulka, and R. Layard, 183–212. Boston: MIT Press.

Xue, Lan, and Zheng Liang. 2005. "Multinational R&D in China: An Analysis Based on a Survey in Beijing." Paper presented at Global R&D in China: An International Forum, Nanjing, China, May 28–29.

Yang, Mayfair Mei-hui. 1989. "The Gift Economy and State Power in China." *Comparative Studies in Society and History* 31 (1): 25–54.

———. 1994. *Gifts, Favors, and Banquets: The Art of Social Relationships in China*. Ithaca, N.Y.: Cornell University Press.

———. 2002. "The Resilience of *Guanxi* and Its New Deployments: A Critique of Some New *Guanxi* Scholarship." *China Quarterly* 170:459–476.

Yao, Shujie. 2005. *Economic Growth, Income Distribution, and Poverty Reduction in Contemporary China*. Oxford: Taylor and Francis.

Ye, Lin. 2008. "*Chuan Tie Tong Zong Jing Li Zhang Yong Ping Chu Ren Tian Jin Yu Dong Zong Jing Li*" [Transfer of Tietong General Manager Zhang Yongping to Take Responsibility at Tianjin Mobile General Manager." CCTime.com. August 14. http://www.cctime.com /html/2008-8-14/2008814920494178.htm (accessed March 2, 2009).

Yeung, Irene Y. M., and Rosalie L. Tung, 1996. "Achieving Business Success in Confucian Societies: The Importance of Guanxi (Connections)." *Organizational Dynamics* 25 (2): 54–65.

Yoshida, Junko. 2003. "China Unveils Its Own Video Format." EE Times, November 18. http://www.eetimes.com/showArticle.jhtml;jsessionid=PENCN1RAJRG3KQSND LOSKH0CJUNN2JVN?articleID=18310016 (accessed June 27, 2008).

Yuan, Yufei, Wuping Zheng, Youwei Wang, Zhengchuan Xu, Qing Yang, and Yufei Gao. 2006. "Xiaolingtong versus 3G in China: Which Will Be the Winner?" *Telecommunications Policy* 30:297–313.

ZGC Park [Zhongguancun Science Park]. 2008. *2007 Nian 1–12 Yue Yuan Qu Gao Xin Ji Shu Qi Ye Fa Zhan Shu Ju* [January–December 2007 Park High and New Technology Enterprise Development Numbers]. Beijing.

Zhang, Danwei. 2008. "China to Issue 3G Licenses Tonight." TMT China. December 31. http://tmt.interfaxchina.com/news/1158 (accessed January 23, 2009).

———. 2009. "Government Announces Further Support for TD-SCDMA." TMT China. January 23. http://tmt.interfaxchina.com/news/1250 (accessed January 23, 2009).

Zhang, Qian. 2005. "Zhongguancun Science Park: China's Hi-Tech Park in Beijing." PowerPoint presentation by a member of the Zhongguancun Administrative Committee.

Zhang, Wei, and Barbara Igel. 2001. "Managing the Product Development of China's SPC Switch Industry as an Example of CoPS." *Technovation* 21:361–368.

Zhao, Dianchuan. 2008. "*Dong Guan Shi Zhang Li Yu Quan: 10 Yi Yuan She Li Zhuan Xing Sheng Ji Zhuan Xiang Ji Jin*" [Dongguan Mayor Li Yuquan: 1 Billion RMB Establishes Reform Promoting Specialized Fund]. Nanfang Wang. August 18. http://news.southcn .com/dishi/dsrdzt/content/2008-08/18/content_4550807.htm (accessed on January 19, 2009).

Zhao, Xiao. 2006. "*Sheng Shi Wei Yan: Yi Zu Zu Ling Ren Xin Jing De Shu Zi Bei Hou*" [Flourishing Exaggeration: Behind One Form of Statistics Alarming People]. Xinhua, October 20. http://news.xinhuanet.com/newmedia/2006-10/20/content_5227379.htm (accessed December 17, 2008).

Zhicheng Champion. 2008. "Ji Tuan Jian Jie—Corporate Profile" [Group Introduction—Corporate Profile]. http://www.zhicheng-champion.com/about.html (accessed January 19, 2009).

Zhong, Jing. 2004. "China's EVD Standard Becomes the Industrial One." China Economic Net, July 21, 2004. http://en.ce.cn/Insight/200407/21/t20040721_1285100.shtml (accessed June 27, 2008).

Zhou, Tao. 2004. "China's Home-Grown CDMA Systems: SCDMA/TD-SCDMA/LAS-CDMA." Paper presented at the Southern California Monte Jade Science and Technology Association Advance Program Workshop: Emerging Technologies of Wireless Communication, Newport Beach, California.

Zhou, Wenlin. 2008. "*Yun Ji Suan Jiang Qu Dai Yi PC Wei Zhong Xin De Ji Suan*" [Cloud Computing to Supplant PC Centric Computing]. ZD Net, March 19. http://server.zdnet .com.cn/server/2008/0319/774358.shtml (accessed December 11, 2008).

Zhou, Xiao. 2008. "Service Outsourcing to Drive Shanghai's Economy." *China Daily*, December 26. http://www.chinadaily.com.cn/regional/2008-12/26/content_7343316.htm (accessed February 3, 2009).

Zhou, Yu. 2005. "The Making of an Innovation Region from a Centrally Planned Economy: Institutional Evolution in Zhongguancun Science Park in Beijing." *Environment and Planning A* 37:1113–1134.

Zhou, Yu, Yifei Sun, Y. H. Dennis Wei, and George C. S. Lin. 2010. "De-centering 'Spatial Fix': Patterns of Territorialization and Regional Technological Dynamism of ICT Hubs in China." *Journal of Economic Geography* (January 12, 2010): 1–32. http://joeg.oxfordjournals .org/content/early/2010/01/12/jeg.lbp065.short?rss=1 (accessed August 8, 2010).

Zhou, Yu, and Xin Tong. 2003. "An Innovative Region in China: Interaction between Multinational Corporations and Local Firms in a High-Tech Cluster in Beijing." *Economic Geography* 79 (2): 129–152.

ZHTP [Zhangjiang Hi-Tech Park]. 2006. "Statistics on Biomedicine Manufacturer at the Park" (in Chinese). http://www.zjpark.com/zjpark%5Fen/nr.aspx?id=25 (accessed January 6, 2009).

———. 2008. "About Zhangjiang: Introduction." http://www.zjpark.com/zjpark_en/zjgkjyq .aspx?id=7 (accessed January 13, 2009).

Zhu, Tianbiao. 2010. "Political Economy of the Chinese Flexible State." Working Paper series no. 1, Department of Political Economy, School of Government, Peking University, Beijing.

ZhuLu. 2008. "China Analysis, Strategy and Entry." World ZhuLu http://www.worldzhulu .com/index.cfm/event/cnAnalysis (accessed August 9, 2008).

Zimmer, Jeff. 2006. "PC Maker Lenovo Announces Plan to Move U.S. Headquarters to Morrisville, N.C." *Durham (NC) Herald-Sun*, March 17.

Zysman, John. 1983. *Governments, Markets, and Growth: Financial Systems and the Politics of Industrial Change.* Ithaca, N.Y.: Cornell University Press.

———. 1994. "How Institutions Create Historically Rooted Trajectories of Growth." *Industrial and Corporate Change* 3 (1): 243–283.

Zysman, John, Niels C. Nielsen, Dan Breznitz, and Derek Wong. 2007. "Building on the Past, Imagining the Future: Competency Based Growth Strategies in a Global Digital Age." Berkeley Roundtable on the International Economy (BRIE) Working Paper 181. http://brie.berkeley.edu/publications/WP181.pdf (accessed June 14, 2010).

Index